"McPhee is an old-fashioned, hard-working, street-smart investigative journalist who is determined to get to the bottom of things."

— Prof. John D. Woodward, Jr., Boston University (retired CIA officer)

"McPhee's reporting clearly proves the government at best lied or covered up, at worse falsified, the facts of a terrorist attack on American soil. A great read for those of us who are fascinated with the truth."

— Jerry Flynn, president United Federation of Police Officers

"McPhee's latest true crime narrative takes the story of the Boston Marathon bombing to new levels . . . even readers familiar with the contours of the tragedy are likely to find McPhee's narrative terrifying and moving."

— *Publishers Weekly*

"McPhee is no armchair journalist reporting from the remove of the newsroom with facts gleaned from Google. She takes you there, to the scene of the crime: a horrendous bombing at a marathon finish line, a pitched gun battle between cops and terrorists in suburban streets — all conjured with vivid, taut prose that gives the reader a deeper look beneath the surface carnage to uncover the disturbing complexities of federal law enforcement.

— Richard Stratton, author of *Smuggler's Blues*

"McPhee, like all great investigators, well understands that one of the keys to unraveling a major case is the ability to recover unseen and seemingly irretrievable facts through the use of well placed sources. Her chronicling of the staggering details surrounding this act of terror is light years ahead of the standard Hollywood crime drama."

— Sean Foley, retired NYPD detective first grade

"Our nation's leaders would do well to wise up and pay attention to the lessons Michele teaches us about the Boston bombing and the serious gaps in intelligence and law-enforcement collaboration."

— Scott Mann, former Green Beret

MAYHEM

Unanswered Questions About
the Tsarnaev Brothers,
the US Government, and
the Boston Marathon Bombing

Michele R. McPhee

STEERFORTH PRESS
LEBANON, NEW HAMPSHIRE

For information about permission to reproduce
selections from this book, write to:
Steerforth Press L.L.C., 31 Hanover Street, Suite 1
Lebanon, New Hampshire 03766

Cataloging-in-Publication Data is available from the Library of Congress

Printed in the United States of America

ISBN 978-1-58642-261-5

1 3 5 7 9 10 8 6 4 2

Contents

Author's Note

When two bombs were detonated on Boylston Street, 550 feet away from the finish line of the Boston Marathon on April 15, 2013, a familiar sense of dread came over me. There was no cell phone service. Loved ones were unreachable. At 2:49 PM, the area just yards from where I'd had coffee earlier that day was a war zone: body parts, pools of blood, broken glass — inexplicable mayhem. Tragically, it was not the first time I had been on hand for a terrorist attack on American soil.

When Al Qaeda fanatics hijacked two planes from Boston's Logan Airport and flew them into Manhattan's World Trade Center Towers on September 11, 2001, I was the police bureau chief for the *New York Daily News*, working out of One Police Plaza, and on the scene at Ground Zero when the towers collapsed.

I began investigating the marathon bombings for ABC News almost immediately after they occurred, continued writing exclusive cover stories for *Boston* and *Newsweek* magazines, and have not stopped since, even after leaving Boston to work on the scripted side of television in Los Angeles. I was there as crime scene detectives and federal agents collected evidence on blood-splattered Boylston Street and when the FBI released photographs of the suspects referred to as "Black Hat" and "White Hat" four days later. Just hours after that release, I raced to Cambridge, where those same suspects were believed to have murdered an MIT police officer and then carjacked a getaway vehicle. The carjacking victim escaped but left his cell phone behind in his Mercedes SUV. Police used its GPS to track it to Watertown, my next stop. Reporters ringed the streets, then dove behind cars when a wild battle involving explosives and sustained gunfire erupted between the suspected bombers and police.

After the bullets stopped flying at 1:01 AM on April 19, investigators recovered more than two hundred spent rounds from the streets and nearby homes. One suspect was dead. The other was on the run. The FBI had publicly identified them as Tamerlan Tsarnaev, twenty-six, and his brother, Dzhokhar, nineteen, two Russian immigrants who had been living in a subsidized apartment in Cambridge. I remained in the paralyzed city of Watertown for the next sixteen hours as SWAT teams searched door-to-door, telling terrified residents to stay put. One family had the surreal experience of a bullet piercing their television set while they watched news of the insanity occurring outside their house. Just after 6:00 PM a Watertown man went out for a smoke and found drops of blood that led to his boat, the *Slip Away II*, dry-docked in his yard. When he pulled back the tarp covering the vessel, he saw a bleeding man in the bottom of the boat and scrambled for his phone. Within minutes cops ringed the boat, and after one of them believed he saw movement, they opened fire. The first shot was followed by a twelve-second barrage into the side of the boat and flash-bang grenades whose hum could be heard blocks away. Then came the cease-fire order. Dzhokhar was captured alive — barely alive. Grateful residents of Watertown lined the streets to cheer the police officers as they later pulled out of the city. I know a lot of cops who got free drinks that night.

Since then I have attended every arraignment and court appearance of the accused bomber, Dzhokhar Tsarnaev, and four other men charged in the attacks, his college friends who were imprisoned for lying to investigators in a terrorism case.

The very same homeland security flaws that I investigated as a *Daily News* reporter were partly to blame for the success of the Boston attacks. In a congressional hearing weeks after the deadly bombings in 2013, former Boston Police Commissioner Ed Davis told federal lawmakers that the lack of information sharing between the FBI and Boston Police Department detectives assigned to work with the FBI on the Joint Terrorism Task Force, all of whom had top security clearance, hindered his officers from investigating allegations that counterterrorism counterparts in Russia had made about the Tsarnaev brothers. In other words, the FBI didn't share intelligence with their BPD partners on the task force — not exactly the spirit of cooperation that experts had urged in the aftermath of 9/11. In fact, to this day the FBI has not answered congressional calls from both sides of the aisle to release details about the warnings the Russians sent, twice, in 2011 in the months before Tamerlan took an unusual trip back to his motherland, managing to get out of the United States, and back in, while on two terror watch lists.

Following 9/11, New York Police Department Commissioner Ray Kelly repeatedly warned me and other reporters who worked out of One Police Plaza that it was "not if, but when" the United States would be attacked by Islamic extremists again. The biggest threat, Kelly said, would be homegrown terrorists. He was right. Researchers with the George Washington University Program on Extremism released a report on the Islamic State of Iraq and Syria (ISIS) in America in 2015 that included startling numbers: More than 900 Americans were under investigation in the United States for connections to terrorism; 250 had traveled abroad to join the jihad; and 56 had been arrested for terrorism-related activities in 2015 alone.[1]

The Tsarnaev brothers, their parents, and two sisters — all of whom had fled Russia in 2002 and settled in Massachusetts — received asylum as refugees from a war-torn area, making them eligible for generous benefits such as housing, cash assistance, and education. Dzhokhar even became an American citizen, sworn in alongside other immigrants on September 11, 2012, in the arena commonly known as the Boston Garden. Despite all that the United States had given the family, the two brothers became the very threat counterterrorism officials had feared since 9/11: homegrown terrorists.

The story, however, is not so simple. I believe the federal government played a direct role in enabling and inspiring Tamerlan

Tsarnaev's monstrous behavior and in blocking local authorities' ability to identify and stop his evolution into a killer. Tamerlan's younger brother, Dzhokhar, in turn, looked up to his older brother. I also believe the federal government actively impeded a full investigation of the marathon bombings, as well as other crimes potentially involving Tamerlan and associates of his, and continues to do so today through a variety of means, including repeated motions to suppress information in Dzhokhar's efforts to have his death sentence reduced to life imprisonment.

In her own book on the Tsarnaevs, titled *The Brothers*, Russian American journalist Masha Gessen writes that questions remaining unanswered in the Boston Marathon bombing case include: "Where were the bombs made? And what had been Tamerlan's relationship to the FBI?"

I spent three years researching this book, and continued digging for another three since. In it I have outlined my theory that the FBI recruited Tamerlan as an operative in late 2010, months before the Federal Security Service of Russia (FSB) warned the FBI's Boston field office that he had become radicalized and planned to obtain training from "bandit groups" in his native Russia.[2] In fact, Dzhokhar's defense attorneys have stated that the FBI attempted to recruit Tamerlan to inform on fellow Muslims, writing, "We base this on information from our client's family and other sources that the FBI made more than one visit to talk with Anzor, Zubeidat and Tamerlan, questioned Tamerlan about his internet searches, and asked him to be an informant."[3]

It is no secret that the FBI has relied heavily on Islamic informants to thwart terrorist plots, a practice that has been condemned by the American Civil Liberties Union and other organizations. Tamerlan would have been the perfect recruit, a handsome multilingual Muslim with ties to both the drug world and a controversial mosque in Cambridge blocks from his house, one that was started and built by a man now serving a federal sentence for terrorism and that counted several convicted terrorists among its congregants. And it was certainly not a secret that Tamerlan would have been motivated to work with the FBI as a cooperating informant out of a desire to become a US citizen. In 2009 he posed for an online photo essay, "Will Box for Passport." In 2010 he was barred from fighting in the National Tournament of Champions, even though he had twice won the title of heavyweight champion of New England, because he was not a citizen. Then there was the issue of money: Tamerlan didn't have any, at least not on paper. For occupation on his death certificate the medical examiner wrote, "Never Worked."[4] Yet he drove a Mercedes without holding a job. He also got married and had a little girl. History has shown that working for the federal government as an informant can be lucrative. Tamerlan got away with so much villainy that only a hands-off policy formulated at the local level by one or more agencies responsible for national intelligence could have engineered it. His probable situation with such agencies was eerily similar to the relationship between James "Whitey" Bulger and the Boston office of the FBI.

Evidence suggests that in 2011 Tamerlan secretly worked on an investigation that dismantled a ring of crack cocaine dealers who moved the drug from Boston to Portland, Maine. Federal investigators called the investigation Operation Run This Town, and its targets were Eritrean gang members, including an eventual defendant, Hamadi Hassan, a native of Cambridge who had grown up with Tamerlan. In fact, the Bureau of Alcohol, Tobacco, Firearms and Explosives (ATF) would trace the gun used to murder Sean Collier, an MIT police officer, four days after the Tsarnaevs detonated the marathon bombs, back to that crew of Eritrean drug dealers, who loaned the gun to Dzhokhar along with the bullets, which he called "food for the dog."[5] It will be shown that Tamerlan's assistance in Operation Run This Town is the likely reason he was never investigated for a grisly triple homicide later in 2011, in which he was clearly implicated.

Four months after the brutal murders, on January 21, 2012, Tamerlan traveled to Russia for six months without a valid passport, even though he was on two terror watch lists. There is evidence that while there he acted at the behest of both American and Russian intelligence to finger Chechen rebels, some of whom were quickly killed. On his return he was guided through customs at John F. Kennedy International Airport, still on the watch lists and still without a passport. It remains unclear how he traveled to New York to fly out of JFK Airport or how he got back to Boston upon his return from Russia.

The *9/11 Commission Report* made tightening border security a key recommendation.[6] Apparently that recommendation did not apply to Tamerlan. There may be a reason — perhaps a deal was made, with promises of mutually advantageous cooperation — that goes beyond lax security.

This book lays out the evidence that I collected over more than six years of reporting, using court documents and police interviews and tracking down dozens of people connected to both the investigation and the Tsarnaev clan. Did US authorities make Tamerlan a promise — if you help us, we will help you — and then renege on it? Did they so embitter their informant that they led him to change sides?

As for where the bombs were made and by whom, it is almost certain the brothers had accomplices who remain at large. In the pages that follow I provide details, ranging from circumstantial evidence to named suspects, that local law enforcement knows about but has not pursued — or perhaps more accurately, has been prevented from pursuing. I don't pretend to have all of the answers, but this story has not gone away, and should not be allowed to go away, until the truth that is needed to protect US citizens and to punish perpetrators is revealed.

Patriots' Day

Amber Woolfenden was running in the Boston Marathon for the first time, a goal she had joined the Wicked Runners Club in Salem, Massachusetts, expressly to achieve. Her husband, Steve, was excited for her as he maneuvered their three-year-old son, Leo, in his stroller — a three-wheeler specially designed with bicycle motocross (BMX) tires for hard-core runners — toward the finish line.

The crowd up and down Boylston Street near the finish line swelled after the Red Sox game ended at 2:08 PM. Leo was happy in his stroller, and Steve found a spot near the Marathon Sports store where he hoped Amber might actually see them as she finished her run, even though roughly twenty-seven thousand runners had left the starting line in Hopkinton, Massachusetts, in several waves since 9 AM. The mobility-impaired athletes had taken off first, followed by the wheelchair racers and then the racers on hand cycles. The elite women were launched at 9:22, followed by the elite men at 9:32. At 10:00 AM the first wave of nine thousand regular runners took off; twenty minutes later the second wave of nine thousand began, and then the final wave of nine thousand left Hopkinton at 10:40 AM.[1] By 12:36 PM the winners had been declared: Ethiopia's Lelisa Desisa won the men's race with a time of 2:10:22, and Rita Jeptoo of Kenya won the women's race with a time of 2:26:25. But thousands of runners were still on the course at 2:49 PM, including Amber.

Steve had planned to meet some friends in front of M Bar, but that wasn't going to happen. It was on the other side of Boylston Street, and there was no way he could cross. So he pulled out his phone, sent them an update via text, and pushed Leo from the store's doorway toward the international flags that lined the last leg of the 26.2-mile race and settled in closer to the finish line. Focused on the runners and waiting for Amber, he didn't notice the backpack on the sidewalk just to the left of Marathon Sports. Then came the boom. It sounded like one of the cannon blasts on the Esplanade on the Fourth of July or at the start of a New England Patriots game. No one knew what it was at first.

Boston Police Department (BPD) Sergeant Dan Keeler knew it wasn't good. He transmitted an urgent message over his police radio: "Stop the race! Stop the race! Send me everything you have to Boylston."[2] Many runners were stopped in Brookline, before they made their way into Boston's Back Bay. Amber Woolfenden was one of them.

"I was in shock and disbelief," Steve would later recall. "It registered that we needed to get out of there. The most logical choice would be to take a one-eighty and go the other way. And we didn't get that opportunity."[3]

Steve spun around and hustled away from the first explosion, headed southwest on Boylston toward the Forum restaurant. He made it exactly 183 feet, moving right into the zone of the second bomb, which detonated thirteen seconds after the first one. This bomb produced an ugly orange fireball more deadly than the first because of the way it was detonated: It was inside a backpack that had been set down sideways so that the fireball from the explosive device inside, improvised from a pressure cooker, blew outward instead of upward. The first bomb had been placed upright and still created the maximum harm intended when it was detonated with a device fashioned from a remote control for a toy car, the sort of thing with which a little boy like Leo might play.

A video would later reveal that in the seconds before the second bomb was detonated, Steve was jostled by a skinny man in a white baseball cap who had been standing near a tree in front of the Forum restaurant and behind a row of children lined up along a metal barricade. Some kids had been leaning on the barricade. Others, like

Martin Richard, had put their feet between the grates and hoisted themselves higher for a better view. With the second blast Steve recalled being hit with an intense heat, a pressure that made him feel like "every part of my body was being punched." He thought he was still standing because he was holding fast to the stroller, but he soon realized that he had been blown to the ground. He yanked back the stroller's cover and saw Leo bleeding. The toddler was screaming over and over again: "Mommy! Daddy! Mommy! Daddy! Mommy! Daddy! Mommy! Daddy! Mommy! Daddy!"

"Leo was conscious. He was alive. He was bleeding from the left side of this head," Steve recalled. He was nauseated by the smell of burning hair and flesh and by the odor of sulfur that enveloped him — a smell like rotten eggs, which cops all around him recognized from their time on the firing range. He heard screams and sirens and saw body parts littered like puzzle pieces. The air was so hot that he felt like he was in front of an opened pizza oven. Steve's main focus was to get his son the hell off Boylston Street.

He reached for Leo and realized that his fingers, oddly, were numb. "That's when I discovered my leg had been severed off." He recognized his boot on the ground, with his sheared-off limb inside. He realized that a glob of what looked like bloodied Scotch tape was in fact his Achilles tendon and knew he had to stop the bleeding. He ripped off his belt and tied it tightly around his thigh.

The buckles on the stroller were mangled, and Steve couldn't unstrap Leo. A stranger knelt next to him, and Steve implored him to help Leo, saying: "My son's bleeding from his head. You need to get him out of here. Please get my son to safety." And the man said, "I will do that but first I'm going to put another tourniquet on your leg."

Then another man, also a stranger, came to Steve's side. Leo was gone, and Steve had no idea whether he would die right there on the sidewalk. The stranger got in his face, Steve remembered, and kept him conscious. "You're going to fucking make it," the man said. "You're going to fucking make it."

Across the street BPD Officer Tommy Barrett didn't know where to start. "There was so many people that were hurt seriously that it was hard to choose who to begin helping first . . . Everybody was hurt really bad, but I was trying to pick who I could help first," he remembered.[4] Barrett ran toward the toppled metal barricade, where the most seriously maimed people — those directly in the blast zone — were fighting for their lives. The Boston cop used his gloved hands to beat out the flames around a man on fire. Another man helped by dousing the man's smoldering flesh with the contents of a beer bottle that had been abandoned on an outside table, and a woman tried to use a cloth napkin as a tourniquet around his critically wounded upper thigh. Three strangers desperately tried to keep one man alive. The man on fire was Marc Fucarile. His flesh was pocked with scalding-hot BB pellets, shrapnel from the bomb. Barely conscious, his body engulfed in flames, his instinct to survive was so strong that he had grabbed for his belt and got third-degree burns on his hands as he pulled it off in desperation, knowing he had to stop the bleeding from his severed leg.

When Fucarile was no longer on fire, Barrett's attention turned toward someone yelling, "There's a kid over here!"

The kid was Leo. Barrett ran toward the child, pulled him to his chest, and carried him like a football across Boylston Street toward Dartmouth Street, where a medical tent had been set up to treat any runners who might be in need of care. Within minutes it transformed from a site for massages and treatment for heatstroke and sprains to a mass casualty response site staffed by a team of doctors, nurses, and volunteers so skillful that every one of the 264 critically injured patients who would be transported to area hospitals survived, including the 17 who had suffered traumatic amputations.[5] Boston Emergency Management Services (EMS) Chief James Hooley set up a system for tagging the wounded: 30 people received red tags, indicating that they were in critical condition and therefore were the first to be transported; 25 patients who were seriously wounded but not at risk of dying immediately got yellow tags, and another 35 who were badly hurt got green tags. In all 118 people were raced to Boston-area hospitals, most within a two-mile radius of the bomb blasts.[6]

A block before Barrett made it to the tent, one of the seventy-three ambulances that would eventually flood the bloodstained street stopped. "I have a young boy," Barrett told the paramedics inside and handed Leo to them before running back toward the boy's father and the mess of charred flesh and congealing blood around him.

"It was brutal," Barrett recalled. "I stepped on somebody's leg. People were missing legs, and you know, the legs were ripped off. It wasn't anything clean or neat. A lot of people had, you know, clothes that were torn, shredded."

He saw a woman sitting up, desperately trying to keep her eviscerated insides within her body. She screamed, her arms flailing, before she went limp. A medical examiner would later determine that she had been conscious for only a minute between being injured and dying. Her name was Lingzi Lu, a twenty-three-year-old Boston University student from China, and her entire body was ripped apart by bomb shrapnel. A jagged, twisted piece of metal was lodged in her leg; another piece of the bomb would later be found in her purse. Lingzi went to the marathon with another Chinese student, Danling Zhou, who would recall holding her own intestines in, her stomach a gaping messy hole of burning flesh, while trying to comfort her friend. "Everyone is panicked. Everyone is asking what's happening. I never think it's a bomb. I tried to calm Lingzi down. Lingzi is holding my arm. I'm about to tell her it's okay, let's go. I never get to say that," Danling recalled, crying.[7]

Observing the young woman in her death throes, Barrett told himself, "There's nothing I can do for her. There were other things I could help people with. Those are the people I had to move to."[8]

Those people included Steve Woolfenden, who at this point had no idea whether he was going to live or die or where his son had been taken. For that matter, Steve had no idea where his wife was. But he was distracted from his own panic by the cries of Denise Richard, who was keening, "Please, Martin. Please, Martin," over her little boy, a piece of shrapnel embedded in her right eye. Steve would later learn that Martin was only eight and, as Mayor Martin Walsh — who succeeded Thomas M. Menino, mayor at the time of the blasts — would come to say repeatedly, had a smile "that could light up Fenway Park."

Martin's entire fifty-three-inch-tall body had been blasted with small nails, tiny pieces of black plastic, round metal pellets, small fragments of wood, and metal pieces of the bomb. He was wearing a Boston Celtics jersey over a New England Patriots T-shirt. Both garments were charred, stained with smoke, ripped, peppered with holes, and blood-soaked.

Martin's father, Bill Richard, was also in a bad way, his pants shredded and a large piece of metal embedded in his leg. He couldn't hear the screams of his family due to ringing in his ears. He could smell the vile odor that filled the air, the scent of spent gunpowder and burning hair. The hair of seven-year-old Jane Richard, Bill's youngest child and only daughter, had been on fire and was smoking. Bill watched, horrified, as she tried to get up but fell back down because her leg was gone. A firefighter would later recall that the little girl's limb looked like it had been put through a meat grinder. Bill made the difficult decision to leave Denise with their dying son and get Jane and their oldest boy, Henry, to a hospital.

"When I saw Martin's condition I knew he wasn't going to make it. I just knew from what I saw that there was no chance, the color of his skin," Bill would recall later, on the stand in the trial of the man who killed his son.[9] "I knew in my head that I needed to act quickly or we might not only lose Martin, but we might lose Jane too." He shielded Jane's eyes as he carried her, Henry clinging to his side. Shock had drained the color from Henry's face.

Steve Woolfenden winced as he watched Martin's eyes roll into the back of his singed head: "I saw a little boy and his mother . . . I saw Martin's face. And I could see a boy that looked like — he was fatally injured." Steve was close enough to reach out and put a comforting hand on Denise Richard's back. She turned to him in a moment of pure humanity to ask, "Are you okay?" He nodded. Denise turned back to Martin as he died.

Not far away Adrianne Haslet-Davis's husband, Adam, was holding her severed lower leg. His own calves were missing chunks of flesh as big as scoops of ice cream, which had been seared away. He was in shock. Adrianne crawled over shattered glass to reach him and began to shout his name, her arms shredded and bleeding. "I screamed Adam! Adam!" she remembered. "I thought that because I couldn't hear myself scream I was dead."[10]

Although the first bomb was not as powerful as the second, it was powerful enough to kill twenty-seven-year-old Krystle Marie Campbell, her daddy's "princess, every father's dream," who — with her best friend, Karen Rand McWatters — was part of the throng of people who pushed their way down Boylston Street after leaving the Red Sox game. Before leaving home, she had given her father a hug, their ritual, and then went with her girlfriend to the game, where they met the men they were dating.

Sometime around 2:00 PM the women had stopped on a bridge in the Boston Public Garden and let a stranger snap their picture. "It was a beautiful day. We were being silly and touristy," Karen recalled.[11] Less than an hour later came the blast that hurled both women to the ground. "I remember lying on the ground wondering if I was dreaming, if I had really made it to the marathon." The force of the explosion snapped Campbell's femur. Her body was covered in burns, and her hair was singed and smoking. She had a BB pellet embedded in the back of her ear, cuts and scrapes on her neck, and contusions on her tongue. Internally, she suffered thermal injuries. Her entire body was hit with pellets, which lodged in her clothes.

Krystle was moaning, and when Karen tried to move closer to her friend she found that her own leg was gone. She used her cut, burned hands to drag herself over shattered glass and white-hot BB pellets to Krystle's side. "I got close to her head, we put our faces together," Karen remembered. "She said very slowly that her legs hurt. Her hand went limp in mine and she never spoke again." A photograph shows a marathon volunteer standing over both women in that very moment with her rubber-gloved hands pressed against their hearts.[12]

Leo Woolfenden wasn't the only child crying for his mother. All Rebekah Gregory could hear, over the incessant ringing that filled her head, was her son, Noah, screaming for her. "I looked down and I couldn't see my legs. My bones were literally on the sidewalk next to me. I thought that was the day I would die," Rebekah would remember.[13] Her eardrums were perforated. She barely felt the skin on her arms being ripped apart by shards of glass on the sidewalk as she tried to crawl to her bleeding son. "I could hear Noah. I don't know how. I could hear my little boy. 'Mommy! Mommy! Mommy!' Over and over again."

Nicole Gross was a tourist, a physical therapist from North Carolina who had come to cheer her mother across the marathon's finish line. She didn't notice the man in the black baseball cap who was behind her right before she fell back in "slow motion." On the ground, she propped herself on her elbows and looked down. It was eerily silent. She could see people's mouths opened in horror, but she couldn't hear anything. "I just screamed for somebody to save me, hear me!"[14] Her eardrums had burst, her left leg was shattered, her right leg had been blown apart, and her right ankle was mangled, her shoe dangling from her severed Achilles tendon. She was in terrible, unimaginable pain. She wasn't alone.

When the first bomb went off, Gillian "Ginny" Reny, an eighteen-year-old high school student, was blown back and saw the "bodies everywhere, blood everywhere." She tried to get up to run but couldn't. "My leg was completely torn apart," she remembered.

"I had nothing to stand on. I was one hundred percent sure I was going to die."[15]

Celeste Corcoran later wished that she could block out what she experienced at 2:49 PM on that Patriots' Day. "I, unfortunately, remember every single detail," she would later say. "I remember being thrown into the air. Landing hard. Not being able to breathe. I remember this thick, thick black heavy smoke. I was choking. There was this deafening silence. My eardrums got blown out."[16] Her husband, Kevin, was terrified but also furious. He held his wife's hand tight, not telling her both of her legs were gone. "This is a terror attack," he said.

He caught himself and began to comfort her: "I love you. You are going to live. I'm not leaving your side. Hold on. Hold on. It's going to be okay." With what little breath she had left, Celeste began to scream.

Kevin was right. People at the Boston Marathon had been attacked in an act of premeditated bloodletting of a sort not seen on US soil since 9/11 — only the 2013 atrocities were committed by homegrown jihadists whose family had emigrated here seeking a better life. On that terrible spring afternoon, no one knew who the perpetrators were. Certainly not Steve Woolfenden, who held hands with a woman he had never met before, Gina DiMartino, as an ambulance transported them to Boston Medical Center. "I wanted to hold someone's hand," Steve would explain.

A cacophony of screams and moans, including some from Steve, filled Boston Medical's emergency room. Then he heard a voice saying, "I'm looking for my husband, Steve," he remembered. "It was my wife's voice. Amber's voice. Amber came and grabbed my head and said, 'Leo is at Children's Hospital. He's okay. He's alive.'"

It would be one of the last two things he'd remember before being raced into surgery; the other was someone tugging his wedding ring from his finger. He woke up in a recovery room, having had his lower left leg amputated. Across town at Boston

Children's Hospital, Leo was suffering from a skull fracture, head laceration, and perforated left eardrum.

———

Things like this didn't happen in Boston, the amputated limbs of seventeen people scattered on sidewalks alongside the lifeless bodies of a child and two young women. This was a scene Americans were familiar with only from footage taken in the aftermath of bombings, usually suicide attacks, in Middle Eastern markets or Israeli cafés. The City on a Hill, birthplace of liberty in America, had never endured such an assault. And its perpetrators were alive and at large.

PART ONE

The Hunters

The Five-Day Search for the
Boston Marathon Bombers

CHAPTER ONE

These Motherfuckers Are Here

The bombs detonated along the finish line left behind "a river of blood," as Assistant US Attorney Steve Mellin would later say.[1] The fireballs came from weapons designed and built to cause maximum harm, intended "not to just kill but destroy." And destroy they did. MBTA buses transported terrified runners and spectators from the bombing site to the Castle at Park Plaza to be reunited with their loved ones, and the area was cordoned off. Business in the Back Bay came to an abrupt halt, and everyone who worked there had to vacate the area. Hundreds of bartenders, waitresses, and retailers were temporarily put out of work because stores, restaurants, and other businesses were damaged or shuttered as a large swath of Boylston Street became a crime scene. Bomb technicians from the Massachusetts State Police (MSP) and the BPD searched the sixty-one bags that had been left at the scene and detonated a suspicious backpack found under the grandstand at the finish line. Crime scene technicians solemnly processed the thousands of BB pellets and pieces of bomb that covered the street. Technicians from the Massachusetts Medical Examiner's Office recovered body parts. Witnesses were interviewed. Video footage was secured. The FBI commandeered an entire hangar at South Boston's Black Falcon Cruise Terminal to set up a makeshift lab to process the evidence. More than twenty different agencies were involved in the hunt for the marathon bombers, and investigators took over two floors of the Westin Copley Place hotel to set up a command post. Residents of Boston and all of its suburbs and surrounding cities and suburbs were afraid to leave their homes. Uncertainty about what would happen next was reflected in the "terror on the faces of the people of Boston," remembered BPD Superintendent Billy Evans.[2]

Evans had been among the thirty thousand runners, the eighteenth time he had participated in the Boston Marathon and his forty-seventh marathon overall. He ran the 26.2-mile course from Hopkinton to the Back Bay hearing the cheers of his officers who whooped for him along the entire route until he reached the finish line, where his wife, Terry, and their son, Will, welcomed him with hugs and congratulations. He had made good time, he noted, smiling — three hours and thirty-four minutes. Not bad for a beat-up old guy from Southie whose fifty-four-year-old wiry frame had taken plenty of abuse when he had been a patrolman chasing bad guys down Boston's streets. Evans liked to say that he was more runner than cop. His superintendent's office at One Schroeder Plaza — which serves as BPD headquarters and is named for two murdered police officers (the brothers Walter and John Schroeder, both of whom were shot and killed on the job) — is decorated with his marathon medals, dozens of them in frames on the wall. Evans was reminded of the Schroeder brothers every working day, and the terrorist attack on Boylston Street was a gruesome reminder of how Walter had died at the hands of a domestic terrorist group.

In 1973, John Schroeder was shot dead when he interrupted a pawnshop robbery in the Roxbury section of Boston. It was a horrible loss for his family and the entire city, whose residents knew the story of Walter Schroeder, a Boston patrolman who had been murdered by the notorious group of anarchists known as the Weather Underground.

In a 2004 press release about its history, the FBI described the group this way:

> The Weather Underground — originally called the Weathermen, taken from a line in a Bob Dylan song — was a small, violent offshoot of the Students for a Democratic Society (SDS), created in the turbulent '60s to promote social change. When the SDS collapsed

in 1969, the Weather Underground stepped forward, inspired by communist ideologies and embracing violence and crime as a way to protest the Vietnam War, racism, and other left-wing aims. "Our intention is to disrupt the empire . . . to incapacitate it, to put pressure on the cracks," claimed the group's 1974 manifesto, *Prairie Fire*. By the next year, the group had claimed credit for 25 bombings and would be involved in many more over the next several years.[3]

Those bombings were expensive, and in the late 1960s and early 1970s many members robbed banks to fund attacks. Those who styled themselves as worthy successors to the Islamic extremists who orchestrated 9/11 had the same goal — to "disrupt the empire."

Walter Schroeder's killers were two women from wealthy families who attended Brandeis University, a male classmate of theirs studying social work, and three other men, career criminals, who had met at the state prison in Walpole and then been paroled. The Weather Underground used bombs and bullets to protest the Vietnam War; Islamic extremists used bombs and bullets to protest US interventions in the Middle East. In both cases innocent people died.

On September 23, 1970, Walter Schroeder, a World War II veteran with nineteen years on the police force and a wife and nine kids at home, responded to a silent alarm at the State Street Bank and Trust in the Brighton neighborhood of Boston. He arrived at the bank minutes after Katherine Power and Susan Saxe, both twenty-one, and their Brandeis classmate Michael Fleischer, twenty-two — along with the parolees William "Lefty" Gilday, forty-one; Robert Valeri, twenty-one; and Stanley Bond, twenty-six — had broken in and stolen $26,000 from a bank vault. Gilday had been a minor-league baseball player from Amesbury when he went to the Walpole state prison for bank robbery. While he was behind bars, he met Bond, a Vietnam War helicopter pilot with a lengthy rap sheet for petty crimes; and Valeri, a small-time hood from Somerville. The three crooks entered a program that helped convicts get into prestigious universities — which was how they met their wealthy coconspirators. The Brighton bank robbery was intended to help fund a revolution, and it was not their first.

When Schroeder climbed out of his cruiser just before midnight, Gilday fired his rifle, shooting and killing the officer, and the perpetrators fled. The murder triggered an unprecedented police response involving every law enforcement agent and National Guardsman in the vicinity. Bond, Fleischer, and Valeri were apprehended within days. Saxe was on the lam for five years before she was arrested and sentenced to seven years in prison; Power eluded authorities until 1993, when she turned herself in and served six years in prison.

The search for Gilday has been described as the largest manhunt in New England history.[4] After a wild firefight and a long police chase using MSP helicopters, Gilday was captured. He was later convicted and sentenced to death, a sentence that would be commuted only when Massachusetts abolished the death penalty in 1982.

More than three decades later, Superintendent Billy Evans, who was called "Mousy" by his closest peers, would be involved in the same sort of hunt that his predecessors had undertaken for Gilday, one that — like the 1970 hunt — would end in a wild firefight with a domestic terrorist.

———

When the first bomb detonated at 2:49 PM, Evans was soaking in the hot tub at his neighborhood gym, the South Boston Athletic Club (known as the BAC). He had earned the indulgence after running the marathon and was looking forward to having a few beers. Thirteen seconds later came the second blast, and within minutes one of his men, Detective Cecil Jones, ran into the gym to break the news: "Superintendent, I think two bombs just went off in Copley Square." Evans jumped out of the hot tub, showered, double-parked in front his South Boston home, kissed his wife, put on his uniform, and raced back to the finish line. The scaffolding with the massive blue-and-yellow emblem for the Boston Athletic Association was shredded. The windows of businesses were blown out. Body parts were strewn on the street he had run down a short time before. Bomb parts were everywhere. The entire street stank of burned flesh and sulfur's rotten egg smell. "It was unbelievable. Surreal. I could see the terror on people's faces, the fear." Evans remembered thinking, "Stuff like this only happens in a movie."

But there was work to do. An unknown enemy had attacked the city, and no one knew why. Only the names of the dead were known: Martin Richard, Lingzi Lu, Krystle Marie Campbell. The victims' bodies remained on Boylston Street for hours, part of the active FBI crime scene, but the remains were not left alone, not even for a moment. "They were ours," BPD Captain Frank Armstrong, who had been a street cop and commander in Dorchester, would say.[5] He stood guard over Martin's body, making sure that the FBI forensic experts were respectful of the smallest bombing victim and, more important, that his body was not unattended for even a second.

Armstrong would not stand guard alone. As investigators from the FBI and the BPD crime scene squad analyzed the carnage and looked for the attackers around the clock, chasing down every lead and even using overhead drones, BPD Officers James Scopa and William Zubrin honored little Martin alongside their captain, staying with the body into the night. Lingzi had her own sentry: BPD bomb technician Frank Deary stood by her body near the ruins of the Forum restaurant, which was an eerie sight with blood-splattered lunches and melted drinks still set up on the white tablecloths covering patio tables. Not far away — near Marathon Sports, the site of the first blast — BPD Officer Paul Downing watched over Krystle's body. Other police officers joined the uniformed Boston cops as they waited until after midnight, when the medical examiner's staff finally moved the victims from Boylston Street to the morgue on Albany Street.

As his officers watched over the dead, Evans met BPD Commissioner Ed Davis and Deputy Superintendent Dan Linskey, and together they went to work taking care of the city and its panicked residents, tourists, and the officers under them. Evans had been up since 5:00 AM on Monday for the race and was afraid to stop moving. "As long as my legs were active, my mind was active," he would later say.

The FBI took over Boylston Street, but it was still the BPD's job to secure the crime scene. "That means nobody gets into it. No one touches evidence," Evans commanded his twenty-one hundred police officers. It wasn't easy. Main roads through Boston such as Newbury Street and Huntington Avenue had been shut down. The hotels near Boylston Street had to be evacuated, along with many of the homes in the Back Bay. "It had to be emptied out to preserve the integrity of all that evidence."

The last thing anyone needed was more people in the city. The Boston Bruins canceled Monday night's hockey game at the TD Garden, although some players had already arrived. All Boston police officers were ordered to start working twelve-hour shifts, which they were happy to do. Everyone wanted to catch whoever was responsible. By 4:54 PM on Monday, Mayor Menino had checked himself out of Brigham and Women's Hospital, where he had been getting cancer treatments (he had also undergone surgery just days earlier for a broken leg), and made his way to the ballroom at the Westin hotel, which was serving as a makeshift, and chaotic, command center. The ballroom had only one hardwired landline, which was commandeered by Richard DesLauriers, the FBI special agent in charge of the Boston field office, so he could talk to people in Washington. There were also calls from President Barack Obama to Menino and Governor Deval Patrick to express his condolences. By 8:50 PM on Monday, the last patient injured in the blasts had been tended to. But the bloody aftermath was far from over.

The next four days would be a blur of evidence collection, asking anyone with pictures or video footage of the marathon to turn those items over to the FBI, and dealing with the belongings that runners and others had left behind in their panic. So many cops and federal agents flooded into the city that many of them were forced to sleep in their cars in the FBI garage at One Center Plaza. By late Monday night a charity, the One Fund, had been set up, and donations from all around the world began pouring in.

On Tuesday the FBI searched a Revere Beach apartment belonging to a young Saudi they initially called a "person of interest" and were photographed by multiple members of the news media as they carried large bags out of the Ocean Avenue apartment building, sparking wild speculation about the apartment's occupant. In fact, twenty-two-year-old Abdulrahman Ali Alharbi was living in the Boston suburb on a full scholarship from Saudi Arabia to study in America. The second blast had blown him into the street, and he had arrived at the hospital covered in other victims' blood. Boston police officers and the FBI grilled him there, and uniformed police officers were stationed outside his hospital room overnight. On April 16, less than twenty-four hours after the marathon attacks, Secretary of State John Kerry had a meeting with Saudi Arabian Foreign Minister Saud Al-Faisal, a member of the Saudi royal family, that had been slated to be open to the press. At the last minute, reporters were shut out of the meeting. Matt Lee, an Associated Press reporter covering the State Department, was furious and lashed out at Kerry's spokesperson. "Are you really trying to say that this [meeting was moved] for scheduling reasons? Is that seriously your answer: that because the secretary was tired after ten days on the road and is going to the Hill tomorrow?" Lee asked. "It doesn't wash. I find it hard to believe that you expect us to believe that's the real reason."

The next day, on April 17, President Obama also had an unscheduled meeting with the Saudi foreign minister and his National Security Adviser, Tom Donilon, at the White House. His spokeswoman told reporters the two discussed Syria during the closed-door meeting. There was no mention of the Saudi student being eyed in connection with the Boston Marathon attacks. But hours later authorities announced that the Saudi student hospitalized under police guard, whose apartment was searched by the FBI, with boxes of materials removed, was a witness and not a suspect. On April 18, Homeland Security Secretary Janet Napolitano would testify to Congress that Ali Alharbi had been put on a watch list by her department but then removed. "He was never a subject. He was never really a person of interest," she said.[6]

Also on Tuesday the FBI announced that the bombers had carried heavy black bags or black backpacks that had contained bombs made out of pressure cookers. Agents had recovered a vital piece of evidence: the bottom of one of the converted pressure cookers. It had been blasted a hundred feet into the air and found on the rooftop of a hotel. Stamped onto the bottom of the six-quart container was its brand name, Fagor. The pressure cooker was made in Europe and sold at only one department store in the United States, Macy's. That night the NBA canceled the Boston Celtics basketball game at the TD Garden.

On Wednesday, Mayor Menino returned to Brigham and Women's Hospital for cancer treatment, and his cabinet held a meeting there to discuss recovery priorities for the city, including getting people back to work. Napolitano announced that the FBI wanted to speak with individuals seen in at least one video recovered from the Boylston Street crime scene, but she did not elaborate. Then at around 1:00 PM, CNN reported — erroneously — that a suspect was in custody, which sparked a rush to the John Joseph Moakley United States Courthouse in South Boston. As the media surrounded the building, a bomb threat was called in, and the courthouse was evacuated. Once the threat was determined to be a hoax, the building reopened — but by then all proceedings had been canceled.

————

By Thursday, Evans hadn't stopped moving for four days. At 5:20 PM the FBI held a press conference at the Westin. FBI agents had identified two men wanted in connection with the horrific blasts. "We consider them to be armed and extremely dangerous," DesLauriers told reporters.[7] As he spoke, grim-faced agents flanked two massive posters of the wanted terrorists — with ARMED AND DANGEROUS written at the bottom. "No one should approach them," DesLauriers said. "No one should attempt to apprehend them except law enforcement. Let me reiterate that caution. Do not take action on your own."

The release of the suspects' photos did nothing to soothe frayed nerves. In fact, in some ways the pictures just heightened fears. The bombers, still images taken from a grainy security camera feed at Whiskey's bar on Boylston Street, looked like a thousand other Boston college kids in frat-boy weekend wear. The suspects were white boys with baseball caps and black backpacks jostling through a crowd of other white boys with baseball caps enjoying the spring sunshine and cheering friends and relatives toward the finish line. They could be anywhere. They could be anyone. Nerves had been frayed before DesLauriers's announcement, but after the press conference, strangers were eyed with additional suspicion. Unattended vehicles were seen as potentially explosives-packed weapons of mass destruction.

Not surprisingly, residents of Cambridge began calling 911 to report suspicious idling vehicles near their homes. The first call came at 6:02 PM from a woman who told a Cambridge police dispatcher that a green Ford Explorer was parked near her home at Hamilton and Magazine Streets. After making the call she stood in the street to wait for the officer the dispatcher said would be coming. She flagged down Sergeant Rob Lowe when he arrived at the scene.

The last thing any police officer wanted to do that night was spend the shift following up on unsupported tips from terrified Cambridge residents. Even before the pictures were released, there

had been nonstop calls about unattended bags and tips about innocent Muslims. It had been an exhausting four days, and the FBI's
press conference was a clear signal that no one in the law enforcement community would be getting rest anytime soon. Every police
radio was crackling nonstop with calls to 911, reports of suspicious vehicles, transmissions from fellow officers, and orders from
dispatchers — all becoming a confusing stream of white noise.
Lowe was responding to one of those calls.

"This car has been parked in front of my house forever. It looks
suspicious. There was another one earlier. Can you come check it
out?" the woman who made the call asked Lowe, pointing to the
Ford Explorer with a man behind the wheel. A Cambridge Police
Department report of the dispatch details the actions Lowe took:

Lowe ran the license plate on the computer in his cruiser, but it
came up as obstructed — a sign that the person in the vehicle may
have been working in an undercover capacity. He approached the
vehicle. "We got a report of a suspicious vehicle," Lowe told the
driver. "Can I ask why you are parked here?"

"Just waiting for somebody. I'll be leaving in a little bit," the
driver said. He then drove off. The person he was "waiting for" was
apparently not going to show up.

At 6:15 PM, after the Ford Explorer had pulled away, Lowe
spotted another SUV around the corner on Erie Street. This
one was a Chevy Tahoe with smoked-out, or intentionally dark-
tinted, windows. This vehicle's license plate number was strange,
too, partially covered by a bicycle rack mounted to the back. The
rear window on the passenger side slid down as Lowe got close,
congressional investigators would later learn when they interviewed multiple Cambridge police officials who had concerns
about what had happened that night.

"Sir," Lowe said, "can I ask why you are parked here?"

The driver twisted his upper body toward the sergeant at his
passenger-side window and grunted, "I'm with the FBI."

"Okay, I need to see some ID."

The driver fumbled in the vehicle's console next to him and pulled out a wallet, flipping it open and holding it out to Lowe with the ID extended.

"Can you hand it to me?"

"No."

The sergeant was taken aback. "Sir, I need to see your ID."

"I'm with the FBI. Can you please leave?"

"I need to see your ID," Lowe repeated.

"I'm not giving it to you, dude," the driver said.

Lowe climbed back into his cruiser and reported in, according to the Cambridge Police Department report. "STOPPED A VEHICLE. PARTIALLY OBSTRUCTED PLATE. PERSON INSIDE ID'ED SELF AS FED AGENT. WOULD NOT PRESENT ID TO CAR 18." As Lowe spoke with the dispatcher, the SUV took off.

Then at 6:35 PM Cambridge Police Officer Peter Vellucci spotted a vehicle near Allston and Brookline Streets, just a few blocks away, that matched the description Lowe had called in. He followed it, calling his location in to the dispatch officer. According to the report, ten minutes later another SUV with a "sketchy guy" began to follow Vellucci's cruiser. Both SUVs had obstructed license plates. That meant only one thing to local police: The drivers were feds.

That kind of outright disrespect was unnerving, even given the fact that the FBI and law enforcement agencies in Massachusetts had never fully enjoyed a courtesy-filled relationship. There had been the James "Whitey" Bulger debacle, in which leaders of the FBI's Boston field office had put a murderous drug dealer on their payroll as a way to advance their own careers. There had also been a congressional investigation into an unholy alliance between the FBI and an East Boston mob-boss-turned-informant that had been made public months earlier, despite the bureau's efforts to keep the arrangement a secret from the MSP, the Essex County District Attorney's Office, and even the attorney general of Massachusetts.

Clearly something was going on in Cambridge that night that the feds did not want to share with local law enforcement officials. All week there had been whispers about arguments at the Black Falcon Cruise Terminal evidence center. Ten separate viewing stations with computer terminals had been set up there along three rows to review the 655 videos that the FBI had collected as part of the investigation. Cops and agents sat side by side looking for anyone in the footage who seemed out of place or nervous, or who was carrying a black backpack — pieces of which had been found in the flesh of some of the marathon bombing victims and collected by FBI forensic examiners at hospitals all over the city. Off to one side, remembered one veteran BPD homicide investigator, two FBI agents sat alone. They didn't introduce themselves. They didn't mingle. Instead they compared photos in their laps with photos on their computer screen, a detail corroborated by other witnesses who requested anonymity. The FBI had sent an expert from its Forensic Audio, Video, and Image Analysis Unit, Special Agent Anthony Imel, from his lab at Quantico, Virginia, to Boston to oversee the data collection. Imel did not appear to have any oversight of the FBI agents sitting by themselves, the witnesses said. A local FBI special agent, Kevin Swindon, who supervised the Boston division's Computer Analysis Response Team, didn't either. He was too busy analyzing a security tape taken from inside the Forum restaurant, which in a clear and horrifying way showed the second blast. "We had numerous amounts of employees watching this video over and over and over again," he would later tell ABC News. "We couldn't see anything that stuck out."[8]

One man from the US Drug Enforcement Agency (DEA) finally could not take it any longer. He stood up and confronted the duo: "What are you guys looking at?" There was no response. A retired investigator who was there later recalled in an interview conducted on background that the DEA agent said, "Fuck you guys. You know who these mutts are and you're not sharing!" The agent stormed out. But his words stuck with the other officers and agents still looking at videos at their separate viewing stations. Those FBI agents were not seen at the evidence center again.

Multiple police officers assigned to work at the Black Falcon Cruise Terminal but not authorized to speak on the record have told me: "They knew. They held it [the information] for days. They knew."

———

The story about the strange encounters between the Cambridge Police Department and the FBI would be repeated over and over again, reaching police officers in Cambridge by Thursday and eventually being recounted to investigators from Senator Charles Grassley's office. After the release of photos of "Suspect Black Hat" and "Suspect White Hat," as the two perpetrators were now labeled, Cambridge cops surmised that FBI surveillance in SUVs with obstructed plates meant the bureau had a lead on the identities of the bombers they did not share with the city's police department, their purported law enforcement partners.

Among the cops concerned about what the FBI knew was Rob Lowe, who called his lieutenant, Chris Bertolino, on the Cambridge Police Department's primary dispatch line and asked him to switch over to a supervisory channel, according to radio transmissions.

"Do you know anything about the FBI being around here?" Lowe asked.

Bertolino didn't. Neither did anyone else. Nothing mattered more to local law enforcement than catching the marathon bombers, and if the FBI knew the bombers might be in Cambridge, they should have taken advantage of the eyes, ears, and expertise of the uniformed personnel in the city. Even if FBI agents didn't want to share their information, they didn't need to be belligerent.

At roughly 9:30 PM on Thursday, traffic on Brookline Street, which was used as a way to get from Memorial Drive to Central Square, was at a standstill. Even the police couldn't get through. Another Cambridge police supervisor, who asked not to be identified, drove the wrong way down Brookline Street to find an MBTA bus stopped in the middle of the street. Cambridge detectives were standing nearby.

"What the hell is going on?" the supervisor remembers demanding.

"We have no fucking idea," a Cambridge police officer answered. "The FBI asked us to stop the bus."

An MBTA bus stopped in the middle of a main drag was a problem. Police would later say that FBI agents climbed aboard and escorted someone off. To this day no one knows who, and the FBI isn't talking about it.

"Tell that fucking bus driver to move the fucking bus," another Cambridge police supervisor barked. Traffic was backing up all the way into Central Square, causing commotion along another main thoroughfare, Massachusetts Avenue. That's when a man approached the group of Cambridge officers, several witnesses recalled, and introduced himself as John Foley, the assistant special agent in charge of the FBI's Boston field office.

Foley was apologetic. He tried to smooth things over and explained that there were agents from all over the country working in Cambridge, and he couldn't control some of them. There was nothing to worry about, Foley said.

Cambridge Police Commissioner Robert Haas arrived on the scene. Rank-and-file cops watched as the men talked excitedly in the street. There was mass confusion in Cambridge. Agents from the FBI's mobile surveillance team scowled at police officers and vice versa. Tensions were high and getting higher.

"These motherfuckers are here," cops began to muse aloud to one another. It was clear to the Cambridge police officers on duty that the FBI had likely identified the two baseball-cap-wearing lunatics who had left the bombs on Boylston Street. They just weren't sharing the information — as usual.

Lowe drove home, but he didn't have a chance to change out of his uniform or talk to his wife or four kids before the next tragedy was broadcast over every police radio in the vicinity of Cambridge. The voice of Massachusetts Institute of Technology (MIT) Police Sergeant Clarence Henniger, recognized by many of his police partners in the city, screeched, "Officer down! Officer down!" Sean Collier, an MIT police officer, had been murdered in cold blood, shot in the head as he sat in his cruiser on campus. Could the perpetrators be Suspect Black Hat and Suspect White Hat, the very men many Cambridge police believe the FBI had been searching for in Cambridge? If in fact the FBI had known the identity of the baseball-cap-wearing bombers and had shared that information with local law enforcement agents, would Sean Collier be alive today?

That was a question that would eventually be asked on Capitol Hill by federal lawmakers — in particular, Senator Grassley. After meeting with multiple MIT police officers and Cambridge police officials, Grassley fired off a letter to FBI Director James Comey, new to the job after replacing Robert Mueller, that contained some pointed questions. Grassley wrote, "Uniformed members of the Cambridge Police Department encountered multiple teams of FBI employees conducting surveillance. It is unclear who the FBI was watching." He then asked Comey: "Was the FBI conducting surveillance in the area of Central Square in the City of Cambridge on the night MIT Officer Sean Collier was shot dead?"[9] Finally he said, "Continued reluctance for the FBI to share information with local law enforcement . . . would be extremely troubling."

The outrage was bipartisan. Congressman Bill Keating of Massachusetts, a former Norfolk County district attorney in the state until his 2010 election, also wrote to Comey. He was a man who understood the machinations of ongoing investigations, but, he would fume, there was no excuse for the FBI to obstruct congressional inquiries. "As a former District Attorney, I understand the sensitivities surrounding an ongoing investigation," he wrote to Comey. "However, none of the questions I have would compromise the integrity of the investigation into the bombings.

I'm not looking to place blame. What I am looking to do is identify our security shortcomings and change them. Without forthright information from the FBI, we are prevented from taking the critical steps needed to protect the American public. It is my hope that Director Comey makes this a priority because I intend to keep demanding answers until I receive them."

Those answers would not come. To this day the FBI categorically denies knowing who the bombers were before one of them was killed in the gun battle that famously ensued later that night. On October 18, 2013, the FBI's Boston field office released a strongly worded statement after Grassley's letter became public: "There has been recent reporting relating to whether or not the FBI, Boston Police, Massachusetts State Police, or other members of the Joint Terrorism Task Force knew the identities of the bombers before the shootout with the alleged marathon bombing suspects and were conducting physical surveillance of them on April 18, 2013. These claims have been repeatedly refuted by the FBI, Boston Police, and Massachusetts State Police. To be absolutely clear: No one was surveilling the [bombers], and they were not identified until after the shootout. Any claims to the contrary are false."[10]

Local law enforcement officials were highly skeptical of the FBI's denials. Cops from all over the country had flooded Boston as part of a manhunt for the terrorists who detonated two bombs at a sporting event and the FBI claimed to have sent a team to Cambridge for an unrelated event? In the very same neighborhood the world would soon learn the Tsarnaev brothers had lived since 2002? The night of Collier's death the question became not just what the FBI might be trying to hide, but also who. And of course, why?

That speculation became more urgent at 12:51 AM on Friday, April 19, when two of their own, BPD Detective Ken Conley and MSP Lieutenant Dan Wells, were nearly shot to death by friendly fire when their unmarked MSP pickup truck was mistaken for a vehicle that had been erroneously reported stolen. Both men were assigned to the North Shore Gang Task Force; they had been on duty in the area of Cambridge when the "officer down" call came through, and they had responded to it. Then came another urgent message from a Watertown police officer: "Shots fired." As they made their way toward Watertown on Adams a "be on the look-out" (BOLO) warning was issued for "an unmarked black MSP pickup truck."[11]

An MSP trooper spotted an unmarked black MSP pickup truck traveling on Adams Street and opened fire. The trooper's twenty-one shots pierced the vehicle, but miraculously the two cops inside were not hit. One of the bullets was lodged in the headrest on the driver's side, just inches from where Conley was sitting (both men were later honored at the White House by President Barack Obama). Still, no explanation was ever given of how the two members of the NSGTF made it to Watertown so quickly. And multiple law enforcement agents noted that on Thursday night the same vehicle had been in the same area of Cambridge where the FBI vehicles had been spotted, an area that police would soon learn was the bombers' neighborhood.

Commissioner Davis would soon raise his own questions about the FBI very publicly at a congressional hearing, at which FBI agents steadfastly refused to show up to provide answers.

CHAPTER TWO

Get on It

April 18 started early and ended late for all Massachusetts law enforcement officials. With the marathon bombers still at large, President Barack Obama came to town that morning for an interfaith service to honor the bombing victims at the historic Cathedral of the Holy Cross in Boston's South End, the mother church for Boston Catholics. More than two thousand people crowded the pews — many of them dignitaries and politicians, including Governor Deval Patrick and his predecessor, Mitt Romney; and Secretary of State John Kerry, a Bostonian. Massachusetts Senators Elizabeth Warren and Ed Markey were there as well, along with most of the congressional delegation from the commonwealth and officials from every Massachusetts police agency. The politicians sat among relatives of the first bomb's victim, Krystle Marie Campbell, and teachers from the Neighborhood House Charter School, where the marathon bombing's youngest victim, Martin Richard, had been a beloved student.

Both the president and First Lady Michelle Obama had spent time in Boston as Harvard University students, a point that the president referred to in his remarks from the altar: "Boston is your hometown, but we claim it a little bit too."[1] At that point the president looked at Boston Mayor Thomas Menino, whose longtime friend BPD Deputy Superintendent Dan Linskey had wheeled him into the service, his broken leg in a cast. He had repeatedly checked himself out of his cancer treatments at Brigham and Women's Hospital to attend briefings at the makeshift command center at the Westin Copley Place hotel. Officers told me on background that the mayor refused to take painkillers for his broken leg or the fast-moving cancer — which would take his life in October 2014 — so he could be clearheaded. During the service he hoisted himself out of his wheelchair, his face twisted with pain, and talked about his beloved city. "We are one Boston. Nothing can tear down the resilience of this city."[2]

As uplifting as the service proved to be, it had been a security nightmare for police department heads who had put in long hours every day since the deadly blasts. To make matters worse, there was the awkward matter of disinviting Suhaib Webb from appearing on the dais with the president and other dignitaries, though he still attended the service. Webb was the imam of the Islamic Society of Boston Cultural Center, a conglomerate that includes a large mosque in Roxbury and the smaller mosque on Prospect Street in Cambridge, but he could not pass a Secret Service background check. In the end another leader of the Muslim community took his place. Webb publicly complained on his Twitter page about being disinvited, telling his followers that he had been replaced but not explaining why. In the previous days Webb had been an outspoken critic of the Boston Marathon attack and had condemned the cowards who dropped the bombs as "criminals and enemies of society" on his Twitter page. The Islamic Society of Boston Cultural Center had offered trauma counseling and urged congregants to cooperate with the FBI if agents came calling. Still, Webb could not shake off some of his past associations with radicals like so-called Lady Al Qaeda, Aafia Siddiqui, who had been convicted in 2010 of attempted murder and armed assault on US officers, and with other convicted terrorists who had prayed at his mosque.[3]

The Siddiqui situation led to nagging concerns for MIT Police Chief John DiFava. Siddiqui had been an MIT student, and it was clear that the bombings had been an act of terrorism. DiFava knew that Webb, an imam familiar on the MIT campus because of the Cambridge mosque's proximity for Muslim students, had just been disinvited from a position near the president of the United States. DiFava was also receiving demands about every fifteen minutes from MIT administrators for updates on the bombing investigation and manhunt. Calls from panicked parents of students (both Americans and foreigners) were flooding his department's phone lines. When DiFava finally pulled out of the Stata building's parking garage just after 9:35 PM on Friday, expecting to head home for the night to care for his ailing mother, he was tired. That's when he saw one of his officers, Sean Collier. DiFava pulled alongside Collier's cruiser to say hello.

———

Collier was a born cop. When he was three years old, he told his mother that he was going to be a police officer. When he played cowboys and Indians, he was always the sheriff. Even as a little boy, one of six children in a blended family, he would squeal when he saw a police car and make whooping siren noises until one of his siblings begged him to shut up. By the time he graduated from high school he was already on his way toward achieving that goal, working as a volunteer auxiliary police officer in his hometown of Somerville, Massachusetts. He would become the youngest Somerville Police Department auxiliary officer ever to be promoted to sergeant. He paid his own way through the MBTA's Transit Police Academy, knowing that despite his high score on the civil service test, veterans received preference on civil service hiring lists, and he had not served in the armed forces. With veterans on the list ahead of him, Collier knew that going through the academy on his own dime would help him with police commanders doing the hiring. His self-funded police academy training would save any department that hired him from having to pay for it. To this day he holds the record for the highest grade point average of any graduate of the academy, an accomplishment that led to his hiring by the MIT Police Department.

DiFava liked Collier. He was a go-getter, willing to jump into any fray, without being a hothead. He was the type of cop who would quietly let homeless people into a warm basement on campus. Against the rules? Sure, but it was still the right thing to do. He was good at bantering with the college kids and had solid relationships with other officers. DiFava would be sorry to lose him, though he was happy for Collier, who was just three weeks away from realizing his childhood dream of becoming a full-time Somerville police officer.

DiFava and Collier chatted in their cars for about three or four minutes about the bombers, whose photos had been released hours earlier. Then DiFava said good-bye.

"Be safe," the chief called out his window.[4] Collier nodded.

Earlier Collier had been in the dispatch area with his buddies David Sacco and Joe West, watching the press conference the FBI held at 5:20 PM. A video of the suspects had been released and posted on the FBI's website. It had been found among the footage reviewed at the Black Falcon Cruise Terminal, and within hours of its release it had been seen by millions. It showed a taller man in a black hat walking down Boylston Street, with a shorter man in a white hat behind him. The FBI said that the two men were the bombers, and they were armed and dangerous.

At roll call that night, MIT officers would later recall, Collier pointed to Suspect Black Hat and remarked, "This guy looks familiar. I think I have seen him around campus." Other officers looked at the image and shrugged. Both suspects looked like typical MIT students: white guys wearing baseball caps and carrying backpacks.

Collier was assigned to sector 1–2, two sections of the east part of MIT's campus. The assignment included walking a route around some of the main buildings. He climbed into cruiser 285 and started the routine business of the night: having improperly parked cars towed and making sure suspicious characters weren't lurking around the campus. Sacco was working the desk, monitoring 911 calls and radio traffic from nearby police departments.

"This lady's not too happy her car's gone," Collier texted Sacco not long after he and DiFava parted company. Everything seemed mundane, routine — just another night as a campus cop. Collier and Sacco made plans to meet after their shift and waited for 11:00 PM to come.

Then Sacco received a 911 call at the desk: "MIT Police. Call recorded. Officer Sacco."[5]

"Hi. Umm . . . we're in the Koch Institute," postdoctoral student James Van Deventer said. "We're hearing a lot of loud noises outside of our window. They don't sound exactly like gunshots but they're sharp quick noises. There is a police officer who seems to be, umm, seems to be in the vicinity in a car but we really don't know what's going on. So yeah, do you have any information?"

Sacco asked for more information. "On the Stata side or the Main Street side?"

"On the Stata side."

"And you're hearing — how do you describe the noises?"

"It sounds like somebody's hitting a trash can really loud. Something along those lines."

"There's an officer in a cruiser near there?"

"There's a cruiser that's right by there," Van Deventer answered.

"Okay, we will check it out."

The Stata side of the building was in Collier's patrol area. Sacco picked up the radio to dispatch him to the scene. "Sector 1–2 respond to suspicious noises or loud noises near Koch building, Stata side."

No response. He tried again. Silence. Sacco then tried calling Collier's cell phone. The radio had been acting up lately, ever since construction to expand the campus had begun. The call went right to voice mail. Sacco sent Collier a text. No response. Another call over the radio. No answer.

"Other units, I am trying to raise sector 1–2. No response."

Sergeant Clarence Henniger keyed his radio microphone. "What is the nature of the call?"[6] He had worked with Collier since the latter joined the MIT police force. It wasn't like Collier not to answer. He was not the type of cop to "take a slide"— leave early, hoping the bosses wouldn't notice. Nor was he the type to chat up a young female student and ignore the radio.

"We just got a call about loud noise, drums, some sort of loud noise coming from the direction where Collier was," Sacco responded.

"Use the emergency alert button," Henniger instructed Sacco and turned his cruiser around to head back to Vassar and Main Streets, sure that Collier was already answering the call. He dialed Collier's cell phone, twice, and got voice mail both times. And Collier made no response to the emergency alert tone, especially odd for a cop like Collier. Henniger's stomach twisted. Something was wrong.

He saw Collier's parked cruiser. Its lights were on, the driver's-side door and window were open, and the engine was running. Henniger threw his own cruiser into park and ran up to the driver's side of Collier's car. Collier had been shot three times in the head and three times in the right hand. His body was leaning toward the passenger seat, which was soaked with blood. Blood was everywhere: splattered all over Collier's radio and shining slickly on his gun belt, pooled in the front seat, and even spotted on the can of sugar-free Red Bull in the cup holder. A 9-millimeter shell casing sat in a pool of congealing blood on Collier's seat, and there was another on the passenger seat and a third lodged under the carpeting. Copper projectiles littered the cruiser floor. Collier's handheld microphone had been ruined by gunfire. His police hat rested on the passenger seat.

"Oh my goodness! All units respond!" Henniger shouted into his own radio. "Officer down! Officer down! *All units*, officer down!"

He checked for a pulse and knew that Collier wasn't going to make it. He screeched his last order for an ambulance. "Get on it!"

West responded, sickened: "Sarge, we got everything on it."

Henniger noticed a gunshot wound in Collier's left temple and another one in his neck. Clearly Collier had been shot as he reached for his microphone, because there was a hole through his right hand. Henniger looked around, panicked. The scene might still be hot — whoever was responsible for executing a cop, his friend, might still be nearby, perhaps even in a bush somewhere, waiting to ambush another cop.

Henniger reached over and took Collier's pulse again, hoping his heart was still thumping. The pulse was slight, and Collier was barely breathing. Blood was gurgling out of his mouth.

Another cruiser screeched to the scene forty-five seconds after Henniger's arrival. West, momentarily stunned, froze in place, and Henniger looked at him: "Let's get him out."

West grabbed Collier's shoulders, Henniger his legs, and the two men tried to lift their friend gently out of the car. The slickness of blood everywhere made it hard for the two men to get a grip.

"You'll be okay," West repeated to Collier over and over. "Just hang in there. Hang in there. You'll be okay." But everyone knew Collier would not be okay. He had been shot at such close range that there were muzzle burns on his head, including one from a bullet that had been fired directly between his eyes. Collier never had a chance to pull the .45-caliber Smith and Wesson locked in the gun holster of his duty belt. There was a bullet still in the service weapon's chamber, and its magazine was loaded with ten more. His killer or killers had tried to yank the weapon out of his gun belt, but service weapons for police officers are holstered in specially made retention systems so that they cannot simply be pulled out.

Another magazine was attached to Collier's duty belt, which was bloody and — investigators would later discover — covered with his killer's fingerprints. There were spent rounds from a 9-millimeter Sig Sauer everywhere in and around Collier's cruiser: Rounds were recovered behind the vehicle, one from the front passenger seat, and another from the blood-soaked driver's seat. Projectiles and fragments were scattered all over the car from the close-range shots.

Angrily, West asked his friend, "Who did this to you?"

There was no response. A medical examiner, Renee Robinson, would later explain that Collier "just died. Essentially rather quickly."[7] He had been shot six times. The fatal blast had been the one right between the eyes.

———

When DiFava had been appointed to head the MIT police force two years earlier, he had seen the position as a step toward retirement, a way to stay in law enforcement without the violent chaos and political maneuvering he had experienced as colonel of the MSP, where twenty-three hundred troopers worked. The MIT police force consisted of only sixty-two officers, but that did not mean that his life as university police commander was sleepier than his role as a state trooper colonel. There were roughly eleven thousand students at any given time on MIT's Cambridge campus. Though the student population boasted more than its fair share of geniuses, many of the students had a staggering lack of common sense or street savvy, making them targets for all kinds of shenanigans. And the politics of dealing with the governor and state lawmakers as a colonel in the state police was easy in comparison with navigating the ever-shifting landscape of an elite university obsessed with ensuring that the school's reputation for safety remained intact — especially among the parents and students who shelled out or borrowed more than $60,000 a year for tuition and housing.

In the days after the Boston Marathon bombing, more than a few of those parents had grown concerned. DiFava had, too. One of the three people slain on Boylston Street was Lingzi Lu, a Boston University student who, like so many students at MIT, had come to Boston from China to pursue higher education. Parents all over the world were looking for answers. The phones rang nonstop.

In the months before the marathon bombings, MIT had its own set of problems that did not, at first glance, appear to have anything to do with the bloodbath on Boylston Street. They came from a group of anarchist hackers who belonged to an underground network known as Anonymous. One of the group's heroes, Aaron Swartz — a technology visionary, political activist, and cofounder of the website Reddit, which he helped launch in 2005 out of an apartment in Somerville — had been found hanged, a tragic end to a two-year saga that began when the millionaire was arrested on charges of violating the Computer Fraud and Abuse Act. The Secret Service, which was among the multiple federal agencies prosecuting Swartz, had noted his suicide with a memo to federal prosecutors, now part of the public court filing, that read: "On 1/11/13 Aaron Swartz was found dead in his apartment in Brooklyn, New York — an apparent suicide." It continued: "A suppression hearing in this had been scheduled for 1/25/13 with a trial date of 4/1/13, in U.S. District Court of the District of Massachusetts." A suppression hearing meant that the charges would be dropped — in this case, because the target of the criminal charges was dead.

Swartz had first attracted the interest of investigators in 2008, when he and other internet activists published the now-infamous "Guerilla Open Access Manifesto" that began: "Information is power. But like all power, there are people who want to keep it for themselves."[8] It was a public lament about how expensive it was to be an academic these days. Swartz had a solution: He would steal the books that students historically had to pay for, not with a heist but with a computer.

All it took was a cheap Acer laptop, one that was registered in the name of Gary Host (a clever wordplay on the term "computer server host" and an indication that Swartz thought of himself as a ghost, according to prosecutors[9]), an encrypted email address, and a break-in at an MIT closet. Then Swartz began downloading thousands of articles from JSTOR — a pay-for-use site used by the university — using MIT's own network. It worked, at least temporarily. When officials at MIT caught on, they blocked Gary Host's network access, but that move did little to stop the technological genius.

On January 4, 2011, he sneaked into the basement of MIT's Building 16, hid an electronic notebook connected to a hard drive under a box in a dusty wiring closet, and began to download material. Two days later he went back for the hard drive, hiding his identity hacker-style. "As Swartz entered the wiring closet, he held his bicycle helmet like a mask to shield his face, looking through ventilation holes in the helmet," federal prosecutors said in a court document. Swartz, who was not affiliated with MIT, was arrested on federal charges. When Secret Service agents showed up at his apartment with an arrest warrant, he asked, "What took you so long?" On January 19, 2011, he pleaded not guilty and posted a $100,000 bond. Because Swartz had exhibited such nonchalance and swagger, his suicide came as a shock to the technology community, and even to the law enforcement officials who were prosecuting him.

US Attorney for Massachusetts Carmen Ortiz announced on January 14, 2013, three days after his suicide, that her office would drop the case against Swartz and released a statement reading:

> As a parent and a sister, I can only imagine the pain felt by the family and friends of Aaron Swartz, and I want to extend my heartfelt sympathy to everyone who knew and loved this young man. I know that there is little I can say to abate the anger felt by those who believe that this office's prosecution of Mr. Swartz was unwarranted and somehow led to the tragic result of him taking his own life.
>
> I must, however, make clear that this office's conduct was appropriate in bringing and handling this case. The career prosecutors handling this matter took on the difficult task of enforcing a law they had taken an oath to uphold, and did so reasonably. The prosecutors recognized that there was no evidence against Mr. Swartz indicating that he committed his acts for personal financial gain, and they recognized that his conduct

— while a violation of the law — did not warrant the severe punishments authorized by Congress and called for by the Sentencing Guidelines in appropriate cases. That is why in the discussions with his counsel about a resolution of the case this office sought an appropriate sentence that matched the alleged conduct — a sentence that we would recommend to the judge of six months in a low security setting. While at the same time, his defense counsel would have been free to recommend a sentence of probation. Ultimately, any sentence imposed would have been up to the judge. At no time did this office ever seek — or ever tell Mr. Swartz's attorneys that it intended to seek — maximum penalties under the law.

As federal prosecutors, our mission includes protecting the use of computers and the Internet by enforcing the law as fairly and responsibly as possible. We strive to do our best to fulfill this mission every day.[10]

Her apology did little to appease the twenty-four-year-old hacker-activist's supporters. In the days after the bombing on Boylston Street in April 2013, even as the mayhem resulting from that attack made international headlines and the hunt for the bombers continued, Ortiz was still receiving death threats from Swartz supporters who blamed her office and what they called "overzealous prosecution" for his suicide. The threats were part of an ongoing battle against the government and MIT that had begun three days after his death, when Anonymous hacked the university's website and posted a memorial to Swartz followed by a list of demands.[11]

On January 26, 2013, weeks after hacking into the MIT network, Anonymous defaced and dismantled the website of the US Sentencing Commission, disrupting for days the work of that government agency — one that ironically had nothing to do with the sentences meted out to hackers. Anonymous members dubbed that action Operation Last Resort. Anonymous hackers announced in a YouTube video that the attack on the government website was part of what would become a prolonged protest of unfair prosecution against technology programmers like Swartz, intended to "engage the United States Department of Justice and its associated executive branches in a game of a similar nature."[12]

The hackers carried out their threat. On February 23, 2013, the Cambridge Police Department received an email reporting that a "male with a large firearm and wearing body armor" was on the MIT campus, a threat that caused immediate panic and sent university police, Cambridge cops, and state troopers to the campus. As the manhunt for the gunman was under way another email was sent and a phone call was made, both of which warned that the gunman on campus was "retaliating against the people involved in the suicide of Aaron Swartz" and named an MIT employee as a possible target. Anonymous, it seemed, wanted to point the finger at an MIT employee whom they felt had been complicit in the investigation of Swartz. But there was no gunman. It was a hoax, and a dangerous one at that, as MIT Executive Vice President Israel Ruiz explained in a campus-wide email: "As we all know by now, there was never a gunman on campus. This hoax also involved a malicious allegation against a member of our community and direct threats of physical harm to MIT staff. We should all understand that this is not a game."[13]

Anonymous's orchestrated stunts would only get worse. In March a group of people wearing the trademark Guy Fawkes masks adopted by Anonymous members showed up at Ortiz's tony suburban home carrying WANTED posters showing her face along with the word MURDERER. The guests left a cake on her stoop decorated in frosting that read JUSTICE FOR AARON.[14] Her neighbors were horrified and called police. The cake was collected by the FBI for investigation.

Ortiz was furious. In a terse written statement, she said, "I respect the rights of individuals to express their views, [but] when they came into my neighborhood wearing masks, my neighbors and young children were frightened. Some of those neighbors called the local police, who responded and handled the situation. I think it would have been more appropriate for them [the protesters] to have expressed their views at the courthouse."[15]

Anonymous would express its views over and over again. There were written threats to federal prosecutors. The home address of Stephen Heymann, the lead prosecutor in the case against Swartz, was published online, along with the names of his family members. Email threats and taunts became commonplace. "Just saw you were totally dox'd [referring to having one's real personal identity publicly revealed] over the weekend by Anonymous," read one email sent to Heymann. "FYI, you might want to move out of the country and change your name."[16] Then a postcard was mailed to his house that depicted his father's head decapitated by a guillotine.

It got so bad that the US Attorney's Office complained to a federal judge about the "various harassing and potentially threatening emails directed at United States Attorney Ortiz and the United States Attorney's Office following Mr. Swartz's suicide."[17]

The harassment continued even after the jihadists bombed the finish line of the Boston Marathon. In fact, four separate unfounded bomb threats were made in Cambridge on the day of the marathon bombing, including on one of MIT's campuses — threats that officials have since blamed on hoaxers like the members of Anonymous.

Not only was every cop on high alert looking for the bombers, but there was also chatter from Cambridge cops about federal agents inexplicably setting up surveillance teams all around MIT's campus. As the former head of the state police, DiFava was all too familiar with the FBI being uncooperative — even abrasively evasive — with local police. He thought his biggest problem would be dealing with a turf war between the feds and the Cambridge locals.

———

That same night another incident sent Cambridge police officers racing to the area around MIT. Around 10:20 PM, around the same time Collier was murdered, a bearded man in a floppy hat pulled a gun on a clerk at a 7-Eleven — while talking on his cell phone. The robber held up the convenience store while calmly chatting with someone.

Today multiple law enforcement officials say — but only privately, for fear of reprisals because there have been no charges — that they believe the robber was a man named Daniel Morley, an anarchist who was photographed by the New York Police Department (NYPD) as he led an Occupy Wall Street march through Lower Manhattan. His activities that day led to his arrest in New York, though the charges were later dropped. His rabid anti-establishment politics led him to join groups like the Free Staters, and he had links to Anonymous.

DiFava had no idea that Collier's murder was connected to the Marathon bombing three days earlier. At 11:20 PM, about fifty minutes after Collier was found shot to death in his cruiser, a man named Dun Meng was carjacked in Cambridge. Two assailants kidnapped the young businessman at gunpoint and made him drive them around.

"Do you know about the Boston Marathon explosion?" the larger of the two men asked.

Meng answered, nervously, "Yes, I know."

"Do you know who did it?" the carjacker then asked. He was a hulking man, roughly six feet tall and weighing more than two hundred pounds. He was the guy with the gun.

"No, I don't," Meng answered.

"I did it," the gunman said and then pointed a 9-millimeter gun at Meng's temple. "And I just killed a policeman in Cambridge."[18]

CHAPTER THREE

Good Job, Boy. Good Job.

Dun Meng loved his Mercedes-Benz SUV 350, black and chrome with top-of-the-line features. He leased it for $652 a month and had no problem paying the bills. After a long day working as a transportation engineer in Kendall Square, he liked to drive along the Charles River, see the lights, and pull over and just think for a while or answer a few text messages. That's what he was doing on April 18, 2013, just after 11:00 PM, when he heard a car screech to a halt on the curb behind him. He looked in his rearview mirror and saw a green Honda Civic. A tall man emerged from the car and approached Meng's passenger-side window, motioning for Meng to open it. When Meng hesitated, the man knocked — insistently.

"I thought he was trying to ask for directions," Meng later recalled.[1] He rolled down the window just enough for a hand to reach inside and snap open the door. The man was suddenly inside the car, pushing the 9-millimeter Sig Sauer against Meng's temple.

"Where's the cash?"

Meng rooted around in the car for his wallet. "First after I give him the cash," Meng recalled later, "'You only have that amount of cash? That's not enough.' He asked me, 'Where's your wallet?' So I give him my wallet too. And there's no cash in the wallet."

Meng heard the metal sound of a magazine being slid partway out of the gun. He didn't want to look, but he turned and saw the bullets lined up in a deadly row in the clip before the gunman shot it back into place.

The carjacker confessed to Meng that he was one of the two "armed and extremely dangerous" subjects of the massive manhunt for the perpetrators of the marathon bombing.

"Drive!" the gunman yelled.

Meng was trembling as he drove. Meanwhile his kidnapper started making small talk.

"What's your name?"

Meng gave him his American nickname, "Manny."

"He said, 'Money?'." Meng recalled. "So he laughed about it. 'Money? You must got a lot of money.' So I said, 'No, not Money.' I said, 'My name is Manny, M-A-N-N-Y.'"

"Where are you from, Money?"

"China. I'm Chinese."

"Okay, you are Chinese. I'm Muslim. Muslims hate Americans."

Meng thought for a second and answered, "I'm Chinese. Chinese are very friendly to Muslims."

"Okay. I love you are Chinese. Just be relaxed and keep driving."

The gunman directed Meng, having him turn left, then right, then left again. Some of the streets were familiar, like Commonwealth Avenue and Market Street in Brighton, but then Meng found himself driving down a warren of dark, dead-end streets not far from Watertown's Arsenal mall. "How long have you been in the United States? What do you do?" the gunman asked.

"I came here for study," Meng answered. "I went to Northeastern University. My English is not very good."

"Who do you live with?"

Meng told his carjacker he shared a Cambridge apartment with roommates.

"Is there anyone you care about?"

Meng hesitated, and his hesitation bought him just enough time to avoid having to reply. As he pulled up in front of a house on Dexter Avenue in Watertown, the gunman became distracted and did not press him for an answer. The number on the house was 89. It was a two-family house similar to many other homes on the labyrinth of streets surrounding it. A smaller man emerged from the right-side door of 89 Dexter Avenue. According to law enforcement officers, the building housed English-language students from all over the world, including Saudi Arabia, Pakistan, and Chechnya.[2]

The gunman climbed out of the car and began chatting with the smaller man. One of them opened the rear hatch of the Mercedes SUV, and Meng felt the weight of heavy items being loaded into the back. He thought about running, but he looked around at the deserted street and thought better of the idea. It turned out the smaller man had driven the green Honda that had pulled up behind Meng originally — the one that the gunman had gotten out of — to Watertown and parked it on Dexter Avenue. Now the smaller man slid wordlessly into the backseat of Meng's car.

"I'll drive," the gunman said, motioning for Meng to move over. The large man with a boxer's build climbed in behind the steering wheel and pulled away from the curb. Within minutes they pulled in front of a Bank of America ATM in Watertown. The smaller man got out and rapped on Meng's window. Meng noted he was wearing a hooded sweatshirt with ADIDAS across the front in neon lettering. Dark curls peeked from beneath a cream-colored scally cap. He was unshaven and younger than the other man, probably only in his early twenties.

"What's your PIN?"

Meng told him the four-digit code, his girlfriend's birthday. It ended with 86 — the year he was born. The driver started to chat again.

"Do you — do you think all the white people look the same?"

"What?" Meng remembered asking. "What was the question? I'm sorry."

"Do you think all white persons looks like same, like do you think the black person looks the same? And so you won't remember my face, right?"

"I don't remember anything," Meng answered. And then the smaller, younger man was back. The door slammed, and the Mercedes headed back toward Dexter Avenue. As they drove there was a tense moment when one of Meng's roommates called him, the number showing up on the SUV's GPS panel. No one moved to answer the call, and Meng let it go to voice mail. Then Meng's iPhone text-message tone pinged. The text was written in Mandarin, and the driver demanded a translation. Meng told him his roommate had written, "Where are you? It's dangerous outside."

The driver asked him how to say "no" in Mandarin, and Meng told him. The driver was suspicious and asked Meng to pull up an English-Mandarin dictionary app on his phone. Meng gave him the phone, and the driver responded to the roommate's text.

That prompted a phone call from another roommate, the first roommate's boyfriend. Tamerlan got rattled. He pulled his gun from the driver's-side pocket and for a second time that night pointed it at Meng's head, telling him: "You have to answer the phone right now. If you say any single word in Chinese, I will kill you right now."

Meng later told investigators, "I pick up the phone, answer in English, 'How you doing?' Which is very weird because my room-mates are Chinese too . . . I say, 'I feel sick. I am going to stay at friend's house.'"

"What?" Meng's roommate answered in Chinese. "Why are you speaking English?"

Meng said, using English again: "I'm staying at a friend's house. I have to go right now." He hung up, and the driver's face softened.

"Good job, boy. Good job."

Meng knew he had to find a way to escape. The driver's demeanor had gone from friendly and understanding to angry and volatile. Eventually, Meng asked, "Are you going to kill me tonight?"

The driver laughed. "I'm not going to kill you. Just relax, man. Maybe we will drop you off at someplace very far away from any person and you will have to walk about five or six miles to find any person."

Then the driver steered the SUV into a Shell gas station near Memorial Drive in Cambridge. Throughout the ride the smaller man never spoke, except when he asked Meng to pop in a CD he had brought with him from the green sedan, a disc of jihadi *nasheed*, which Meng later described as eerie "religious" music. The smaller guy slipped out of the SUV to go into the convenience store and made his way back to the vehicle, weighed down with packages of Doritos and cans of Red Bull. The driver was preoccupied with a portable Garmin GPS device, which had been retrieved from the Honda Civic. Meng decided it was now or never, and he quietly unbuckled his seat belt.

In his head he began to count: *One. Two. Three. Four.* Then he yanked open the door and ran faster than he had ever run in his life across Cambridge Street and into an adjacent gas station. He felt the breeze from the gunman's hand brush his left hand and heard him yell *"Fuck!"* as he dashed across the street. The half-block sprint felt like a mile.

He ran into the Mobile station on Cambridge Street, very close to where the FBI had pulled the unknown suspect off the city bus and across the street from a building that housed two Tsarnaev friends who would later be charged in the case, and held the door shut behind him, sliding down toward the floor in case shots came in through the windows. The tension of the night overwhelmed him, and he begged the confused clerk to call 911. He put his hands together in prayer and began to sob: "Please, please, please call 911."

"I have a man who says he was carjacked," the clerk explained to the dispatcher.[3] Meng grabbed the phone and screamed at the dispatcher that the men who had his car "did the marathon explosion!" The dispatcher was stunned: "What? What did they say when they took your car?"

Meng answered, "They have guns."

The dispatcher kept Meng on the phone with mundane questions as Cambridge detectives raced to the gas station; some of them had been nearby at the MIT crime scene. Meng explained that his carjackers might be Middle Eastern. "They are Muslims," he told the dispatcher. "One guy is pretty skinny." And he said, "They have guns. They want to shoot at me."

Meng told the dispatcher that he had left his iPhone, which had a GPS tracking device, in the Mercedes and said that he wanted investigators to "find them quickly" so they didn't come back for him.

Then he waited for the police to arrive.

CHAPTER FOUR

BOLO

Late on the night of April 18 the murder of Sean Collier became a cautionary tale at police roll calls all over Massachusetts. Duty sergeants stressed the need for extra vigilance, especially for officers in one-man cruisers. In Watertown a blue-collar city adjacent to Cambridge, this was the message delivered to officers gathered for an 11:00 PM shift change just three miles away from the active crime scene. At that time it appeared that Collier's murder could be connected to a robbery at gunpoint of a 7-Eleven in Central Square, Cambridge.

As he readied for work as a Watertown patrolman that afternoon, Officer Joe Reynolds had watched the FBI's press conference. Like most of the cops in the Watertown Police Department, he was the epitome of a townie. He had graduated from Watertown High School then taken the civil service test and joined the police force. Reynolds had the midnight shift, and his assignment was to patrol the east end of Watertown, a residential neighborhood abutting upscale Belmont, Brighton, and Cambridge. At 12:28 AM his sergeant, John MacLellan, dispatched a BOLO warning — "be on the lookout" — over the radio:

"Suspect One is five-seven, the second with darker skin, both suspects armed with firearms, driving a Black Mercedes SUV registration 1-3-7-N-Z-1. Carjacked at 816 Memorial Drive at the gas station in Cambridge. Suspects are two Middle Eastern males, one with darker skin, no description on clothing yet, both are armed with firearms. They fled in the vehicle towards Harvard Square. Victim said one of the suspects went into the Shell station and paid cash for gas, put gas in the car before they fled, and that was when the victim was able to get out of the vehicle."[1]

The radio traffic started to get intense, with police officers on the frequency from neighboring towns weighing in with questions. Reynolds listened in Watertown, while MSP Trooper Chris Dumont listened from Logan Airport, where he had worked on President Barack Obama's arrival and departure the day before.

BPD officers and Cambridge Police Department detectives were at the scene of both gas stations: the Shell station where the younger suspect had gone on the junk-food-buying spree and the Mobil station where a terrified Meng was "trembling" as BPD Officer Michael Nickerson interviewed him about his ordeal.[2]

"I believe they have video in that Shell station; I am with the victim and believe they have video in the station," Nickerson reported to the dispatcher. (There was a Shell station directly across the street from the Mobil with security cameras.)

"Does the victim report the operator, that was operating the vehicle, was armed with a firearm, but he was unsure about the passenger?" the dispatcher asked.

"He said the operator of the vehicle displayed a firearm."

As more information became available from Dun Meng, the dispatcher continued to advise cops that the carjacking could be connected to Collier's murder and that the perpetrators could be headed to New York City.

"The victim is stating 137-NZ1 Mercedes 350, possibly heading to New York and involving that shooting at MIT," the dispatcher repeated over the channel that every cop in the vicinity was tuned in to.

———

At the moment there was no such thing as days off or downtime for any law enforcement officer in the commonwealth. Everyone was tired, anxious, and working mandatory overtime, and until the bombers were caught, most of the officers didn't mind a bit. Dumont had watched the FBI press conference at his Logan Airport barracks. Given the quality of the pictures of Suspects Black Hat and White Hat, he'd thought that they would have been caught by the time he heard the 10:36 PM report of Collier's murder. But they hadn't been. And when he arrived at Main and Vassar Streets to assist in the perimeter search for the cop killers, he couldn't help but wonder if the bombers had anything to do with Collier's murder.

Meanwhile, Joe Reynolds, the Watertown cop, had headed to Mount Auburn Street, the main drag that connected Cambridge to Watertown, and was waiting there. He, too, was wondering whether Sean Collier's murder and Dun Meng's carjacking by men who claimed to be the marathon bombers were connected when the radio crackled again.

Dun Meng's GPS locator in the Mercedes had pinged in the area of 61 Dexter Avenue and then again at 89 Dexter Avenue. It was on the move, and the narrow street it was moving along was just a hundred yards from Reynolds's location.

"I'm headed in that direction," Reynolds radioed in. It had been twenty minutes since the original BOLO warning had been issued.

MacLellan heard his transmission and issued an immediate caution: "I believe there is a gun in that vehicle. Please wait for backup before you take any action or pull it over." MacLellan had written the license plate number on his hand with a black Sharpie when the first BOLO warning was transmitted. He looked at the number again and memorized it as he drove toward Reynolds's location.

"Affirmative," Reynolds acknowledged as he made his way to Dexter Avenue.

A green Honda Civic with a black hood came creeping along slowly with another vehicle driving directly behind it. "It was very suspicious," Reynolds would remember. They were going only "five to ten miles an hour."[3]

The Honda drove past him first, followed by a black Mercedes. As the second vehicle passed his marked Watertown Police Department cruiser, the driver stared at the cop. "We locked eyes at each other," Reynolds remembered.

The Honda turned onto Laurel Street, and the Mercedes followed. Reynolds made a three-point turn and began pursuit. "As I was following them, they both sped up for a bit. I thought they were going to take off; it might be a car chase." He radioed his dispatcher that he had spotted the vehicle everyone was looking for. MacLellan, his sergeant, immediately got on the radio and reiterated that Reynolds should wait for the backup that was just minutes away. The driver had bragged that he had just killed a policeman in Cambridge. MacLellan knew he'd do it again if given the chance.

Suddenly both cars stopped in the middle of Laurel Street. Reynolds was two car lengths behind when a hulking man opened the driver's-side door of the Mercedes and stepped out, his right arm outstretched and holding a gun. He walked fearlessly toward the cruiser and began firing. Reynolds ducked down behind the dashboard and threw the cruiser into reverse, while grabbing his shoulder radio. "Shots fired! Shots fired!" he yelled into the mike. Surrounded by darkness, Officer Reynolds was suddenly amid chaos. Shards of glass showered him, and the metallic sound of bullets ripping into metal was disorienting. All he could see were muzzle flashes, over and over again. The bullets came nonstop. He stopped the cruiser, leaned across to open the driver's-side door, and then dove onto the street behind it to return fire.

MacLellan heard the unrelenting explosion of bullets even before he rounded the corner and pulled up to the left side of Reynolds on Laurel Street. Bullets had pocked Reynolds's cruiser door and continued to rip through metal and glass — too many rounds to count. MacLellan yelled into his radio: "Shots fired! Shots fired! Shots fired!" just as Reynolds had. It was unusual to hear multiple 10-13 radio calls (the code for a police officer in trouble), and the cries for help brought a cavalry of uniforms racing toward Watertown from surrounding departments.

As MacLellan pulled alongside Reynolds's cruiser a bullet smashed through his own windshield, spraying him with broken glass. The bullets kept coming, and the gunman made no move to retreat. He stood right in the middle of the street like a cowboy in a black-and-white western standing his ground. That's when MacLellan had an idea: put his own cruiser into drive and let it roll toward the gunman.

"Maybe I could gain some time," MacLellan remembered thinking. "Try to figure out how many suspects we had. I let the vehicle go, and I stepped to the side of it and used it as cover as it was rolling and I tried to throw some rounds down range."[4]

Reynolds dashed out from behind his cruiser door and crouched behind the sergeant's slow-moving cruiser. Both men emptied their guns at the suspect, who didn't go down but instead ran behind the Mercedes for cover. That's when it became clear to both cops that there were two men firing at them. One was taller than the other, and both fit the description in the BOLO warning: Middle Eastern men with dark hair and scraggly beards. "I could see muzzle flashes," Reynolds would say later. "And at that time I saw Sergeant MacLellan run into the side yard, so I followed him over there to communicate what he wanted."

Residents on the leafy block peered out windows and live-tweeted about the two suspects, whom they could see crouched for cover behind the stolen Mercedes with bags and backpacks — similar to the ones used to conceal the bombs on Boylston Street — at their feet. They came in and out of cover as they retrieved ammunition and other bags from the nearby green Honda. MacLellan and Reynolds took cover behind a small tree. They emptied the magazines of their .40-caliber Glocks, reloaded, and emptied their magazines again. "I had two spare mags on my belt as well as the one in my gun, and I used all my bullets," Reynolds would say later.

The gun battle lasted eight or nine minutes, but it felt like hours. And the situation was about to get worse.

MacLellan and Reynolds saw the smaller of the two men light something and fling it their way. It was a pipe bomb, and it landed next to MacLellan's cruiser. Boom!

"I think they are throwing M-80s at us," MacLellan reported over his radio. "They keep coming."

He moved from behind the tree to see what the suspects were doing and realized they were both grabbing materials from the back of the Mercedes. Then came another flash of light and an explosion. Then a third and a fourth. The bigger man was throwing the bombs like baseballs, while the smaller one used a hook shot. The explosions shook the street but had no impact on the officers. By this time more cops were arriving on the scene.

Sergeant Jeffrey Pugliese was off duty and had been driving home in the family minivan when he heard the beginning of the firefight transmitted over the radio and drove eighty miles per hour until he was in the cluster of narrow streets exploding with bullets and bombs. Like Reynolds, he was a Watertown native and knew the backyards and side streets of the neighborhood well. He slid open the door of his minivan, grabbed his bullet-proof vest, and began pulling it on as he started jogging toward the gunshots.

In one of the driveways he saw Reynolds and another Watertown police officer, Miguel Colon, who turned and yelled, "Sarge. Sarge! Get down. They're shooting at us."[5]

At that point MacLellan was behind a tree returning fire and shouting at the suspects: "Give it up! Give it up! You're not going to win this! You're surrounded!"

The cops scuttled behind cars in the driveways of Laurel Street. Residents were terrified. Bullets were hitting houses, searing the bark off trees, and ripping through street signs. One family had the surreal experience of seeing a round pierce their television set as it was broadcasting news of the insanity going on outside their house. People forced family members to the floor, shielded their bodies with their own, tried to squeeze into bathtubs or make it to rooms that bullets couldn't reach. The usually sleepy neighborhood had become a war zone. Exploding pipe bombs shook the houses, and bullets pierced clapboard or vinyl siding.

A Laurel Street resident named James Floyd placed his three-month-old son in a crib at the back of his house to protect the baby from the bullets flying outside the front door and peered through a blossoming plum tree to watch the mayhem. He saw lit fuses and heard pipe bombs hitting the ground, like metallic baseball bats connecting with a ball: clink, clink, clink. Two clattered but didn't explode. Two others did, rattling windows. Floyd watched the gunmen continue firing at police and then saw the smaller gunman grab a book bag from the rear of the Mercedes. "That looks heavy," Floyd said to his wife. "This isn't good." The smaller man grabbed the bag by its strap and launched it as far as he could.

Reynolds saw a cylinder flying through the air, a big metal pot, a pressure-cooker bomb like the ones detonated along the marathon's finish line.

"Run, Sarge! Run! Run! Run!" Reynolds yelled.

Looking toward MacLellan, he knew his sergeant hadn't seen the size of the bomb. Reynolds grabbed MacLellan's shoulder and pulled him along. The blast was so powerful it knocked both policemen and Floyd to their knees and terrified everyone in the neighborhood.

MacLellan was so shaken that he holstered his weapon. "It was incredible. It was horrendous. Very loud. I had to reholster my weapon to be able to straighten my head to be able to see." He could feel "debris raining down. For some reason I thought shingles were coming off houses, but it was just stuff landing all around us, smoke, car alarms going off, people screaming."

And the bullets kept flying at Reynolds and MacLellan. "To me there were simultaneous flashes coming toward us. There were two handguns being shot," MacLellan said, although only one gun and a BB pellet rifle would be recovered at the scene, raising questions about possible accomplices. Questions that to this day have never been answered.

Neighbors peered out of windows and watched as the taller gunman started to walk straight toward the cops. He was not firing or hurrying — just walking with the gun at his side. By then Pugliese had flanked the Mercedes from a side yard. He climbed over a chain-link fence and a picket fence and then reached the rear of 89 Dexter Avenue. The sight of a white male with dark hair in a white T-shirt sitting outside the house briefly delayed his progress toward the gunfight.

"Stop right there," Pugliese yelled.[6] The man was not showing any weapons but appeared to be up to no good, since he was just sitting calmly in a shootout, and Pugliese thought he could be connected to the suspects somehow. That suspicion was heightened when, on seeing the cop, the man hopped over a fence and sprinted away. He was the least of Pugliese's worries at that moment, but the man's presence would eventually raise questions when investigators began to look into the actions of anyone who might have helped the Boston Marathon bombers.

"There is an individual fleeing the area," Pugliese radioed the dispatcher, and then he quickly put the unidentified man out of his mind. He and the other officers on the scene had more pressing concerns, such as running out of ammunition. Each standard-issue magazine held only thirteen bullets, plus the one in the pistol's chamber. Two magazines and the single bullet meant twenty-seven shots for each officer on the scene.

Pugliese approached the yard where MacLellan and Reynolds had taken cover. He heard MacLellan yelling at the suspects: "Give it up! Give it up! You don't have a chance."[7] MacLellan was yelling partly because he was out of bullets. But the gunmen didn't know that. They kept firing. Reynolds knelt on one knee, trying to get off a good shot just as Pugliese flanked the gunmen from a side yard. "I drew my service pistol, I took aim at the one individual," said Pugliese. "I took careful aim, and I fired three or four shots at the individual. I thought I was hitting him but I didn't know whether or not I did. I just — you know, I wasn't rushing my shots so I thought I was probably, you know, hitting my target, but it didn't seem to be having any effect."

The suspect just wouldn't go down. Pugliese had been a firearms instructor for more than three decades and decided that he would squeeze off a few "skip shots," aiming at the ground in front of the gunman and hoping that the bullets would bounce back up six to eight inches to hit him. He later explained that he was thinking, "Maybe I could take their ankles out and get them to, you know, stop with the aggressive behavior they were doing."

But the larger man turned and stared directly at Pugliese. He charged toward him, weapon extended, and fired off six rounds. Pugliese wasn't hit. He returned fire until he'd used all fourteen rounds in his gun. He dropped the empty magazine at his feet, quickly reloaded, and continued to fire. Then a miracle happened: The suspect's gun either jammed or ran out of bullets. In a fit of fury, he hurled the useless weapon at Pugliese, hitting him in the left biceps, and ran. Pugliese holstered his gun and chased the suspect down the street. He took a running leap and tackled him. The suspect was bleeding and slippery. He was also strong. MacLellan arrived and flipped the suspect over, facedown. The suspect continued to struggle with the cops, flailing wildly as they tried to pull his muscled arms behind his back to handcuff him. Reynolds raced over to help and smashed his gun, which had been emptied, into the man on the ground. Colon joined his colleagues and tried to wrestle the suspect's left wrist from beneath his body to behind his back. No one noticed that the smaller man had gotten behind the wheel of the Mercedes SUV and had pressed the gas pedal to the floor until Reynolds looked and saw the vehicle's headlights as it spun into a U-turn and then pointed straight at the huddle of police officers and the suspect on the ground.

"Sarge, Sarge, look out! The other guy's in the car. He's coming at us," Reynolds yelled.

By then other officers had arrived. Four Boston cops were standing on the northeast corner of Laurel Street, and three others were across the street. Watertown and Cambridge cops had taken positions along Dexter Avenue and Laurel Street. It remains unclear how many officers opened fire on the vehicle as it sped toward the Watertown policemen on the ground wrangling with the suspect. At least one bullet splintered the windshield, and — investigators would later learn — smashed into the driver's jaw. Still he kept advancing at full speed. The car was only thirty yards away, then twenty.

Pugliese tried to pick up the suspect by his belt to drag him out of the way. But the suspect jerked himself out of Pugliese's grasp and directly into the path of the oncoming SUV. The three Watertown cops leaped out of the way just in time. Pugliese felt the breeze of the racing car on his face. Then he heard a thud. The Mercedes rocked as it rolled over the gunman on the ground, smashed into a Watertown cruiser, and took off. The larger suspect had been caught in the undercarriage of the SUV and was being dragged along. The Mercedes slammed into MacLellan's bullet-riddled police cruiser, dislodging the body.

As officers continued to fire at the now-fleeing SUV, Reynolds asked the stunned Pugliese, "Are you all right?" Pugliese answered, "I'm okay."

The Mercedes crossed Dexter Avenue, proceeded down Laurel Street, and was soon out of sight. Two BPD officers assigned to the gang squad, Sean McCarthy and Scott Pulchansingh, were ordered to pursue the Mercedes, which had managed to get away despite the fact that up to a thousand cops from at least twelve different jurisdictions had responded to the firefight.

The bomb blast left BPD Officer Dennis Simmonds stunned with what would later be called a "severe head trauma"[8] — and which his family would cite as the cause of the aneurysm that took the twenty-eight-year-old cop's life a year later. His name is now etched alongside the names of other fallen heroes killed in the line of duty at the department's headquarters, the fifth victim of the Boston Marathon bombers.

Two officers assigned to the Joint Terrorism Task Force, BPD Detective Ken Conley and Massachusetts State Trooper Dan

Wells, had arrived in Watertown driving an unmarked black state police pickup truck that, inexplicably, had mistakenly been reported stolen. As noted in a previous chapter, their vehicle was fired upon when a state trooper spotted it and thought they were suspects. One of the rounds pierced the detective's headrest but missed him. Detectives recovered twenty-one spent casings around the vehicle. An MBTA transit police officer was grazed in the buttocks by a bullet. They were lucky.

MBTA cop Richard "Dic" Donohue was not. Donohue felt himself staggering and then his partner, Luke Kitto, lowered him gently to the ground as other cops began to radio for help. "Officer down! Officer down!" was heard over the radio channels of multiple police departments. One of the bullets fired at the suspect's getaway car had ricocheted off the vehicle and into Donohue's groin. It was bad. The color quickly drained from his skin. His eyes were open, lifeless.

That's the first thing State Trooper Dumont noted. A medic and combat veteran, like many of the cops on the scene, he knew Donohue didn't have much time. The ambulance was forty-five seconds away, which could be an eternity given the blood loss Donohue had suffered in such a short time.

"Pick him up," Dumont directed.[9] "We'll carry him to the ambulance." Kitto had his partner by the shoulder, and BPD Officer John Moynihan and two others grabbed his torso. A Cambridge cop and Harvard University officers helped hoist Donohue, and together the men hustled toward the back of the ambulance operated by Watertown firefighters and EMTs Patrick Menton and Jimmy Caruso. Caruso applied pressure to the wound, which had stopped bleeding. "He lost most of his blood," Dumont whispered, more to himself than anyone, as he and Menton performed CPR on Donohue. Because both EMTs were in the back of the ambulance, Menton's brother Tim, a Watertown cop, drove it — with the emergency brake still on. Kitto was in the passenger seat, saying, "You're going to be okay, Dic. Hang on. Hang on."

It took just under three minutes to arrive at Mount Auburn Hospital. There doctors performed CPR on Donohue, stabilized him, and transported him to South Shore Hospital. By the time he arrived "he had bled out almost his entire blood volume on the street in Watertown, and . . . because his heart wasn't beating, there's no blood forward flow to cause any bleeding there," Heather Studley, a physician in the emergency room, would later recall.[10] "He looked dead."

By then cops from all over the state had started showing up to donate blood, and every bit of it was needed. Studley was working the overnight shift in the emergency room. When Donohue was brought in, he was unresponsive: he was not breathing, and his heart had stopped. He was dead and had been for roughly fifteen minutes. The only chance he had at life came from the constant breaths of his police brethren who had performed CPR nonstop.

Studley inserted a breathing tube and a large IV into Donohue to start pumping in blood. She gave him a shot of epinephrine to help his heart start beating again. When it did, the blood began to shoot out of the wound. Studley climbed on top of the stretcher and dug her knee into Donohue's groin to stop the bleeding as they raced toward an operating room. "There's no other way," she told the shocked cops. She was right. After hours of surgery and receiving twenty-eight pints of blood, eleven pints of fresh frozen plasma, and six pints of platelets, Donohue had a pulse. Donohue's wife and police brethren would consider what the team at South Shore Hospital had done for Dic to be a miracle.

Donohue had been technically dead for forty-five minutes, Studley would say, explaining that "in the emergency department" his heart had stopped beating for "approximately thirty minutes, I would say, and then add on the pre-hospital time, anywhere — you know, like I said, ten to fifteen minutes." But he lived.

The same would not be the case with the suspected terrorist, who was treated at Beth Israel Deaconess Medical Center in Boston. The burly bomber had been shot nine times and hit and dragged by a speeding SUV, but he was still combative even as he was lifted into the back of a Boston EMS ambulance. Cops wanted to keep him alive, talking. Paramedic Michael Sullivan rode in the back with the wounded man, who had "multiple trauma and road rash," and began to treat "the top" — in paramedic parlance, the upper body — as his partner, Sean Murphy, worked on "the bottom," near the patient's legs.

Sullivan remembered how bad the patient looked. "He was pale. He was sweaty."[11] Sullivan asked the cops what had happened, and they explained that the patient was believed to be one of the Boston Marathon bombers. "All we knew is that he was the suspect. We didn't have a name," Sullivan recalled. "When I asked about the road rash, they [the officers] said, 'No, no, no. It was a blast-type injury from an errant explosive device.'" The man also had been hit with shrapnel. He was alive — but barely.

"We were making eye contact. He was awake. We suspected he was in shock," Sullivan remembered. The patient thrashed violently, though he was handcuffed and secured with seat belts to the ambulance's gurney. "He would lift himself off the stretcher, he would yell and scream and resist us touching him," Sullivan said. "We couldn't get an IV into his arms because he was handcuffed, and he resisted any attempts to put a line into his legs. He was yelling loud. It seemed like he was trying to get out of the seat belts holding him on." Sullivan attempted to dress the patient's head wound and tend to the evisceration across his stomach. All of that would be pointless.

Using its lights and sirens, the ambulance took about five minutes to reach Beth Israel from the bloodstained spot where the gunman's body had been dislodged from the undercarriage of the Mercedes SUV. As the paramedics lifted the dying man out of the ambulance and began rolling him toward the emergency room doors, Sullivan recalled, the patient uttered one last echoing groan while thrashing around. "He was literally yelling GRRRRRRRRRR," Sullivan said — like a bear.

Hospital staffers tried to keep the gunman alive. But at 1:35 AM — roughly an hour after the wild bomb and bullet fight had begun — the suspect was pronounced dead. The cause was listed as "gunshot wounds to the torso and extremities" along with "blunt trauma to the head and torso."[12] An autopsy photo taken by a Boston police officer (who then texted it to another law enforcement officer, who forwarded it in turn, until it was posted on social media) that night showed him on the autopsy table, his body ripped open by the impact of the SUV, and his head crushed and bruised. At that point no one at Beth Israel had any idea who he was other than a suspect in a bloody attack on civilians at an iconic Boston event, a terrorist bombing that had killed two women and a beloved little boy. At that point, hours after the FBI had released the clear photos of the suspects' faces, not a single phone call had come into the FBI regarding the identity of the shooters.[13] They had set up extra phone banks. Agents from all over the Northeast were in Boston to help handle the expected deluge of tips. But the phones didn't ring. The silence was so stunning that Kieran Ramsey — the assistant special agent in charge of the FBI's Boston field office and a military veteran who spoke fluent Arabic — had the phone lines checked to make sure they were working before he went to Watertown to investigate the scene of the firefight there.

The firefight had lasted twenty minutes. A total of 210 rounds had been fired, littering the neighborhood with shell casings.[14] Dozens of bomb technicians had arrived in Dexter Avenue by 1:00 AM to "render safe" the unexploded pipe bombs. Dexter Avenue, Laurel Street, and nearby Cypress Street were shut down as a crime scene.

The 9-millimeter weapon used by the larger gunman and thrown at the Watertown sergeant was recovered. An Airsoft pellet gun that fired .177 BBs was found in a front yard, not far from where the pressure-cooker bomb thrown at cops had embedded in the side of a car. But the second firearm that Watertown police — including Pugliese, the firearms expert — swear was being fired at them by the suspects was never found; as noted, this left lingering questions in the minds of law enforcement officials about possible accomplices. Pugliese would never forget the confrontation with the dark haired man in the white t-shirt who catapulted over the fence and fled into the darkness.

People in Watertown were terrified, especially after the Watertown Police Department issued an emergency alert at 1:57 AM urging the city's residents to "stay in their homes because of an active incident and report any suspicious activity."[15] Meanwhile the FBI enhanced the photos released earlier with clearer shots of the suspects' faces, and 911 calls began to come in: roughly five hundred would be made to the Watertown Police Department by the end of the day. Many of those calls came from residents near the firefights wondering about the ballistics found in their houses — which included a pressure-cooker bomb embedded in the driver's-side door of a car and evidence of other explosives around back-yard swing sets and in children's hockey nets.

By 4:15 AM Massachusetts National Guard military police began to roll into Watertown on twenty-one armored Humvees. The MBTA suspended bus and subway service at 5:15, around the time when Governor Deval Patrick issued a mandatory shelter-in-place order for the more than one million people who lived in the Greater Boston area. Stores were closed and shuttered. The streets were eerily quiet. The only traffic came from law enforcement officials and the military. Black Hawk helicopters flew over-head as SWAT teams went door-to-door throughout Watertown looking for the missing suspect.

"Suspect One is dead. Suspect Two is on the run. We have an MBTA officer who was seriously wounded and is in surgery right now. We have an MIT security officer who has been killed," Patrick announced at a 5:45 AM press conference. "There is a massive manhunt under way. A lot of law enforcement involved in that. To assist in that we have suspended all service on the MBTA. That will continue until we think it's safe to open all or some of that. We are asking people to shelter in place; in other words to stay inside, with the doors locked and not to open the doors for anyone other than a properly identified police officer. That applies here in Watertown, Cambridge, Newton, Belmont, and that includes all of Boston. All of Boston. This is a serious situation. We are taking it seriously. We are asking the public to take it seriously as well. We have every asset we can possibly muster on the ground right now. They are doing a terrific job coordinating with each other. We need the public to help us help them stay safe."[16]

FBI agents then congregated at the two-family house at 89 Dexter Avenue in Watertown, which would soon become a focus of the Boston Marathon bombings investigation, one that would be conducted in top secrecy by the FBI. This was the two-family house from which the carjacking victim, Dun Meng, told investigators the smaller carjacker emerged when Meng pulled up with the larger man. Agents went into the house multiple times that night.

The marathon bombers did not come to live in that Watertown neighborhood by accident. They had friends in the area who were in the United States to study English. One eighteen-year-old resident of 89 Dexter Avenue — Ahmed Al-Ruwaili, from Saudi Arabia — looked so much like the smaller suspect at large that he was handcuffed, spirited out of Watertown, questioned for hours, and later moved from Watertown altogether. He told a Saudi newspaper that the "officers were armed to the teeth. Everything you can imagine, guns, machine guns, electronic devices, etc."[17] Al-Ruwaili was in a common kitchen on the side of the two-family house the students were renting when the officers rushed in. They told the students to get on the floor and put their hands behind their backs. Then they removed their shoes, handcuffed them, and led them outside for individual interrogations. Half an hour later they freed all the students and let them go inside — except for Al-Ruwaili. "They pulled out a picture and flashed it in front of my eyes and asked me if it was a photo of me," he told the Saudi paper.

It was the one released just hours earlier by the FBI of the man known as Suspect White Hat, the one who had escaped the firefight in Watertown, running over his partner, and was on the loose.

Another resident of the house became known as "Naked Guy," because he was videotaped by a CNN news crew sprawled face-down on the ground after he had been ordered to strip in case he was strapped with explosives. He bore a striking resemblance to the older suspect, muscular with thick dark hair and a scraggly beard. BPD Deputy Superintendent Dan Linskey was the one who ordered the man to remove his clothes. A dead man's switch, a device used to detonate suicide vests, had been found in the bushes on Laurel Street following the firefight, and he feared the man might be wearing the corresponding vest. After police questioned him, they released him that same night.

When I visited the house in the days after the gun battle in my job as a reporter, the landlord, an electrical engineer who collected toy car parts like the ones used to build the detonator found on Boylston Street after the bomb blasts, pressed a finger to his lips and warned me, "Be careful what you say. This place is bugged by the FBI." No one from the house was ever publicly identified as a possible codefendant — although some cops have told me that they suspect that members of a larger cell working with the marathon bombers had been living there.

Tom Pasquarello was in law enforcement for thirty-five years, first as a special agent with the US Department of Justice assigned to both the DEA and FBI on cases all over the world, and then appointed to head the Somerville Police Department, where Sean Collier had been slated to become a sworn officer three weeks after he was assassinated on the MIT campus. Retired from law enforcement and now working for an international homeland security company, Pasquarello is one of the officers willing to speak openly about unexamined or unexplained details connected to the two-day crime spree of the Boston Marathon bombers: "Suffice it to say there are a lot of unanswered questions about exactly what happened that night and who might have been involved."[18]

CHAPTER FIVE

Faces but No Names

In the days after the Boston Marathon bombings the FBI set up a command center on the eighth floor of One Center Plaza, the nondescript office building across from Boston's City Hall that serves as the bureau's Boston headquarters. That's where the call center was located, where the phones didn't ring with any substantial tips at first. The Westin Copley Place hotel served as a command post for the twenty other agencies — including the BPD and the MSP — involved in the investigation and ensuing manhunt. Still other investigators worked in the Black Falcon Cruise Terminal, the hangar-size warehouse that the FBI took over to process evidence. It contained two forensic-evidence intake areas as well as ten viewing stations, and there was no hiding the level of activity as personnel came and went. No piece of evidence was too small to be collected and examined. Bomb fragments, often with the blood of victims on them, had been recovered from rooftops, ledges, and on the ground all around Copley Square.

Each bomb, FBI agents believed, contained "thousands of pieces of tiny shrapnel" meant to "shred flesh, shatter bone, set people on fire, and cause its victims to die painful, bloody deaths."[1] The bombs had been packed with BB pellets, sealant, and pieces of cardboard — intentionally placed inside to set the flesh of victims ablaze.

Every fragment of evidence needed to be processed and cataloged. In the first twenty-four hours after the dual blasts, the FBI computer forensics teams had amassed an astonishing ten terabytes of data, enough to fill the hard drives of ten high-end laptop computers.

One of those BPD technicians: Terrence "Shane" Burke, a US Marine who had barely survived a similar attack fighting in

Fallujah, Iraq, in 2006. The scene reminded him of the horror witnessed overseas from fatal IED attacks.

Investigators also recovered evidence from hospitals all over Boston, such as a zipper from one of the two backpacks that had concealed the bombs and was embedded in a woman's leg, molten nylon removed from burned flesh, and BB pellets and shrapnel removed from wounds. Hospital staffers were told that the FBI wanted anything removed from patients' flesh to be set aside. Every hospital in Boston had undergone routine annual training alongside local law enforcement for exactly this type of catastrophe, but nothing could have emotionally prepared the medical staffs for the carnage produced by the blasts in the Back Bay.

By Friday, April 19, the FBI had collected 655 videos from tourists, restaurants, department stores, and news crews. Footage was reviewed over and over in an effort to trace the bombers' paths. Then investigators caught a break. The manager of Whiskey's bar on Boylston Street, a block and a half west of the second bomb blast, called the BPD's main number. Eventually the call was dispatched to Lieutenant Detective Mike McCarthy, a lawyer who now runs the Boston Regional Intelligence Center. The manager told him: "I have something you need to take a look at."[2] The surveillance video from Whiskey's showed a man in a white hat with a black backpack walking with a bigger man who wore a black hat and sunglasses and carried a similar backpack. They were headed in the direction of the first blast site. The footage had been taken twelve seconds before the first explosion. It was the only video that showed them together.

Another video taken from inside the Forum restaurant showed in graphic detail the devastation left after the second bomb detonated: Martin Richard's last breaths, Lingzi Lu's face twisted in anguish, the victims whose flesh had caught on fire, the limbs scattered on the sidewalk next to blood-splattered baby carriages. The Forum video showed something else that would become a key piece of evidence in the case. Behind Martin Richard's family was the man whose face appeared on the wanted poster the FBI had released the day before.

A photo turned in to the FBI taken by a tourist on his iPhone at 2:37 PM on Monday would prove to be the most critical piece of evidence identifying the bombers. It showed Suspect White Hat standing behind Roseann Sdoia and the Richard family on Boylston Street, smirking. He would soon lower his right shoulder and drop his backpack behind a row of children. Three minutes after that, at 2:48 PM, he made a phone call that triggered the first blast. He didn't even turn his head at the explosion.

"Look at this," remarked Kieran Ramsey, the FBI assistant special agent in charge of the Boston field office.[3] "He stood behind that family for five full minutes knowing he was going to bomb that family."

Another video recovered from a surveillance camera inside the Forum restaurant showed the reactions of spectators — who were enjoying drinks and lunch and cheering on the runners — to the first explosion, which sounded like a cannon blast. Everyone turned left, many of them screaming — except White Hat, who turned right, smirked a little, and hustled away up the street. Twelve seconds later came the second explosion roughly 328 feet away, leaving body parts all over the street like gruesome puzzle pieces, blood-splattered store windows, and shattered glass.

The explosion threw Roseann Sdoia over the metal barricade between spectators and the racecourse. She looked down at the blood she felt flowing out of her and saw a foot. She didn't know it was hers until she realized that her strappy sandal was still attached to it.[4] Not far from her was Jessica Kensky and her new husband, Patrick Downes. "I remember being happy. I remember feeling sunlight on my face. I remember feeling really free. I remember holding each other," Jessica said. Then came the BOOM!: "There's smoke, there's blood." She saw her husband with one leg and foot missing. She had no idea that her own legs had also been mangled.[5] They would never be able to return to their Boston apartment because they could no longer climb the stairs.

Tourist Colton Kilgore remembered he was taking a video when suddenly he was airborne, then tumbling to the ground in a tangle of bodies and faces. His camera fell to the ground, still recording. It captured the screams and chaos and actions of Frank Chiola, a BPD cop who as a marine served during Operation Iraqi Freedom. Boston was worse than Baghdad, he remembered. In Boston "you couldn't tell who was alive, who was dead," he said.[6] He raced to a woman who he remembered was wearing blue eye shadow and tried to administer CPR. "She had a friend near her calling out her name. As I applied compression smoke was coming out of her mouth . . . I helped her best I [could]," he said, choking up. "She was suffering. She was in pain. She was in shock. From the waist down it's really tough to describe, complete mutilation. That's as far as I want to say." He later learned that her name was Krystle Marie Campbell.

Sydney Corcoran, a nineteen-year-old psychology student at Merrimac College, had gone with her parents to watch the marathon. Then she was hurled to the ground, her skin on fire, her leg mangled. She couldn't find her mother or father: "I remember thinking, this is it. I'm going to die. I'm not going to make it. I remember feeling like I was just going to sleep."[7] Waking up alive in the hospital was a relief, but Sydney was convinced that her parents had died until a doctor told her that her mother, Celeste, had survived but lost both her legs. Doctors wheeled Celeste into Sydney's room, and they held hands and cried, "just appreciating that we were still alive."

The carnage was too familiar for many of the first responders and investigators on the scene, like the BPD officer who had returned to the force despite having nearly died from injuries in Fallujah; and Lynn, Massachusetts, firefighter Matt Patterson, who had served several tours of combat duty before he jumped over a metal barricade to help seven-year-old Jane Richard in

Boston. Combat veterans made so many comparisons between the war zones where they had served and Boylston Street that when White Hat was finally captured and put on trial, his defense attorneys would successfully argue that all references to Iraq should be stricken from first responders' testimony.

Kilgore's footage also captured Jeff Bauman in one of the more compelling images from the bombings. He was standing near the Corcoran family, waiting for his wife to cross the finish line, when the first bomb went off and he was suddenly on the pavement. He looked down and almost laughed at his macabre predicament: his legs gone, his body mangled, and blood gushing from his lower body. "This is how it's going to end. This is it," he told himself and then comforted himself with the thought that he had enjoyed a great life.[8] A man in a cowboy hat suddenly appeared to hold Bauman's femoral artery, pinched between his fingers, as frantic first responders hoisted Bauman into a wheelchair from the tent set up to treat exhausted or injured runners near the finish line. The man in the cowboy hat was peace activist Carlos Arredondo, whose eldest son, Lance Corporal Alexander Arredondo, had been killed during Operation Iraqi Freedom in 2004, on his father's forty-fourth birthday. In 2011 his youngest son, Brian, who had battled drug addiction and depression after Alexander died, took his own life. Those deaths, Arredondo would later say, motivated him to keep Bauman alive. And he did.[9]

When Bauman woke up in the hospital the next day, his best friend, John Sullivan, was in the room with him. "I knew I wasn't in heaven because Sully was standing there," Bauman remembered. "I knew my legs were gone. I knew my legs were gone instantly."

That was his first thought. His second was that shortly before the explosion a man had abruptly bumped into him and then turned and scowled when Bauman protested with a mild "hey." The rude man was just over six feet tall, wearing a black baseball cap and aviator sunglasses, and sporting what Bauman called "a five o'clock shadow": "This guy, he was about my age, he came up and he was trying to make his way through the crowd, he kind of nudged me, I looked back at him. He was alone, he wasn't watching the race, he didn't look like he was having fun like everyone else. I just thought it was odd." He had noticed the man first and then seen an unattended backpack on the sidewalk, but he didn't really put the two together before the explosion. "I looked back and I saw a bag there unattended. It looked like a regular school backpack." He had paused then shaken off his concern, thinking, "You're in Boston. Stuff like this doesn't happen."

But in the hospital Bauman realized that the man who had bumped him was probably connected to the backpack. Bauman was intubated, so he made a scribbling gesture to Sully, who handed him a pen and paper. The first thing Bauman wrote was "Lieutenant Dan?" a reference to the character in the movie *Forrest Gump* who lost his legs. Sully nodded. The second thing he wrote was more serious: "Sull, I know what happened. I saw the kid. I know what happened."

FBI Special Agent Jeffrey Rowland would view the body of the man Bauman had encountered when summoned to a secured examining room in the emergency area at Beth Israel Deaconess Medical Center. Black Hat's body lay uncovered, the area around him still slick with blood. "His body was very badly damaged. He had been shot nine times. He had been scalped," Rowland said.[10]

Rowland saw how big the dead man was and knew this wasn't Suspect White Hat. Like most law enforcement officials, he had studied the videos. He was looking at Suspect Black Hat. "We had two suspects. We had two faces; faces but no names," he later recalled. But there was one thing that he and others in the FBI were certain of — the explosives thrown at police officers in Watertown were identical to the ones detonated on Boylston Street. This was not just a cop killer or a carjacker who wanted to commit suicide by cop. Rowland was looking at a terrorist, one of the two most wanted men in America.

In a small suitcase Rowland carried a device called Quick Capture Platform, technology that was purchased by the US government in 2003 during the George W. Bush administration and initially used by the military in the war zones of Iraq and Afghanistan. The device allowed intelligence officials to analyze fingerprints of possible terror suspects. For instance, one Iraqi applied to become a US-trained police officer in Baghdad, but when he was fingerprinted as part of the application process, his prints were linked to latent prints recovered on a bomb that had targeted coalition soldiers. The device worked quickly, and well, in combination with a laptop, a fingerprint scanner, and a satellite unit.

The examining room was tiny and narrow, and its shape made for awkward work getting the large man's fingerprints on the pad of the Quick Capture device. Rowland put the device on an office chair and rolled it from one side of the table where the dead man lay to the other, taking prints from both his right and left hands. Rowland connected the device to the Integrated Automated Fingerprint Identification System — a database containing sixty-two million records, including seventy-seven thousand records of known or suspected terrorists — and the Department of Defense's Automated Biometric Identification System. In ten seconds he had identified the dead man. "The world was waiting to hear this name," Rowland later said. "And we had it in ten seconds."

That name was Tamerlan Tsarnaev. The twenty-six-year-old had a Massachusetts driver's license that listed his address as 410 Norfolk Street in Cambridge. He also had a record with the Cambridge Police Department: Four years earlier he had been arrested for slapping a former girlfriend in the face because she dressed lasciviously. It was surprising to learn that the FBI had opened a case on him in 2011 and claimed to have closed it months later. There were other people associated with the Norfolk Street address: Tamerlan's mother, Zubeidat; father, Anzor; sisters Bella and Ailina; and little brother, Dzhokhar — the man on the run.

CHAPTER SIX

Slip Away II

Dzhokhar Tsarnaev was wounded — badly. One bullet had come in through the driver's-side window, hit his left cheek, and exited through his right. His skull felt like it was on fire. His left wrist was useless, its bones shattered by bullets after he raised his arm in an attempt to shield himself from the oncoming barrage of gunshots. Shattered glass had rained into his eyes, which were swollen and bloody. He drove the carjacked Mercedes SUV — smashed and riddled with bullets, it was hardly inconspicuous — to the corner of Lincoln and Spruce Streets, about half a mile from Dexter Avenue, and left it by the curb. A spray of blood stained the driver's-side door, and a small amount of blood was on the floor mat. He was still bleeding, but not profusely.

BPD homicide investigators, along with an MSP trooper with a trained dog, arrived at the scene of the firefight in Watertown, but the FBI ordered them all to keep beyond the perimeter, according to two investigators on the condition of anonymity. No one knew why, since the suspect could not have been far away. And there was a blood trail.

Evidence would later show that Dzhokhar staggered up Franklin Street, leaving droplets of blood on the road. Investigators would find a bloody palm print on the hood of a car at 73 Franklin Street and another on a garage door at 71 Franklin Street. Broken glass was found in the rear of a shed, and two smashed iPhones and an ATM debit card in the name of the carjacking victim, Dun Meng, were found on the floor of the shed — in a slick of blood. The phones would eventually connect the bombing suspects to other men suspected of radical Muslim activity or connections, one of whom would vanish entirely. Nearly two thousand cops were in

Watertown at the time, but in the darkness, none of them noticed the blood trail that led to the backyard of David Henneberry at 67 Franklin Street — where his 1981 Seabird, the *Slip Away II*, was dry-docked under a tarp.

Dzhokhar used the last of his strength to hoist himself onto the swimming platform at the boat's stern, peel back the plastic tarp, and climb into the boat. His blood-streaked fingers stained the covering as he pulled it back over himself and then curled up in the fetal position on the bottom. He was sure he was going to die, but he had some things to say first. He found a pencil emblazoned with the name of Henneberry's son-in-law's business, Duffy Plumbing, in a toolbox on the floor. He gripped the pencil in his right hand, the one that wasn't mangled, and began to write on the boat's fiberglass walls. He produced a neatly written anti-American missive that would be discovered fifteen hours later, streaked with blood and pocked with gunshot holes.

> I'm jealous of my brother who has received the reward of *jannutul Firdaus* heaven *inshallah* before me. I do not mourn because his soul is very much alive. God has a plan for each person. Mine was to hide in this boat and shed some light on our actions. I ask Allah to make me a *shahied*, to allow me to return to him and be among all the righteous people in the highest levels of heaven.
>
> He who Allah guides no one can misguide!
>
> I bear witness that there is no God but Allah and that Muhammad is his messenger [hole] r actions came with [hole] a [hole] ssage and that is [hole] *ha Illalah*. The U.S. Government is killing our innocent civilians but most of you already know that. As a M [hole] I can't stand to see such evil go unpunished, we Muslims are one body, you hurt one you hurt us all, well at least that's how Muhammad (pbuh) wanted it to be [hole] ever, the *ummah* is beginning to rise/awa [hole]

has awoken the *mujahideen* [*sic*], know you are fighting men who look into the barrel of your gun and see
heaven, now how can you compete with that. We are
promised victory and we will surely get it. Now I don't
like killing innocent people it is forbidden in Islam but
due to said [hole] it is allowed.[1]

Dzhokhar also scratched a message into the portside wooden
slats under the railing of the boat. Ingeniously, he then sprayed
a fire extinguisher onto his messages so that the carved-out
letters would be highlighted by the extinguisher's white powdery
discharge.

As the wounded man wrote, SWAT teams were hunting him.
Police in protective gear raided a house in Chelsea that was home
to a Chechen family close to the Tsarnaevs. The youngest son had
posted photos of him shooting off fireworks with Dzhokhar in
the months before the blasts. The son wasn't at home, and there
was no sign of Dzhokhar. Pot dealers in Watertown who lived
on the block where Dzhokhar had received a parking ticket for
leaving the green Honda on the street overnight during a snow
emergency were dragged out of their apartment in handcuffs. The
dealers were the sons of prominent Boston restaurateurs and had
smoked weed with both Tsarnaev brothers. Members of the FBI's
elite Hostage Rescue Team (HRT) arrived outside an off-campus
housing apartment used by many University of Massachusetts–
Dartmouth students. They trained red laser sights on the occupants inside after a cell phone connected to Dzhokhar pinged off
a nearby cell phone tower, an indicator that he could be nearby.

At the same time, evidence teams were counting the bullet and
bomb remnants that were sprayed across Laurel Street and Dexter
Avenue, placing as many as three hundred small yellow evidence
cones in front yards, alongside scattered children's toys. Members
of the teams marked the fifty-six 9-millimeter bullets fired by the
suspects from a Ruger P95 during the twelve-minute gun battle

and the rounds fired by multiple police agencies. Markers were put near the remnants of the exploded pressure-cooker bomb, including one next to a sedan in which the pot had become embedded. Investigators found what they believed to be one of the transmitters used to trigger at least one of the bombs on Boylston Street — a modified FlySky transmitter ordinarily used for a remote-control toy truck but altered as a way to detonate a device from a distance. They also found a dead man's switch, sparking concerns that Dzhokhar was wearing a suicide vest.

Because bomb technicians were afraid that the Tsarnaevs had left unexploded devices at the scene, they decided not to use X-rays to determine whether abandoned bags or packages were explosive. Instead they used what is known as a general detonation, a technique in which a water cannon is used to determine what might have been hidden in any unattended box or bag.[2] The pipe bombs that the bombers had hurled at police — the two that exploded and the two that didn't — needed to be "rendered safe," a procedure that involved deploying specialized robots to blast the devices with water cannons. And that's when the cops at the scene heard someone yell, "There's a bomb!"

Bobby McCarthy, a trooper with the MSP Hazardous Devices Unit, was among the bomb-scene technicians who approached the stolen Mercedes. The SUV's doors were open, and a plastic container with a long piece of green hobby wire could be seen in the floorboard behind the driver's seat. Hobby wire is used to ignite fireworks or toy rockets. It burns down and then hits an explosive charge to spark a blast.

The device would be referred to by investigators as a Tupperware bomb because of the kind of container in which it was kept. (Tupperware released a statement in 2015 pointing out that the description was inaccurate because the device was actually constructed in a Rubbermaid-brand plastic container, but the name *Tupperware bomb* stuck.) It was not an item that anyone wanted to handle. It was too heavy for a bomb robot to disarm, so the specialists on scene donned their bomb suits and attached a heavy clamp to the device. McCarthy attached the clamp to a rope, wrapped the rope around a tree limb, went behind a house to take cover, and pulled the rope. The Tupperware container flew out of the vehicle and into the street, where the specialists examined it. Three pieces of hobby wire had been snaked into three pounds of explosive powder. The long piece of green hobby wire appeared to have been specifically designed to allow someone to detonate the bomb from a distance.

Though the FBI and MSP bomb experts would later describe the Tupperware device as possessing "all the components, the non-electrical fusing system, the main charge and the container," including three pounds of explosive powder, needed to create an extremely powerful IED,[3] strangely, no one would ever be charged with possessing it. Dzhokhar would be charged with possession of the four pipe bombs, two of which had been detonated and two of which were duds, and the four-quart Fagor pressure-cooker bomb detonated in Watertown, as well as the weapons of mass destruction that exploded on Boylston Street — but not with possessing the Tupperware device. Bomb investigators, including McCarthy, found this highly unusual. Forensics would later show that the bomb had the fingerprints of both Tsarnaev brothers but did not indicate if there were other prints on the plastic container.

David Henneberry was a retired phone company employee who had the patience to stay in his house and wait for the shelter-in-place order to be lifted while viewing the chaos outside through his window. At one point he looked out and noticed that two of the chafing guards had fallen from his boat and the plastic tarp looked a little loose, but he let that discovery go uninvestigated until authorities lifted the shelter-in-place order around 6:00 PM.

"I'm going to go out and see what's going on," Henneberry told his wife. It would also give him a chance to enjoy his first cigarette of the day. He remembered that he wanted to "put the pads back up. Simple." He figured the wind must have loosened the tarp, but as he got closer he saw that it was looser than it should have been, even from a strong gust.

He grabbed a stepladder, and as he climbed it he noticed the loosened strap. "Oh my God. Is that blood?" he said aloud to no one in particular.[4] Blood was smeared all over the boat's interior, and some dripping streaks of it had dried. His eyes followed the blood trail, and that's when he saw the body — a man in black shoes, khaki pants, and a hooded sweatshirt lying on his side. Henneberry scrambled down the ladder and rushed into the house. Wordlessly his wife handed him the phone, and he called 911. BPD Deputy Superintendent Bill Evans was six blocks away in Watertown when he heard about the 911 call that had been placed from 67 Franklin Street. He grabbed a Watertown cop. "Take me to this address," he ordered.[5] BPD Commander Bobby Merner, a hard-charging cop who led the city's homicide unit, joined them in the car.

"I'm at the boat," Evans transmitted to the dispatcher less than a minute later. "We have it secure. All we need is a tactical team. Send the tac team."

Dzhokhar Tsarnaev was poking at the plastic tarp from underneath with what looked like a gun. Evans had been all over the Watertown crime scene. He knew there had been two muzzle flashes but only one gun recovered, so he had to assume that the suspect in the boat was armed. Then there was the dead man's switch that had been found in the bushes near the scene of the shootout. Cops had been so paranoid during the daylong manhunt that a Watertown cop stopped and frisked an old Armenian man with a Walkman. The cop was too young to recognize the device and thought it might be an arming mechanism.

Troopers from the MSP Air Wing hovered overhead and pointed a forward-looking infrared camera, which can detect a heat source, at the boat. Images created by such cameras normally look like a blob, but in this instance the pilot clearly saw a person inside the boat. The air wing troopers needed to be the eyes for the tactical team on the ground, but thirty-knot winds were bouncing them mercilessly. "No movement," a dispatcher transmitted, "no movement from the boat on the last pass from the air wing."[6]

Police on the ground began evacuating the residents of surrounding homes. There were cops everywhere as commanders from different departments tried to take control at the scene.

"Any vehicle in front of 67 Franklin with lights on: Shut down your lights. You are backlighting the crime scene," a dispatcher transmitted. Then came a call for radio silence.

Revere Police Department Chief Joseph Cafarelli, a former US Marine, commanded the North Metro SWAT team that on this day consisted of roughly a dozen officers from the Everett, Malden, and Revere Police Departments. The officers were already outfitted in what they referred to as their "call-out gear": helmets, M4 rifles, bulletproof vests, protective eyewear, extra magazines for pistols and rifles, and plastic cuffs. The North Metro SWAT team worked with officers from the transit police, who were also geared up, and some team members moved to the right side of the Henneberry house. BPD SWAT officers took up positions at the left side of the small white house. Everett Police Department Officer Matt Cunningham — a trained sniper who had served in the US Marine Corps during Operation Iraqi Freedom and in the US Army in Sarajevo during NATO's intervention into Bosnia's bloody internecine war — took up a position with his fellow SWAT team member Revere Police Department Officer Joe Turner at a window on the second floor of the Henneberry house. The owners had invited them in, and they trained their rifles' red laser sights on the boat below.

All of the cops on the scene had been working for at least fourteen hours, since responding to the scene of MIT Police Officer Sean Collier's murder. The North Metro SWAT team had sprinted with their heavy equipment roughly a quarter mile to the Franklin Street address.[7]

SWAT team commanders decided to flush out the suspect with flash-bang and stun grenades, both nonlethal devices designed to disorient with bursts of light and noise. "All units do not return fire," an FBI supervisory agent broadcast over his radio. "There might be a flash bang from the FBI. Do not return fire."

There was a blast and then a flame in the stern of the boat. "The suspect is sitting up in the boat. Repeat. The suspect is sitting up in the boat inside the stern," a dispatcher broadcast over the police radios.[8] He was trying to set what he thought was a can of gasoline ablaze, raising a new concern: fire combined with the boat's forty-gallon fuel tank. Darkness, then floodlights from a Lenco BearCat — a small armored tactical vehicle that provides cover for police officers in urban environments much as a tank would in warfare — suddenly illuminated the boat. Cafarelli's brother John, also a Revere Police Department officer assigned to the North Metro SWAT team, was driving the vehicle.

"Air Wing reporting no movement in the back of the boat," a dispatcher transmitted. Evans listened to every word and asked once again for radio silence from officers so that the commanders in charge of the scene could communicate with one another. "There is movement on top of the stairs. Beware of booby traps," a dispatcher transmitted over the radio.

The movement sparked chaos. Thinking the suspect was armed, a police officer opened fire, prompting more gunshots — all fired by cops. The suspect, it would turn out, was unarmed. No one knows who fired that first round, but the fusillade lasted for ten to fifteen seconds while 126 bullets were fired into the boat.

"Shots fired! Shots fired," Evans screamed into his radio. Furious — a cop was more likely to be hit than the suspect — Evans jumped out of his car with a megaphone in his hand: "Hold your fire! Hold your fire! There are friendlies all around this boat!"[9]

When the bullets stopped, an FBI supervisor named Derek Bailey approached Evans and told him: "From now on every decision at this scene will be made by you." Evans nodded. The standoff continued until finally, more than an hour and a half later, at 8:30 PM, the BearCat was sent in to rip back the plastic tarp. A voice emerged from inside the bullet-riddled boat. It was weak, but Cunningham could hear it from his perch at the second-floor window. So could the FBI negotiator from the HRT, who was standing next to him.

With a distinct Russian accent, the teenager yelled, "They're going to kill me! I don't want to die. They're going to kill me. I need help. They're going to kill me."[10]

The HRT negotiator responded over his bullhorn: "Come out! No one is going to hurt you. Keep your hands visible. You have to climb out. No one is coming in."

Dzhokhar Tsarnaev's leg came out first. He slung it over the side of the boat and slowly hoisted himself to the deck, blood dripping from his wounds, his face smeared with blood and highlighted with red laser sights from multiple rifles, including Cunningham's. The negotiator ordered him to lift his shirt. He did so, feebly.

"He lost so much blood he started wavering. He was bleeding from everywhere. No one wanted him to fall back into the boat. No one had any idea what was inside it," Cunningham remembered.

Cafarelli's team was ready to act and got into what SWAT teams referred to as a "stick formation," officers in a line. This line consisted of Cafarelli, Malden Police Department Sergeant Rich Correale, and Revere Police Department Officer Mike Trovato (another combat veteran; he had served in the US Army during Operation Iraqi Freedom). Then, on three, they swarmed the boat.

"I grabbed a leg," Cafarelli remembered. "Everyone had a limb, and we pulled him to the ground and he landed on his back."

Trovato ripped open the suspect's shirt, looking for a suicide vest or IEDs, and patted him down for weapons. Nothing was found. A North Metro SWAT officer held the teenager down as a transit officer handcuffed him. Tactical EMTS and medics from the FBI and ATF swarmed in to treat the bomber's wounds.

"North Metro SWAT has one in custody," was announced over the radio, and the cops who had massed along the streets and in the backyards of the homes surrounding 67 Franklin Street sent up a roar.

Having a transit police officer cuff Dzhokhar was a sign of respect for Dic Donohue, who was still fighting for his life. Two Boston EMS paramedics were called in to take custody of the suspect and transport him to Beth Israel Deaconess Medical Center, the same hospital where his brother had been pronounced dead that morning.

Paramedic Laura Lee took a position at Dzhokhar's head and "grabbed a pulse."[11] He was still breathing but bleeding. Lee and her partner rolled Dzhokhar onto a "scoop board" and hustled him into the back of the ambulance, followed by several cops who tried to crowd inside "the bus." "Everybody wanted to get in. But, you know, there was only room for that many," Lee recalled. The paramedics needed room to work, but investigators wanted to keep the suspect talking.

Lee assessed his wounds: "His hair was all matted, so we didn't really sort of examine it very, very closely or it might have started to bleed again. He had a wound along the jaw here that was open. It looked like one of the fragments had probably gone off. His cheek looked a little deformed." At some point, Lee remembered, Dzhokhar's eyes rolled up into the back of his head, but she and her partner kept him alert by asking him a series of questions, intentionally using a loud voice. One of the questions they asked the bleeding teenager who was suspected of an imaginably evil act was whether he had any allergies.

"He said he was allergic to cats," Lee recalled.

As Dzhokhar was raced to the hospital, the BPD posted a tweet: "CAPTURED!!! The hunt is over. The search is done. The terror is over. And justice has won. Suspect in custody."[12]

Governor Patrick, Mayor Menino (still in his wheelchair), and public safety officials from all over the state met a massive swarm of reporters to deliver the extraordinary news that the manhunt was over. "We have a victory," announced MSP Colonel Tim Alben. "We got him," said BPD Commissioner Davis.[13] The mood was jubilant but chaotic at the Watertown mall's makeshift command center. By then reporters and cops had been gathered there for more than twenty-four hours, with political big shots and police brass jockeying for position in front of the cameras.

Evans wanted no part of it. He turned to Merner and said, "Let's go get a beer."[14] They had earned it. And when they arrived at Doyle's — a bar in Jamaica Plain popular with civil servants — no one would let them pay for anything.

Dzhokhar arrived at the hospital just after 9:00 PM in critical condition with gunshot wounds to the side of his head, face, throat, jaw, left hand, and both legs. He was intubated and rushed into surgery. The next morning, when Dzhokhar woke up in the Surgical Intensive Care Unit heavily medicated, his jaw wired shut, deaf in his left ear, and handcuffed to his bed, agents from the High-Value Detainee Interrogation Group (HIG), a cooperative effort among the FBI, CIA, Department of Defense, and other government agencies, were in the room. Agents from the FBI handed him a notebook and paper.

He wrote his address, incorrectly, on the first page. The agents asked him if there were any more bombs. He wrote "NO!" Then he wrote "lawyer" — ten times.[15]

"Is it me or do you hear some noise," he wrote.

At another point he scribbled, "I am tired. Leave me alone," and his pen trailed off the page. For hours the terrorist wrote short notes complaining of his pain or exhaustion. He also asked questions about his brother, whose death he had caused by dragging him under the wheel well of a stolen Mercedes. The agents wouldn't tell him if Tamerlan was alive or dead until he answered some questions about "danger from other individuals, devices, or otherwise."

"Is my brother alive? I know you know. Is he living? Is he alive?" Dzhokhar wrote on his second day in the hospital. "Is he alive? One person can tell you that."

The next day he wrote, "Is he alive? Show me the news. What's today? Where is he? Can I sleep? Can you not handcuff my right arm? Where is my bro????"

PART 2

Timeline of Terror

Who Are the Marathon Bombers?

CHAPTER SEVEN

Growing Up Tsarnaev

Raisat Suleimanova remembered the last time she saw her Aunt Zubeidat Tsarnaeva, which was in 2010. Zubeidat was wearing a black hijab and a burka that covered her body. It was unnerving for Raisat: "It was a shock for me. Knowing what kind of person Zubeidat used to be, it was very strange to see that. She used to be such a fashionable person. She loved to wear bright clothing; and now to see her wearing a hijab it was a shock, and not just for me, but for my mother and everyone else."[1]

Raisat said that Zubeidat used to be known as a flamboyant dresser, with her fur coats, leopard-print bags, big sunglasses, and magenta lipstick. Zubeidat even put highlights in her hair, a rarity in the Republic of Dagestan. She "had this bright personality," Raisat remembered. "She's a strong person. She's a very determined person. She always wanted everything excellent, to be ideal in her life, to be beautiful."

Her niece remembered Zubeidat's garrulous nature, saying that she was "very social, very loud" and drove her husband, Anzor Tsarnaev, batty. He was a quiet man, hardly the life of the party, and what little personality he possessed seemed to drain out of him when his wife was around. Still, he followed her like a puppy, Raisat explained, not exactly a trait that Russian men are known for. "Anzor was crazy in love with Zubeidat, crazy, crazy in love. He was worshipping her. He wouldn't go anywhere without her. He was very jealous of her." But she could not be tamed, not even as a little girl.

Zubeidat Khiramagomedovna was born May 8, 1967, in Chokh, a village in the Gunibskiy District of Dagestan, in the mountains along the Caspian Sea. Her native village is now a hotbed of an ultraconservative strain of Islam known as Salafism, which declares that Salafi Muslims are the only true interpreters of the Quran and that moderate Muslims are kaffirs — nonbelievers or infidels. When she was growing up under Soviet communism, however, Salafism did not yet have a toehold in Dagestan. After the borders opened in the 1990s, young men traveled to Saudi Arabia and other conservative Sunni Muslim states and brought it back home with them. Recruiters followed to help introduce radical Salafi views to a part of the world where they previously held no sway. The most visible proponents of Salafism today are the barbarous Islamic State of Iraq and Syria (ISIS) militants.

Zubeidat was seven years old when her mother died of breast cancer. After that she was shuffled from brother to brother and from region to region. By the time she reached college age, she was eager to leave Dagestan and moved to Novosibirsk, Siberia, where yet another brother had made his home. There she met Anzor, who was serving his mandatory military term in the early 1980s. They married in 1986 — exactly one day before their eldest child, Tamerlan, was born. A photograph of the baby and his parents shows Zubeidat's wild, Western style: Her raven hair is piled haphazardly atop her head, and streaks of bright color highlight her face. Other family photos from that era show her in low-cut dresses and wearing red lipstick. The couple settled in Kyrgyzstan, where more children were born: Bella in 1988, Ailina in 1990, and Dzhokhar in 1993. A bloody, internecine war ravaged the region, and the Tsarnaev family moved to Chechnya, another cauldron of ethnic violence, and then back to Kyrgyzstan before finally following Anzor's brothers to the United States.

By then, though, the tensions between the husband's and wife's families were already palpable. Zubeidat's family, which belonged to the Avar Muslim ethnic group, felt that Anzor, who was of Chechen ethnicity, was weak and underemployed, chasing odd jobs all over Russia to the detriment of his children. "Unfortunately they moved around a lot, and the children had to switch schools a lot. So the children didn't have time to adapt to the new school when it was time to move again," Raisat recalled. "So they always lived out of suitcases, so to speak. We would even say, 'You're like gypsies. You always move around. You never stay in one place for a long time.'"

In one family photo Zubeidat had erected a Christmas tree filled with lights and ornaments and served wine, all considered by her family a sign that she was falling away from Islam. "They would celebrate the major Muslim holidays, but they wouldn't pray five times a day," Raisat remembered.

Everywhere they moved, the family struggled to make ends meet. In 2002 the odd jobs dried up for Anzor, and there was friction with local government officials. Anzor and Zubeidat successfully applied for a ninety-day tourist visa and left the country to visit family members in the Boston area.[2] Zubeidat met her family for a last good-bye before she left. The mood was subdued. For once Zubeidat was quiet and acting like a dutiful wife to Anzor. They would be relying on his family for help once they were in the United States. In particular they would lean on his younger brother Ruslan, who had shortened his last name to Tsarni, to provide the resources and connections they would need to stay in the United States. A lawyer, Ruslan had moved to the United States in 1995 and had become an American citizen after marrying the daughter of a Russian-speaking CIA official, Graham Fuller, a Harvard University graduate who had served as the vice chair of the National Intelligence Council, a prestigious post reserved for the most revered agents.

In Chechen families older brothers did not usually seek help from younger brothers. Traditionally the eldest son would take care of his younger siblings, as Zubeidat's older brothers had taken care of her after their mother died. Anzor was ashamed that he needed Ruslan's help. Not only did he need Ruslan to pave the way for them in the United States, but he also needed him to take care of their three older children, Tamerlan, Bella, and Ailina. Ruslan was settled in Kazakhstan at the moment as an American working abroad, and his nephew and two nieces were sent to stay with him.

Anzor and Zubeidat would travel with Dzhokhar, the baby of the family, who, according to multiple family members, was an unusually happy eight-year-old. Dzhokhar's presence could prove helpful when his parents applied for political asylum as refugees from a war-torn region of the former Soviet Union.

Zubeidat's family hated to see Dzhokhar go. They called him Jahar, and everyone loved him. "He was a very sunny child," Raisat said. "Very kind, very warm." She has a cherished memory of watching him cry when Mustafa died in *The Lion King*.

Ruslan helped the family find a place to live in the United States. For the first month eight-year-old Dzhokhar and his parents stayed in the home of famed Chechen surgeon Khassan Baiev in Needham, Massachusetts. By the time the other three children arrived, the Tsarnaevs had found a taxpayer-funded apartment in Cambridge. Political refugees were eligible for subsidized housing benefits through the Department of Housing and Urban Development's Housing Choice Voucher Program (Section 8).[3] The Tsarnaevs moved into a cramped top-floor apartment at 410 Norfolk Street in Cambridge, owned by the wife of a friend of Ruslan's, a Russian émigré named Alexander Lipson who taught Russian and Slavic linguistics to Harvard University students. Graham Fuller, who went on to become a longtime CIA operations officer and had acted as the station chief in Ankara, Turkey, had been one of Lipson's brightest students. His biographical information states:

> [I] first became smitten with the Middle East at age 16 while reading *National Geographic* magazines and being enticed by the exotic landscapes, the culture, and the crazy shapes of the Arabic language that I decided I had to learn. I studied a lot about the Middle East, and Russia, when I was in university. I always expected

to become an academic, but my draft board deemed otherwise; I was drafted and sent into intelligence work. I had an extraordinary chance to learn about the Middle East first hand while serving as a CIA operations officer all over — Turkey, Lebanon, Saudi Arabia, Yemen, Afghanistan and Hong Kong for two decades. It was an education in itself, and a chance to travel and learn a lot of languages, which I loved. I then "came in from the cold" and was appointed a top analyst at CIA for global forecasting.[4]

He retired from the CIA in 1987 but continues to write about the Middle East for various think tanks.

According to some of Fuller's writings, he advised the administrations of both President Ronald Reagan and President Bill Clinton to use Muslim extremists to fight the former Soviet Union. The Northern Caucasus region had many young Muslim men who hated the Russians and could be recruited along with jihadists from Saudi Arabia, Pakistan, and other Middle Eastern countries. These recruits, who could be trained in techniques of guerrilla insurgency and sent to fight against the Soviets in occupied Afghanistan, were called mujahideen. CIA-trained mujahideen later fought against the Russians in their own republics of Chechnya, Dagestan, and other areas of the former Soviet Union with large Muslim populations. One of them was a Saudi who would go on to mastermind the attacks on New York and Washington, DC, on September 11, 2001: Osama bin Laden.

Although it is unclear how Ruslan and Fuller met, there is no question they became close. Fuller says that his daughter was married to Ruslan for about five years and spent a year living with him in Bishkek — one of the cities where the Tsarnaev family had lived before immigrating to the United States.[5]

Immigration officials believed Anzor's story that his life was in danger because of his Chechen heritage and granted the family refugee status within weeks of their arrival in 2002. That meant that Tamerlan, Bella, and Ailina — then sixteen, fourteen, and twelve, respectively — would also be invited into the United States as refugees. Inexplicably, the siblings traveled to Turkey to make the trip to the United States, rather than flying out of Moscow. They arrived in the United States on July 19, 2003.[6] Fuller had lived in Turkey extensively and wrote a book about the region, *The New Turkish Republic: Turkey as a Pivotal State in the Muslim World*, that was published five years later.

A strange question would emerge in 2016 when a Freedom of Information Act request led to the release of Tamerlan's immigration records. Nearly three years earlier, Department of Homeland Security (DHS) Secretary Janet Napolitano had denied a similar request made by members of Congress. The records, which included dozens of pages of entirely redacted material, contained two "Medical Examination for Immigrant or Refugee Applicant" forms for Tamerlan. Both listed the same name (Tamerlan Tsarnaev) and date of birth (October 21, 1986). Both had been filled out at the US embassy in Ankara, Turkey. Both noted that Tamerlan did not have an "apparent defect, disease, or disability" or HIV 1 or HIV 2.[7] After arriving in Cambridge, however, he did test positive for tuberculosis and received medicine for the condition. TB is often cited as a reason not to admit an immigrant seeking asylum in the country. Both were dated July 10, 2003. But the photo attached to one form showed a blue-eyed man who did not resemble Tamerlan at all. The photo stapled to the other form showed the sixteen-year-old Tamerlan. Both men were photographed wearing identical patterned shirts with black collars, something the State Department has yet to explain. Despite repeated requests by Dzhokhar Tsarnaev's legal team, the State Department has steadfastly refused to release the A-files for Tamerlan's family.

Shortly after the older three Tsarnaev children left for the United States, Ruslan moved to the Washington, DC, area with his second wife, Zalina. He still interacted with his nieces and nephews and continued to despise his brother's wife and to blame her as his brother began to spiral into a dark depression. "I helped that family. I raised that family. I tried to save those children. But they are all like their mother. Evil spawn from an evil woman," Ruslan said after Tamerlan and Dzhokhar were identified as the marathon bombers.[8]

By 2006 everyone in the Tsarnaev family had obtained legal permanent alien status and green cards, which made them all eligible for employment. But not a single member of the family has held a permanent job in the United States, including Anzor. The federal subsidy covered their rent; the Supplemental Nutrition Assistance Program (SNAP) helped pay for food, and cash withdrawn through Electronic Benefits Transfer (EBT) cards was used for clothing. The only income-producing work performed by family members was done off the record, so no income taxes were ever paid. Zubeidat did facials in the cramped apartment for cash. Tamerlan delivered pizzas, his immigration paperwork said. Dzhokhar sold drugs, according to court testimony.

Sam Lipson, Alexander's son, remembers Anzor as a reserved, strong man — a former boxer in Russia who pushed his eldest son into the ring, too. But in America, he seemed to wither, especially in the presence of Zubeidat. Her English was better than his, and she was "loquacious," Sam remembered. Anzor "was a person of few words, is kind of the way I imagined, you know, sort of a cowboy. He made good eye contact, was very warm, but didn't speak much. She spoke a fair amount. Her English was fairly good."

When Alexander died, his wife, Joanna Herlihy, grew closer to the Tsarnaev children and tried to watch out for them, her son said — especially the girls. Ruslan, too, was worried about the corrupting influence of their mother on Bella and Ailina.

No one could stop the girls from following their mother into a world of welfare dependency and unmarried pregnancies. The older daughter, Bella, had attended Cambridge Rindge and Latin School but dropped out after becoming pregnant at sixteen. She was briefly married to a Chechen Muslim named Mamakev Rizvan — a marriage her father arranged after she became pregnant. After the marriage ended she had a series of boyfriends.

On December 11, 2012, police were called to the home in Fairview, New Jersey, that Bella was sharing with her then-boyfriend Ahmad Khalid, after she allegedly scratched him. The officers smelled pot and raided the house. They found drugs and $537 in cash and arrested both Bella and Ahmad on the spot. She pleaded not guilty to drug charges a month after the Boston Marathon bombings, and a judge allowed her to enter a rehabilitation program that would wipe her record clean if she stayed out of trouble. The FBI raided the same New Jersey house again, during the manhunt for Bella's brother Dzhokhar.

Ruslan became a national figure four days after the marathon attacks, when he held a press conference on the lawn of his home in Montgomery Village, Maryland. He denounced his nephews as "losers" and added, "We are ashamed." He also urged Dzhokhar to turn himself in: "He put a shame on this family. He put a shame on the entire Chechnyan ethnicity."[9]

By then Tamerlan was dead. Ruslan had not called the FBI when photos of his nephews — then identified only as Suspects Black Hat and White Hat — were released, according to FBI investigators who spoke on the basis of anonymity.

Ailina was Ruslan's favorite niece. He called her a "sweet, sweet girl, growing up," and wanted to get her away from Zubeidat so badly that he arranged a marriage for her when she was only sixteen. Too young to marry without court approval, she petitioned the Commonwealth of Massachusetts Probate and Family Court on September 12, 2006. The court granted her request the same day.[10] Her husband, Elmirza Khozhugov, was close to Ruslan. "She threw that marriage away," Ruslan said later.

Police records tell a different story. After the wedding Ailina moved with her husband to the West Coast. Months later she called the police and reported that her new husband had tried to strangle her. Khozhugov pleaded guilty to assault charges, and the couple divorced.

On April 6, 2010, Ailina, now twenty and living back in the Boston area, was among a group of diners at an Applebee's restaurant that paid the bill with counterfeit money. Their server picked up on the scam, ran outside, and jotted down the driver's license plate number. Boston police found that the car was registered to Ruslan's second wife, Zalina Tsarni of 410 Norfolk Street in Cambridge. Zalina, of course, no longer lived at that address. She hadn't even been to Boston since 2003. A Secret Service agent and two BPD detectives were sent to the Tsarnaevs' home to investigate. Zubeidat was there, and she was fully aware that Zalina's identity had been stolen and then used to register the family car and obtain an alternative driver's license, thereby qualifying the family for additional EBT funds in Zalina's name. But none of that was mentioned to investigators. Zubeidat told them that Zalina wasn't home, and the police went on their way.

Subpoenas were then mailed to Zalina Tsarni at the Tsarnaevs' address, but they were ignored. In September 2010 an arrest warrant was issued for Zalina Tsarnaeva, the woman police believed had been driving the car used in a counterfeit money crime. Ruslan was livid. He faxed paperwork to the Boston police proving that his wife lived in Maryland with him, and BPD detectives paid Zubeidat another visit. This time she had a different story. She said that her daughter Ailina might have used her aunt's information accidentally, but they couldn't question her because she no longer lived with her. "Zubeidat Tsarnaeva stated that her daughter Ailina had moved about three months ago into a shelter with her son and sister Bella," BPD Detective Robert Kenney wrote in a police report. "Mrs. Tsarnaeva stated the reason was that her daughters felt that she was too strict."[11]

Kenney recalled the arrest warrant for Zalina, and her legal troubles were over. So was Ruslan's relationship with his brother's family: "I officially disowned them from my soul in 2010 after they caused my wife and me so many problems. I did so much for them. Helped them in Russia, helped them here. Took the kids into my home. Gave them money. They disgraced me."

By the time of the bombings, Ailina Tsarnaeva had moved on to a new man, with whom she had a baby. He was also the father of three children with another woman, and that woman was giving him a hard time in a custody battle, according to the NYPD. Ailina took matters into her own hands, allegedly calling the woman and making this threat: "Leave my man alone. Stop looking for him. I have people. I know people who can put a bomb where you live."[12] Considering the charges that Ailina's brother was facing, the woman took the threat very seriously. So did the NYPD. Ailina turned herself in at the 30th Precinct, but the charges were later dropped. She still faced legal proceedings on unrelated issues in Massachusetts, where she appeared in a South Boston courtroom in July 2014. When asked about the charges against her brother, Ailina screeched, "Everyone knows he was framed. Accept it!"[13]

———

Tamerlan Tsarnaev had his own problems with relationships, court records show. In 2009 he was dating two women. One was a pretty, petite brunette named Katherine Russell, who had grown up in the posh Rhode Island town of North Kingston under the watchful eyes of her father, an emergency room physician, and her mother, a nurse. Katherine was attending classes at Suffolk University and working at an Italian ice cream shop, a *gelateria*, in the North End, Boston's Little Italy. The other woman was a neighborhood girl, Nadine Ascencao, who would tell reporters that she had lost her virginity to the muscular boxer and had been in love with him for three years, starting when he was a fun-loving party boy who dressed colorfully in metallic shoes and designer jackets. But then things started to change. He started watching jihadi videos and told her she had to convert to Islam.

On August 12, 2009, Nadine was leaving to go to a family barbecue when Tamerlan told her she was dressed too provocatively and slapped her face. Nadine called 911 from her cell phone, crying hysterically that her boyfriend had "just beat her up."[14] When a Cambridge police cruiser showed up, Tamerlan arrogantly confessed. "Yeah, I slapped her," he said, according to the Cambridge Police Department report of the incident, adding that the two had been arguing about his other girlfriend. The police arrested Tamerlan for domestic violence, but Nadine refused medical attention and declined to file charges, so the case was eventually dismissed.

————

Katherine and Tamerlan were an unlikely pair. Having grown up in a sprawling home in an upscale suburb as the daughter of medical professionals, she was enrolled in college, holding down a part-time job, and sharing a North End apartment with a roommate. Then she met Tamerlan, an overbearing and abusive man who has been accused of hitting her more than once.[15]

Katherine's mother, Judy, was horrified when at some point in 2010 her daughter began to wear a hijab and study the Quran. Her grades at Suffolk University began to suffer, and she eventually dropped out. Gina Crawford, Katherine's best friend from fifth grade on, saw the changes and reached out to Judy. Katherine's roommate, Amanda Ransom, was so afraid of Tamerlan's explosive temper that she moved out.

Judy knew that it was time for her to talk to both Katherine and Tamerlan about where their relationship was headed, and she invited them for dinner in North Kingston. The evening didn't go well. Katherine and Tamerlan were nearly two hours late and had no good excuse for their tardiness. "It really irritated me. It wasn't a good way to start off," Judy recalled. Besides, "it was hard to get to know him, and he didn't really seem interested in getting to know us, so it didn't start off on a really good footing."[16]

Tamerlan was not just verbally and physically abusive; he was also a womanizer who cheated on Katherine repeatedly. The cheating came as a relief to Judy. "I didn't really want her to be with him," she said. "I didn't think they were a good match. He didn't seem to have any — [pause]. The only thing he had passion about, what really was driving him was boxing at that point. So he didn't really have a job."

Judy's concerns increased as her daughter and Tamerlan tried to push their Islamic views on her and the rest of the Russell family, who had never been very religious. All of a sudden her daughter — her little Katie, who loved ballet and jazz and who had worked hard to get into Suffolk University — was quitting college in her junior year, converting to Islam, and talking about marrying the unemployed boxer. "He became much more religious and talked about it much more frequently," she said. "Like anytime I saw him, he would talk about it and try to, you know, show me books and get me to learn about it."

The close relationship she had had with Katherine began to grow more distant, especially when her daughter told Judy on the same day both that she was pregnant and that she was going to start not just covering her head but wearing a burka. Her mother tried to talk her out of marrying Tamerlan, telling her that he was no good. Katherine responded to her mother's criticism by not inviting anyone from her family to her wedding. "No one went," Judy said. The memory made her voice shake with hurt even six years later.

The family didn't miss much. The June 21, 2010, ceremony in Boston's Masjid Al-Qur'aan mosque was anything but romantic. Taalib Mahdee, the imam at the mosque in the hardscrabble neighborhood of Dorchester, recalled that Katherine called him and simply said, "We want to get married."[17] He was quick to agree, because Muslim teachings say it is good to be married. He didn't meet the couple until they showed up on a ninety-degree day, Katherine sweaty and heavy under the burka, Tamerlan in a button-down shirt and dress pants. In the cluttered and carpeted second-floor mosque, they exchanged promises to be good to Allah and each other. Mahdee never saw them again. It was bizarre that they hadn't gotten married in Tamerlan's own mosque, the Islamic Society of Boston's mosque on Prospect Street in Cambridge, just a few blocks from their Norfolk Street home.

In October, Katherine gave birth to a little girl. By then she had adopted the Muslim name Karima, and she and Tamerlan named their daughter Zahira. But there was no room for the new mother and a wailing baby in the Tsarnaevs' cramped Cambridge apartment, so she moved back home with her parents, who welcomed their daughter and granddaughter with open arms. Sometimes Tamerlan would visit his wife and new baby on the weekend, Judy said, but what was supposed to be a temporary visit so Zahira could get acquainted with her grandparents stretched into a ten-month stay, with no financial support whatsoever from Tamerlan. The Russells were paying for diapers and baby food. Enough was enough, Judy told her daughter. "I thought it was time that he supported his — you know, his wife and daughter."

Katherine had told her parents that Tamerlan's father was a lawyer, but that was a lie. Anzor, Judy discovered after she did some checking, had "bought his law degree," which, she was told, "is typical in Chechnya." Tamerlan's sisters — divorced teenagers — had babies of their own. Tamerlan's mother was terrifying, stern and completely covered with a black headscarf and burka. And all of them were living in that tiny apartment on Norfolk Street in Cambridge, decorated with multiple black Islamic flags often associated with jihad.

——

Tamerlan may have started a new life with Katherine/Karima — growing a five-inch beard and beginning to abstain from drugs and alcohol like a good Muslim — but his arrest for domestic violence against Nadine continued to haunt him. In fact, the arrest made him ineligible for US citizenship for five years. The naturalization process that the Tsarnaevs had applied for as political refugees contained a morals clause, and his slapping Nadine constituted an act of "moral turpitude."

It was a devastating blow for someone who dreamed of fighting in the Olympic games as a member of the US boxing team. Tamerlan had been granted a green card in 2006, but legal permanent residents are not eligible for any US team that competes in the Olympics. Tamerlan was a two-time heavyweight Golden Gloves champion, a laudable accomplishment, but green card holders are also unable to compete in the National Tournament of Champions. He was so desperate to change his status that in 2009 he participated in an online photo essay by the photographer Johannes Hirn called "Will Box for Passport." The photo was shot at Wai Kru, a mixed martial arts gym in Brighton that was like a second home to Tamerlan. Mixed martial arts, or MMA, would become the only thing in addition to Islam to which Tamerlan dedicated himself.

Tamerlan started keeping a journal. In one entry he wrote, "Now I live because I'm a warrior . . . and someday I want to stand before the One. The mujahedeen spent a long time living in a dream. And is slowly waking up."[18] Investigators believe that Tamerlan woke his inner mujahideen by committing a grisly triple homicide on the tenth anniversary of the 9/11 terrorist attacks.[19]

CHAPTER EIGHT

It Looks Like an Al Qaeda Training Video in Here

The tenth anniversary of the deadliest terror attack on American soil was especially meaningful in Boston because two of the hijacked planes took off from Logan Airport. The bloodshed began at 8:13 that morning, when Mohamed Atta took control of American Airlines Flight 11 one minute after the Boeing 767 carrying ninety-two people left the ground.[1]

Atta used a box cutter to take out the pilots, as fellow hijackers Waleed al-Shehri and his brother, Wail al-Shehri, fatally stabbed two female flight attendants. The al-Shehris were Saudi but had received terrorist training "in the forests" of Chechnya before joining the 9/11 hijackers. Their victims' screams were heard by American Airlines ground workers after flight attendant Betty Ong managed to call a gate attendant from an air phone before being killed.

"The cockpit is not answering, somebody's stabbed in business class — and I think there's Mace — that we can't breathe — I don't know, I think we're getting hijacked," Ong screeched into the phone.[2] It was one of the last communications from the plane before it hurtled into the North Tower of the World Trade Center.

———

The tenth anniversary of 9/11 was the last thing on Erik Weissman's mind. He was in a lot of trouble. Nine months earlier, in January 2011, his landlord, Paul Thurston, was concerned when he couldn't reach the tenant of his one-bedroom apartment at 10 Brownson Terrace in the Roslindale section of Boston and had let himself into the unit. Drugs were everywhere: twenty-three five-pound bags of marijuana strewn all over the place, cocaine hidden in a suitcase, hashish in hermetically sealed bags, and a shoebox full of pills. Thurston drove straight to the Boston police station in Brighton, and his information prompted detectives to apply for a search warrant. Once inside Weissman's apartment police discovered, in addition to the drugs, two digital scales, a currency counter, and $21,504 in cash. There was even a ledger in which Weissman had jotted down drug transactions. Detectives immediately issued an arrest warrant for Erik, who had been arrested three years prior and had pleaded guilty to possession of marijuana with intent to distribute. The police were lying in wait when he arrived home, and now he was facing far more serious charges. In the months following his arrest, Erik Weissman spent most of his time at the apartment of a buddy, Brendan Mess, on a quiet dead-end street on the second floor of a Victorian house at 12 Harding Avenue in Waltham.

On the night of September 11, he had a quick meal with his sister and then parked his Mercedes SUV in front of Brendan's apartment around 7:30. The apartment had become a more quiet hangout ever since Brendan's girlfriend moved out. Hibatalla Eltilib was stunning — tall and long-legged, with skin the color of warm caramel and captivating green eyes. But "Hiba" was also a real psycho, the type of girlfriend who would get mad and throw knives. It didn't take a lot to set her off, either. She was a Sudanese immigrant who in recent months had become increasingly outspoken. She would argue with Brendan's friends about the wars in Iraq and Afghanistan and began embracing beliefs tied to her faith. She started calling Brendan and his buddies a bunch of lazy, pot-smoking lowlifes and tried to get Brendan to convert to Islam. He refused. She brought some of her Muslim friends to the house to try to convince him to be more pious, but he just laughed. Friends remembered that his response prompted a violent reaction. Hiba hurled knives and beer bottles at Brendan, who kicked her out a few days before September 11. She left Boston and went to stay with friends in Florida.

Erik was excited when he got to Brendan's because it was going to be their first boys' night in a while. Brendan, twenty-five, and Erik, thirty-one, had been friends for a long time. Both were from Cambridge and had graduated from Cambridge Rindge and Latin. The other friend joining them that night was Raphael "Rafi" Teken, thirty-seven. Unlike Brendan and Erik, Rafi had been a rich kid who attended a private high school. All three were regulars at Wai Kru, the MMA gym in Brighton where Tamerlan trained. They liked to record their partying lifestyle in cell phone videos, like one that showed Brendan at a pool party taking a deep drag on a fat blunt and then blowing it out, smiling, and declaring it "extra funky."[3] Brendan had no room in his life for drama — even if it came from a smoking-hot woman, and especially when she started to say what his friends would remember as "a lot of controversial shit."[4] With Hiba no longer around to give them a hard time, the plan was to smoke weed and stay in.

It was a warm, clear night. Neighbors on the leafy block left their windows open to let in the fresh air. So did Brendan. The pot smoke from the second-floor apartment wafted upward and didn't bother anyone below.

All three men were unlikely bad boys. Brendan had graduated from Vermont's Champlain College with a degree in professional writing and was a talented mixed martial arts fighter who made a living training other cage-warrior wannabes. Rafi had grown up on a sprawling estate in tony Brookline and graduated from prestigious Brandeis University. His father was an assistant rabbi, a spiritual leader of a Jewish synagogue in Newton, and his brother was a popular jazz musician. Erik was a devout Jew who took care of his ailing elderly father in his spare time. MMA — and weed — brought them together. All three had police records.

Erik, a bodybuilder, owed a lot of people money for the drugs that he was supposed to sell but had gotten seized by police in the January raid. One of his suppliers was a dangerous Armenian named Safwan Madarati, who turned out to have connections to a group of dirty Watertown cops who had been arrested on May 25 of that year. One of those dirty cops had been captured telling Madarati in a wiretapped phone call: "You need to lie low. Someone is making you out to be the biggest mule in Massachusetts. The rats were talking."[5] That cop, Robert Velasquez-Johnson, was right. The rats were talking. The US Attorney's Office unsealed an indictment after the May arrests of Madarati and eighteen others involved in his distribution network. The group's activities included drug dealing, money laundering, and extortion across the country — in California, Florida, Maine, New York, and Nevada — and into Canada. Madarati mainly worked locally, though. He controlled sales of steroids and hydroponic marijuana in Bedford, Burlington, Newton, Waltham, and Watertown, where he kept an apartment in which to manufacture and distribute marijuana and Ecstasy.[6]

Madarati's arrest had international implications. Velasquez-Johnson had warned him that his case involved agents from the DHS's US Immigration and Customs Enforcement drug unit, an elite squad designed to investigate narcotics trafficking that funded overseas terrorism. Madarati had ties to an Eritrean crew of narcotics traffickers in Portland, Maine, who were of particular interest to the international unit. Agents were concerned that the Portland dealers might be sending proceeds back to relatives connected to Al Qaeda's Somalia-based Al Shabab.[7]

Erik knew that Madarati probably thought he was one of those rats, which was why he and his drug-dealing associates in nearby Waltham were lying low and hiding out. Madarati might have been in custody without bail, but he had reach all over the area. To make matters worse, a high-end bong company Erik had invested in was going belly-up. Unfilled orders meant angry customers. Erik was happy to be surrounded by friends, tough MMA fighters like himself.

Rafi — who worked as a personal trainer — had been arrested for assault on a girlfriend, while Brendan was still facing charges that he had beaten up a group of people without provocation in Cambridge. When the cops showed up to question Brendan about the incident, he had threatened one, saying, "I can knock you out if I wanted to."[8] Three additional officers soon arrived, and the altercation ended with Brendan being hit with a chemical spray, wrestled to the ground, and handcuffed. That case was still wending its way through the legal system.

Erik, Brendan, and Rafi shared more than just a propensity for violence and pot. They were prolific marijuana dealers, and some of their best customers hung out at Wai Kru. That was where they would meet up with one of Brendan's closest friends, Tamerlan Tsarnaev, who usually traveled with another Chechen named Ibragim Todashev. Todashev was a revered fighter with the disfigured nose and cauliflower ears that came with brutal bouts. Brendan and Tamerlan had attended Cambridge Rindge and Latin together, and after graduation they even briefly shared an apartment, back when Tamerlan was a party boy dating more than a few women at the same time and rhyming with a Boston hip-hop crew called the FlyRydaz.

Married now, and living in his parents' home, Tamerlan had been trying to talk Brendan into marrying a Muslim woman, someone like Hiba. In fact, Brendan had met Hiba through Tamerlan, but he strenuously resisted efforts by both of them to get him to embrace Islam. Tamerlan and Hiba were obsessed with 9/11 conspiracies and the wars in the Middle East, blaming the United States for killing Muslims without provocation. Being with Hiba and Tamerlan had become tedious, both of them lecturing constantly about how living a life of depravity was like spitting in the eye of Allah. Tamerlan had even told Brendan that "the FBI is watching me; they think I'm a terrorist"— a story Brendan told his other friends later, giggling.[9] Right around that time Tamerlan, along with his fellow Chechen Ibragim, had started turning heads at Wai Kru by rolling out their prayer rugs and performing their devotions to Allah in the gym.

But Tamerlan was a boxing hero with two Golden Glove heavyweight championships behind him, and Brendan wanted to get better with his fists, so he tolerated the rants. Tamerlan was known to throw his arm around Brendan's shoulders at Wai Kru and declare, "This is my only American friend" — especially when there were other Russian Muslims around, which was often these days. On June 11, 2011, Brendan introduced Tamerlan to his old jujitsu trainer, Scott Wood, a former army ranger who owned Vermont Brazilian Jiu-Jitsu, near the Champlain College campus. They were all at the Shriners Auditorium in Wilmington, Massachusetts, to watch World Championship Fighting 11. As Tamerlan walked around the stadium, people stopped him to take selfies with him and shake his hand, calling him "Champ." He was an idol, a giant who towered over "Irish" Micky Ward, a celebrated professional boxer from Lowell, Massachusetts, in a photograph that hung in a Lowell boxing gym.

"This guy is the man," Brendan said as he introduced Wood to Tamerlan. Wood shook his hand, noting Tamerlan's height, girth, and honed muscles. "Big dude," Wood said to Brendan. They all laughed.

That was the last time Wood would see Brendan alive.

———

"I didn't hear a thing until the girl was screaming," a Harding Avenue resident would tell reporters and police on the evening of September 12, 2011, as police lights lit up the narrow dead-end street with blue and white strobes. "She was in the street yelling, 'they're all dead. There's so much blood.'"[10]

The girl was Hiba Eltilib, and she had run crying out of her estranged boyfriend's apartment, her feet splattered with blood. She had flown back from Florida that morning, hoping to make things right with Brendan. When she landed she called his cell phone. No answer. She rang the house phone — again, nothing. She jumped in a cab to 12 Harding Avenue and walked into the scene of a massacre.

Brendan's body was facedown on the floor near a door in the kitchen. It looked like someone had grabbed his hair as he ran toward the exit and raked a machete or sharp knife against his throat with enough force to nearly cut off his head. Erik's throat had been slashed the same way. Then his penis had been cut off and tossed onto his face. Rafi had been killed in a similar ritualistic fashion, gruesomely sexually mutilated and nearly decapitated by what prosecutors would call a "blunt object."[11] It was likely a machete, multiple police sources said. The Jewish victims were tied up. All of the bodies were sprinkled with marijuana, and five thousand dollars in cash sat atop a table.

"Oh my God," exclaimed a uniformed Waltham policeman who was one of the first officers to arrive on the scene. "It looks like an Al Qaeda training video in here."[12] The date was not lost on the officer, either: the tenth anniversary of the bloodiest jihadi attack on the United States. The marijuana and cash having been left behind, clearly this did not appear to be robbery. The suburban apartment massacre appeared intended to send a message, but what was the message and who was it for? Investigators believed that the murders happened sometime between 9:00 PM and midnight. The last call placed from the apartment had been from Erik's cell phone at 8:54 PM. Erik had called a neighborhood restaurant, Gerry's Italian Kitchen, to order three chicken parmigiana dinners, three meatballs, and three sausages. When the deliverywoman rang the doorbell twenty minutes later, no one responded. Calls placed to Erik's cell phone went unanswered. Hiba discovered the bodies the next morning.

Authorities could not write off the bloodbath at 12 Harding Avenue as the killings of three drug dealers who had pissed off the wrong machete-wielding thugs. It was clearly much more than that — especially given the sexual mutilation of the two Jewish victims.[13]

On the afternoon of September 12, Middlesex County District Attorney Gerard Leone held a press conference about the murders and described the crime scene as "graphic." He also said detectives had information that there had been other people in the apartment earlier but declined to elaborate: "We know there were at least two people who are not in that apartment now who were there earlier."[14]

He went on to describe the slayings. The men were found in separate rooms, all "killed by sharp wounds to their neck area," Leone said. "We don't know how many people were actually at the crime scene when they were killed. But there were many factors that led us to believe there was more than one person at the scene when the decedents were killed."

Waltham politicians showed up at the scene to calm fearful residents, none of whom had heard a thing — not a shout or a scream despite their wide-open windows in the balmy weather. When homicides happen in small, tightly knit neighborhoods, people often say, in disbelief, that such things don't happen there. City Councilor Gary Marchese told reporters: "What's sure is the neighborhood will never be the same. It'll take some time to heal."[15]

The murders quickly faded from the headlines. Brendan came from a fractured family, and his brother, Dylan, was not exactly cooperative with police. Erik was out on bail for dealing drugs — again. Rafi was his wealthy family's black sheep.

On September 19, Brendan's family held a memorial service for him at Ryles Jazz Club in Cambridge. His divorced parents, Derek and Susan, were there, together and distraught. The service was well attended by many friends and former teachers, but his old friend Tamerlan was conspicuously absent from the service and the funeral. "It's no coincidence that the last time I saw my friend Brendan alive he was walking out of that fight with that kid Tam," said Wood. "I really thought I would have been coaching that kid [Brendan] in the Ultimate Fighting Championship. Brendan's no saint; he liked to party. But nothing that he was into should have taken him to his end."[16] That week, Karima Tsarnaeva, Tamerlan's wife, googled stories about the Waltham triple murder, according to court documents unsealed in 2019.

Wood was not the only one who found Tamerlan's failure to pay his respects strange. Brendan's only brother was extremely concerned and passed the information about Tamerlan along to investigators. He also noticed that his brother's girlfriend had left town after the murders, which fueled suspicions about her hair-trigger temper and close association with Tamerlan. "She's shady and she's lying," Dylan said shortly after the murders. "So is her friend Tam."[17]

Furthermore, cops and many customers who used the Gerry's Italian Kitchen's delivery service remembered that Tamerlan was one of the many drivers who worked for the restaurant under the table. Managers of Gerry's denied that, but scores of people — including Waltham police officers — swore that Tamerlan had delivered the restaurant's food to their offices and homes. But for some inexplicable reason, despite his name having been mentioned to the state troopers assigned to the Middlesex County district attorney and to a Waltham detective working on the murders, Tamerlan was never a suspect.

The reason, some seasoned investigators said (on background, because the unsolved triple homicides are an open investigation), is because he was too valuable as an asset working for the federal government on a drug case with ties to overseas terrorism and as an informant who had infiltrated a mosque around the corner from his house with ties to radical Islam and convicted terrorists. The murder victims had played too hard, and their deaths were soon forgotten.

Tamerlan was a handsome multilingual US resident desperate for American citizenship. Federal investigators had been assigned to take down a crew of Muslim multinational immigrants who were selling crack cocaine all over New England and sending the proceeds overseas. The men bought the drugs from Madarati and others in Boston, according to court records, and transported them to Portland, Maine. The undertaking, which the FBI and DHS had dubbed Operation Run This Town, relied on confidential informants.

A former Cambridge resident who had moved to Portland named Hamadi Hassan was one of the operation's targets. Like Tamerlan, Hassan was in his twenties, and he had lived around the corner from the Tsarnaevs until moving to Maine in 2010. Federal records filed in Hassan's case show phone calls between him and an informant that included references to Wai Kru, the place that connected the three murdered men, Tamerlan, and Ibragim Todashev.

Ibragim fled Boston the night of the triple murder and headed to Florida "real fast," as his roommate would later tell the FBI. Tamerlan left the country four months later, in January 2012, for his motherland. Back in March 2011, the Federal Security Service of Russia (FSB), the modern equivalent of the old Soviet KGB, had begun sending the FBI and the CIA a series of warning messages about Tamerlan and his suspicious connections — including one that was sent within days of the triple murder in Waltham.

CHAPTER NINE

Muaz in the Motherland

There had long been tensions between the American FBI and the Russian FSB. FSB agents had been known to break into apartments of American agents stationed there and defecate on their pillows. And they did not trust each other. But both countries were trying to eradicate Islamic terrorism: The enemy of my enemy is my friend.

On March 4, 2011, the FSB sent its first message about Tamerlan and also his mother, Zubeidat, to the FBI's legal attaché (Legat) in Moscow, and later it sent the same letter to the CIA. The FBI still refuses to release the letters, even after FSB officials read it to a congressional delegation that included Representative William Keating, a Democrat from Massachusetts and a former prosecutor. "I asked them for a copy and they said, 'Well, can't you get it from your own people?' They read to me that document . . . and it was amazing in its detail dealing with Tamerlan Tsarnaev," Keating said.[1]

According to Keating, the letter described intercepted text messages among Tamerlan, his mother, and Magomed Kartashov, her second cousin — a former Dagestan police officer who had become a prominent Islamist and leader of a group called Union of the Just, a Muslim advocacy group that has been banned in Russia because of its affiliations with militants who declared war against Vladimir Putin's Russian forces in their homeland. Zubeidat and Tamerlan, the letter said, "were becoming adherers of radical Islam."

The FSB also provided full names, addresses, and phone numbers for many members of the Tsarnaev family and warned that Tamerlan "had changed drastically since 2010" and was preparing to travel to a part of Russia "to join unspecified underground groups" in the Caucasus who formed their own "bandit groups."[2] The FBI's legal attaché in Moscow sent a translated copy of the FSB's warning about the Tsarnaev mother, son, and cousin to the Counterterrorism Division of the FBI's Boston Field Division, telling them "to take any investigative steps deemed appropriate and provide Moscow with any information derived" and promising them that the information would be forwarded to the Russians.

Around the same time the FSB picked up and interrogated a suspected Chechen terrorist named William Plotnikov. Under questioning, Plotnikov gave up some of his fellow English-speaking jihadists. One of them was Tamerlan Tsarnaev.

Five days after the FSB sent its letter, the legal attaché in Moscow sent a letter to the FSB acknowledging receipt of the information and requesting that the FBI be kept in the loop. "According to available information," a report released in April 2014 by the Office of the Inspector General of the Intelligence Community stated, "the LEGAT did not coordinate with or notify the CIA in March 2011 after receiving the lead information concerning the Tsarnaevs."[3] According to a declassified summary of the report:

> In September 2011, the FSB provided the Central Intelligence Agency (CIA) information on Tamerlan Tsarnaev that was substantively identical to the information the FSB had provided to the FBI in March 2011. In October 2011, the CIA provided information obtained from the FSB to the National Counterterrorism Center (NCTC) for watch-listing purposes, and to the FBI, Department of Homeland Security (DHS), and the Department of State for their information. Upon receiving the information, the NCTC added Tamerlan Tsarnaev to the terrorist watchlist.

Months later, with both the CIA and the FBI notified about his increasingly dangerous and radical views, Tamerlan was headed to Russia, where he would meet the very men about whom the FSB had warned the American counterterrorism officials: Plotnikov, the extremist, and Tamerlan's mother's second cousin, Magomed. Evidence would show later that Tamerlan had for some reason clandestinely recorded many of his conversations with Magomed.

Tamerlan departed from Boston's Logan Airport and connected at John F. Kennedy International Airport for a flight to Russia. He landed at Moscow's Sheremetyevo Airport on January 21, 2012. By then he was on two different terrorist watch lists. The first was the Terrorist Identities Datamart Environment (TIDE) database, which is the repository of all international terrorist identifier information shared by the FBI, CIA, Defense Intelligence Agency, and National Security Agency (NSA) and maintained by the NCTC. The NCTC maintains TIDE by adding biographical or biometric identifiers. The second was TECS, a system used by the Department of Homeland Security to manage the flow of people through border ports of entry. DHS describes the program as a way for customs agents to file reports about any "encounter with a traveler, a memorable event, or noteworthy item of information particularly when they observe behavior that may be indicative of intelligence gathering or preoperational planning related to terrorism, criminal, or other illicit intention."[4] Despite Tamerlan's being on both of those lists, he boarded his plane in Boston without a hitch.

Tamerlan's declassified DHS US Citizenship and Immigration Services (USCIS) file reveals that he used an odd list of aliases over the years, including Tamerlan Tsarnaeu. In Russia he introduced himself to people as Muaz Tsarnaev (in tribute to a celebrated Dagestani rebel named Emir Muaz). He also used two birthdates in his USCIS paperwork: October 21, 1987, and October 21, 1988. The FBI says that after receiving the FSB's letter about Tamerlan's and his mother's increasing extremism, Special Agent

David Cedarleaf of its Boston field office counterterrorism unit conducted a "threat assessment," determined that Tamerlan did not pose a threat, and closed the case in June 2011.

As part of his review, Cedarleaf interviewed Tamerlan and his parents, Zubeidat and Anzor, according to the Office of the Inspector General. The IG found that Cedarleaf did not contact Tamerlan's wife, Katherine/Karima, or at least that, if he did, such contact never became part of an official file. Nor did Cedarleaf visit the controversial Prospect Street mosque in Cambridge where Tamerlan prayed, despite its connections to radical Islamists — including its founder, Abdurahman M. Alamoudi, who would later be sentenced to twenty-three years in prison for, among other crimes, giving money to Al Qaeda leaders.

The FBI's Counterterrorism Division wasn't called the "spook squad" for nothing. The agents in it operated with almost total autonomy, sometimes away from the prying eyes of their own bosses. Agent Cedarleaf was part of an even more secretive unit nicknamed "the red brigade," a tight-knit crew with military backgrounds whose members worked and socialized together outside of the circles in which most law enforcement officials moved. They all happened to have reddish hair. Nothing about Cedarleaf's March 2011 investigation into the Tsarnaevs was ever shared — not with the police in Cambridge, where the Tsarnaevs lived, and not with the police in Boston, who ran the Boston Regional Intelligence Center. Cedarleaf didn't even share the information with his JTTF counterparts from the DHS or his local police partners.

The Boston FBI field office sent a letter to the FSB dated August 28, 2011, through its legal attaché in Russia in which it indicated that its agents found "nothing derogatory" about the Tsarnaevs.[5] Still, inexplicably, despite the seeming lack of derogatory information, the customs agent from Boston assigned to the Joint Terrorism Task Force, Jim Bailey, added Tamerlan Tsarnaev's name to TECS on May 22, 2011, with his correct date of birth: October 21, 1986. Russian counterterrorism officials added his name, and the multiple aliases that Russian law enforcement agencies had dug up for him, to the TIDE database in October 2011. That same month a USCIS Form I-912, which would waive fees connected to processing an immigrant's naturalization, appearerd in Tamerlan's A-file. On the form, signed by Tamerlan Tsarnaev on August 28, 2011, there is a column for "Name of Agency Awarding Benefit." The name of that agency is redacted on the form without explanation. The "Date Benefit Was Awarded," however, was not. It reads, "APPX. 10/2011." A month after the Waltham triple murders.

When Tamerlan left the United States for Russia a few months later, in January 2012, his presence on those lists should have raised alarm bells. Somehow it didn't. Defense attorneys for Dzhokhar would later assert in a court filing: "The FBI made more than one visit to talk with Anzor, Zubeidat and Tamerlan, questioned Tamerlan about his internet searches, and asked him to be an informant,"[6] a claim the FBI would quickly deny. "The FBI checked U.S. government databases and other resources to look for such things as derogatory telephone communications, possible use of online sites associated with the promotion of radical activity, associations with other persons of interest, travel history and plans, and education history," lawyers for the government responded. "The FBI also interviewed Tamerlan Tsarnaev and family members. The FBI did not find any terrorism activity, domestic or foreign, and those results were provided to the foreign government in the summer of 2011."[7]

Tamerlan's ability to travel to a hotbed of terrorism without an American passport while simultaneously being on two terror watch lists was extraordinary, especially since the FSB had specifically warned the FBI about him. Law enforcement officials in Massachusetts began to say that Tamerlan was an informant for the feds, a spy sent to Russia to help track and kill the men with whom he was in contact. They believed that he was working for the US government, motivated by the promise of citizenship.

These suspicions soon seemed to be corroborated. Plotnikov was tracked to a terrorist compound in Dagestan and killed. So was another militant with ties to radical Islam. And Magomed Kartashov, the leader of Union of the Just in Dagestan and Zubeidat's second cousin — the man with whom Tamerlan had recorded his conversations — would be prosecuted.

Shortly after the marathon bombings Magomed was jailed in a Russian penal colony, which is where the FBI tracked him down and interviewed him in the weeks following the terrorist attack.

———

Muslim informants have become a controversial topic since 9/11. It is no secret that the FBI used some of the same techniques they had used to flip informants in the drug wars to identify and recruit so-called mosque crawlers who would inform on potential radicals. The practice had led to multiple lawsuits alleging that police had infiltrated dozens of mosques and student groups in a manner that was tantamount to unconstitutional profiling. After then-mayor Rudy Giuliani appointed Ray Kelly to be commissioner of the NYPD, Kelly created a secretive unit that operated alongside the Zone Assessment Unit, Intelligence Analysis Unit, and Cyber Intelligence Unit. It was called the Terrorist Interdiction Unit, and its purpose was to recruit Muslims who took the civil service test to become cops, pull them from the police academy, and turn them into undercover operatives.

These operatives, trained in espionage and surveillance with the help of the CIA, were nicknamed "rakers," a reference that their mission was to scrape up information on anyone espousing radical Islamic beliefs or potentially plotting to commit an act of terrorism. But "create and capture" would become counterterrorism investigators' most useful tool. Create and capture was a practice in which an informant, the mosque crawler, would enter the community being surveilled, "create" conversations about jihad or terrorism, and then "capture" responses from targets and report them back to their handlers. The practice was effective insofar as it led to multiple criminal prosecutions. Repeatedly using this tactic, the vaunted NYPD Intelligence Division — working alongside intelligence officers in the NSA, caseworkers in the CIA, and agents in the FBI — uncovered evidence of jihadi-inspired plots.

Several of the plots that were uncovered intersected with the mosque Tamerlan Tsarnaev began to frequent after undergoing his transformation from a womanizing party boy to a pious Muslim who first began to study the Quran in 2010, at the age of twenty-four.

Tamerlan was a perfect candidate for recruitment by the US government. Broke, desperate for citizenship, and with a new wife and baby girl to take care of, he spoke fluent English, Russian, and a dialect of Chechen. The Islamic Society of Boston's Cambridge mosque had long been a target for investigators because of its ties to the Muslim Brotherhood, along with convicted terrorists like Lady Al Qaeda — Aafia Siddiqui — the MIT-trained neuroscientist who is currently serving an eighty-six-year federal sentence for trying to kill Americans in Afghanistan;[8] and Tarek Mehanna, a pharmaceutical student convicted in 2010 of an Al Qaeda–inspired plot to shoot up a Massachusetts mall.[9] Mehanna's codefendant, Ahmad Abousamra, fled to Syria after his indictment and remained on the FBI's list of ten most wanted terrorists until a drone strike targeting ISIS leaders killed him.

———

When Tamerlan flew to Russia in January 2012, his name should have been flagged at JFK Airport. Why he left the country from New York City and not on an international flight from Boston remains unexplained. He was on TIDE and TECS terrorist watch lists. His travel documents were an American permanent resident alien card that had been issued to him in 2007 and a passport issued in Kyrgyzstan in 2001, when he was fourteen, which would expire in August 2012.

He wasn't stopped at JFK for additional screening, and he wasn't stopped when he arrived in Moscow as a suspected terrorist.

Before long the men at the mosque he attended and his Dagestani relatives gave him a different moniker — "the American" — and connected him with his mother's second cousin, Magomed Kartashov, leader of the Union of the Just.

The Union of the Just did not outwardly preach the use of violence, but neither did its members condemn it. Magomed was outspoken against US involvement in the Middle East, and the Union of the Just shared the goals of mujahideen fighters everywhere: politically unify all Muslims in a caliphate as widely as possible and impose Islamic law (sharia).

Magomed had grown up across the street from Zubeidat's grandmother and had known the Tsarnaev family when Tamerlan and Dzhokhar were small children. Since that time he hadn't seen either boy, until Tamerlan showed up in the Kizlyar region to visit with relatives and Magomed came over to say hello.

"I didn't recognize you, cousin," Magomed said, pulling Tamerlan into an embrace. Tamerlan was dressed "like an American," Magomed later recalled when interviewed by an FBI team in 2013 at the Russian penal colony where he'd been incarcerated. Tamerlan was wearing a long raincoat and eyeglasses, spectacles that he didn't need for reading. He slicked his hair back with olive oil and wore too much cologne for the pious Muslims who surrounded Magomed. "I haven't seen you since you were about ten. Wow. Big guy."[10]

Tamerlan knew a lot about Magomed from his mother, who had been texting with him. He didn't wait long to ask Magomed to help him achieve the goal that had brought him to Russia. He told Magomed: "I want to go into the forests. I want to train. I want to go to Syria. I came here to get involved in jihad."

It sounded at first like boasting from a spoiled American, but Tamerlan was puffed up as if he had already been a mujahideen. He told Magomed that he had followed one segment of the Quran that urged Muslims to follow orders like "cut off their heads and make them kneel in front of you." That is exactly what investigators believe happened to the three men in Waltham months earlier.

Magomed was stunned. To preach radical Islamic viewpoints so openly could get you killed in that part of Russia. Moreover, Tamerlan's talk of training to go to Syria, where brutal young mujahideen were gaining a stronghold, struck him as babble from someone who had been spending too much time on the internet from the safety of America, being wooed by slick propaganda and speeches from the likes of recently slain American Al Qaeda leader Anwar al-Awlaki.

"Brother, there is not jihad in the streets," Magomed told the FBI he had explained to his relative.

"How well do you even know Islam?" he asked, knowing that Tamerlan had hardly grown up in a pious family. His mother, Zubeidat, had left Russia a flighty overdressed woman. His father, Anzor, had never been a devout Muslim and had been laughed at behind his back for letting his wife dominate him.

In courtroom proceedings deciding Dzhokhar's fate back in the United States following the marathon bombings, another cousin, Nadia Suleimanova, would describe the Tsarnaevs as "holiday only" Muslims. "What I mean is they would celebrate the major holidays, Kurban Bayram, Uraza Bayram, but they wouldn't pray five times a day."[11]

Magomed was suspicious of Tamerlan's newfound devotion to Islam, asking him: "How many times a day do you pray?" They talked about the proper way to praise Allah five times a day and about nonviolent jihad, fighting against the Russian aggressors without bullets or bombs.

"I cannot argue with you," Tamerlan answered. He had seen Magomed's lectures posted on YouTube by the Union of the Just. "I am not on your level."

Magomed then lectured him about Muhammad, who had been beaten mercilessly but never responded with violence: "You have to stop or you won't make it to the next tree."

Magomed was not a bomber or a beheader of infidels, but neither did he condemn his Muslim brethren who used violence as a tool. Those men included Mamakaev Rizvan, the former husband of Tamerlan's sister Bella — another person whom the FSB had found was exchanging frightening text messages with his former mother-in-law supporting jihad. The FSB warned the FBI that Mamakaev was considered an extremist, a warning that the FBI would dismiss as questionable intelligence because the text messages had been obtained illegally.

Mamakaev attended the Kotrova Street mosque in Dagestan, where Salafism was preached and a black flag associated with ISIS hung over the door. Russian antiterrorism agents had it under constant surveillance, which is how the Russians learned that Tamerlan had met with Mamakaev at the Kotrova Street mosque for the drive into the rural area where Magomed lived. Tamerlan's former brother-in-law also traveled with him and Mamakaev — Elmirza Khozhugov, Ailina's former husband, to whom she had been introduced by her Uncle Ruslan.

Elmirza had stayed in touch with the Tsarnaev family because Ailina was raising his son, Ziyaudi (called Zia). In fact, he later recalled that the last time he had seen Zubeidat — at the airport where she dropped off his son in 2011 — he had almost laughed in her face because she was wearing a hijab: "It made me laugh. I know that wearing these clothes isn't going to change her, the way she is actually. So I just saw it as an attempt to cover up what she had on her mind as if it could help."[12] Elmirza wanted his son to live with him, and he met with Tamerlan in Dagestan to see if his former brother-in-law could help make that happen. Together they drank coffee, gossiped about the family, and discussed Islam.

Neither of Tamerlan's former brothers-in-law nor his mother's cousin traveled with him to Georgia to attend an event run by the Jamestown Foundation, a think tank in Washington, DC, that was created in 1984 by a former head of the CIA. Graham Fuller, the CIA agent with ties to Ruslan, contributed to the foundation as an analyst. So did Brian Glyn Williams, a former CIA agent who was then an associate professor of Islamic history at UMass Dartmouth, the school Dzhokhar had enrolled in a year before, in September 2011.

Investigative reporters in Russia obtained a document — drafted by Colonel Grigory Chanturia of the main security service of the Georgian Ministry of Internal Affairs — that said that Tamerlan had been spotted at the Jamestown event. The Jamestown Foundation categorically rejected the investigative reports, calling them "entirely false and groundless," and added, "Our organization has never had any contact with the Tsarnaev brothers, and we have no record or knowledge of either of them ever attending any Jamestown event in Washington, DC, or elsewhere."[13]

Nonetheless, when it came to the CIA and the Tsarnaev family, there seemed to be a lot of coincidental overlaps. Glyn Williams even posted photos of his trip to Georgia in the summer of 2012 on the website,[14] where he boasted of his CIA past as a field operative in Afghanistan, Uzbekistan, and elsewhere in Central Asia in the early 2000s, calling himself an expert on suicide bombers. He told *South Coast Today*, a small Massachusetts newspaper, that he had been in touch with Dzhokhar Tsarnaev, who had emailed him to begin a discussion about Chechnya when he was still a high school student at Cambridge Rindge and Latin, saying, "That kid and his brother identified with the Chechen struggle."[15]

Like Fuller, Glyn Williams often sympathized with the struggles of Muslims in Russia's unrelenting fight against Islamic extremists — which, some argued, under Vladimir Putin was violent and overzealous. Those struggles would become common laments of Tamerlan that, before long, were echoed by his little brother, Dzhokhar.

————

Tamerlan's wife, Karima, had moved back in with her husband after living at home in Rhode Island for a short time, and with him gone to Russia for several months, she found herself alone with their baby, Anzor, and Zubeidat. Anzor was unraveling. His doctor, Alexander Niss, would later describe him as a "very sick man"[16] who suffered from panic attacks, anxiety, and post-traumatic stress disorder from his days growing up under the watchful eye of parents who had lived through the regime of Joseph Stalin. Zubeidat had claimed that her husband had been tortured in a Soviet prison camp, and as a result he often hallucinated that KGB agents were following him, the same story that the couple had told US immigration officials in 2002 to get political asylum. They had gone so far at the time as to say that they would be killed if they ever returned to Russia.

Anzor was seeing a psychiatrist and taking a handful of pills every day: Trazodone to help him sleep; Zoloft, an antidepressant; Klonopin for panic attacks; and Zyprexa, an antipsychotic medication to treat his paranoia. On top of that, he took Provigil to counteract the zombie-like state the other medications put him in, a drug to provide "alertness," Niss explained. Some of the medications worked to counteract the injuries that Anzor said he had suffered during a brutal beating outside a Russian social club in 2009. Anzor had been sipping cognac at Arbat, a Russian deli not far from Wai Kru, Tamerlan's gym. One night a week Arbat operated as a clandestine illegal (because it didn't have a permit to sell alcohol) social club for Russian expatriates. Anzor was drinking alone when a Russian came up to him and demanded that he apologize for bumping a woman's chair. Anzor told Tamerlan the story from his bed at Massachusetts General Hospital, and his son then went to the Boston police to report his father's assault. "My father said, 'I'm not apologizing. I didn't do it,'" Tamerlan reported.[17] The unknown man then took the fight outside. Anzor was "punched in the back of the head, and then attacked by the large group including a couple of females," Tamerlan told BPD detectives. Anzor spent a week in the hospital and was never the same afterward.

The beating left Anzor broken, and Zubeidat became bossier than ever. A short time later she underwent a complete metamorphosis, eschewing the fashion she loved for shapeless long clothes and a black head scarf. Anzor couldn't take it. The couple divorced in August 2011, according to family court records in Middlesex County, but continued to live together.

Zubeidat always had some plan to make money on the side, while simultaneously collecting government assistance — whether it was a home health care job under the table or giving facials in her apartment without a license. One of her clients remembered her as funny, swearing at an appointment in 2011. A month later "she was saying that her son taught her the government attacked the World Trade Center towers and she was wearing a burka," the client said.[18]

Despite their claims that a return to Russia would be a death sentence, Anzor went back to Dagestan in June 2012 and has since stayed there. A month later, back in Massachusetts, Zubeidat ran into some legal trouble. She was arrested for shoplifting $1,600 in expensive clothing from the Lord & Taylor department store at the upscale Natick Mall. It seemed a good time for her to leave town, so she went to Dagestan in July — "covered," to use the Islamic term. When her former son-in-law Elmirza saw her, he had to stifle a laugh at her new look and Islamist attitude. "She didn't even know how to cover properly," he would remember. "Her daughters don't know anything about Islam."[19] Still, Zubeidat was his elder, and he showed her the proper respect. Everyone did, even Magomed Kartashov, the respected leader of the Union of the Just.

Sometime in July, Tamerlan and Magomed were chatting on their cells when Zubeidat took Tamerlan's phone. She had a request for her cousin: "Take care of my son."[20]

With Tamerlan, Anzor, and Zubeidat gone, Karima was alone with her daughter in the apartment. Bella and Ailina were living with new boyfriends or in homeless shelters, depending on the day. Dzhokhar had taken up residence in a dorm at UMass Dartmouth, selling weed on campus with two Russian buddies, Dias Kadyrbayev and Azamat Tazhayakov — both sons of rich parents who had sent their sons to the United States for a better education than they could get in Russia. Azamat drove a brand-new BMW 330xi with a UMass bookstore vanity plate affixed to the front that read TERRORISTA. They all smoked weed with two brothers from Eritrea who had graduated from Cambridge Rindge and Latin with Dzhokhar, the twins Stephen and Steven Silva, and an Ethiopian American named Robel Phillipos. (The Silvas' mother would explain why she gave her sons the same name with different spellings by telling a Cambridge police officer that Stephen was pronounced *Steff-an*, two law enforcement sources recalled.) The Silva twins and Phillipos lived in the same Cambridge high-rise building, ironically over the gas station to which the carjacking victim, Dun Meng, would escape on the morning of April 19, 2013, before the Watertown shootout. On July 4, 2012 — just before Zubeidat left Cambridge for good — Dzhokhar celebrated his independence outside a house party in Arlington with Stephen and a man from the Bronx. They sat in Dzhokhar's green Honda, talking and throwing beer cans out the window, until an Arlington police officer showed up. The cop took their names and wrote Dzhokhar a citation for having an open container of alcohol in his vehicle. Of course the officer had no idea that Dzhokhar was asking Stephen to get him a gun, along with "food for the dog" — bullets.[21] Dzhokhar wanted to rob some rival drug dealers who went to a Rhode Island college, he told Silva. Silva knew some Eritrean drug dealers in Portland, Maine, connected to his friend "Icy," who could get Dzhokhar a gun. They were the same narcotics traffickers who were targeted in Operation Run This Town, the case targeting the Eritrean crack dealers. When the Arlington cop showed up the conversation stopped temporarily; the two young men were spooked.

Dzhokhar stayed in regular contact with his brother via email. Tamerlan sent him online links and materials about the jihad in Chechnya and Dagestan and the mujahideen's interpretation of Islam. Tamerlan's screensaver was a picture of Makhachkala, the capital of Dagestan. His password for the files he kept encrypted was *AllahAkbar*. Tamerlan emailed his brother about going "into the forests." Dzhokhar's replies tended to be short, as if he was too stoned to care. "Sounds interesting," he wrote in one.[22]

Karima stayed busy, too. Tamerlan had told her he would be in Russia for just a few weeks, but then he called and said that his passport had been stolen and he had to stay in Dagestan to fill out new paperwork. She spent much of her time searching the internet using phrases like "can women become shaheed," "nasheed jihad," "wife of mujahedeen," and "what are the rewards for wives of mujahedeen?"

———

As Magomed Kartashov watched footage of the Boston Marathon attacks from the penal colony where he was serving time for fighting with police not long after his third cousin had recorded their conversations, he immediately thought of Tamerlan. One of the last things Tamerlan had said to him, Magomed told the FBI, was: "You have convinced my head but my heart still wants to do something."

After Tamerlan returned to the United States in July 2012, he stayed in touch with Magomed using the Russian social networking site VK (that country's version of Facebook), on which he opened an account using Muaz, the name he used in Russia and the one he would try to legally make his American name on January 23, 2013, according to his USCIS file. The last time Magomed spoke to Tamerlan was via Skype sometime in early March 2013. In that call Tamerlan complained that he had become a stay-at-home dad. His wife worked full-time, under the table, while they simultaneously collected taxpayer subsidies including free rent, food stamps, and EBT cash from an ATM card. "I'm home all day watching the kid, or I'm training at the gym," Tamerlan said.[23]

He then complained about two public arguments he had had with an imam at his Cambridge mosque. In November the imam talked about American holidays, like Thanksgiving, being celebrated by Muslims, and Tamerlan lost his cool, stood up, and shouted, "That is not allowed in the faith!" The second time Tamerlan was escorted out of the mosque after the imam lectured about Martin Luther King and compared him to the Prophet Muhammad. "You're a kuffar! You are contaminating people's minds! Hypocrite! Hypocrite!" The congregation had tired of Tamerlan's antics and drowned out his words with shouts of "leave now!" Leaders of the mosque told him that one more such incident would ban him from the mosque for life.

"Why do you need to do that?" Magomed asked, shaking his head in the Skype call. "Why do you keep getting into that kind of trouble?" Tamerlan didn't answer him. Magomed had no idea that conversations they'd had during Tamerlan's time in Russia had been recorded on Tamerlan's laptop, recordings that would later be discovered by investigators.

In a legal brief the government called the recordings "extremely difficult to understand even in translation. They appear to consist of several men talking about religious issues, including the proper form in which to do jihad, which can be violent or non-violent depending on one's religious philosophy."[24] But no one ever explained why Tamerlan was recording his conversations with Magomed in the first place.

Then came the bombings on Boylston Street.

"I saw everything on Russian television," Magomed told the two FBI special agents who visited the penal colony where he was being held on June 5, 2013. The FSB had already been there to interview him weeks earlier.

"I had a thought, it could have been Tamerlan. When Tamerlan arrived in Russia he was already thinking about jihad and looking to do something."

He explained to the FBI agents that he thought the videos

of the American Al Qaeda cleric Anwar al-Awlaki and other posts had inspired Tamerlan long before he traveled to Dagestan. Then Magomed mentioned Tamerlan's going to visit a friend in Utamysh, Dagestan, "in the forests." That visit did not end well for Tamerlan's friend, William Plotnikov.

CHAPTER TEN

Into the Forests

In July 2012, Tamerlan Tsarnaev likely traveled to Utamysh, a small village in the Kayakent District of Dagestan, Russia, not far from the Caspian Sea. He wanted to see his longtime internet friend, a man whom he had exchanged ideas with online as part of a group called World Assembly of Muslim Youth, someone whom he had texted repeatedly — so often that the text messages had raised alarms within Russian anti-insurgency circles. A onetime champion boxer and student at Seneca University in Toronto, the Russian-born man had been reported missing by his parents in Canada. But William Plotnikov wasn't missing at all. He was training to be a terrorist with the Caucasus Emirate, a group that the US State Department had added to its list of foreign terrorist organizations in 2011 because of its allegiance to Al Qaeda. The group's militant jihadists sought to expel non-Muslim Russians from the region and establish an Islamic state.

In Dagestan, Plotnikov was called "the Canadian," just as many people had taken to calling Tamerlan "the American." Both were obsessed with mixed martial arts fighting. Both had earned championship titles in boxing. Both spoke English and Russian fluently. And both had developed a Westerner's fascination with online Islamic extremism through lectures from Anwar al-Awlaki and Tamerlan's relative Magomed Kartashov.

Like Tamerlan, Plotnikov had once been just another Euro trash teenager in a big city, clad in designer clothing, well spoken and well traveled, a man who dated local women and ate at posh restaurants. Plotnikov's first name, William, suggested the Western life that his parents envisioned for their only son when he was born in 1989 at a Siberian hospital in the former

Soviet Union. Calling their son William was an indication of the Plotnikovs' determination to flee the burgeoning violence in their homeland for better opportunities in North America. By the time Plotnikov was fifteen he had twice been a Russian youth champion fighter. This made him a target for underworld gangs; young, strong athletes were perfect recruits for criminal crews. So in 2005, William's father, Vitaly Plotnikov, quit his job as an oil industry executive and moved the family to Toronto. He was willing to stock supermarket shelves to keep his son away from the criminal element in his homeland, he would tell reporters in Canada and the United States.[1]

Nevertheless, while his parents were vacationing in Florida in 2010, Plotnikov slipped out of Canada and into Chechnya.[2] Plotnikov would later tell his parents that he had finally found something outside the boxing ring to fight for: radical Islam. He and Tamerlan were among the hundreds of Westerners recruited on jihadi internet sites. According to James Comey, who served as FBI director from 2013 to 2017, ISIS managed to recruit 250 Americans who were willing to travel overseas to work for the caliphate.[3] Comey also said, at the time, that aspiring jihadists were under twenty-four-hour surveillance in all fifty states.[4]

———

In three years Plotnikov had become a trained killer in Dagestan. Now twenty-three, he was wiry and strong, his sinewy muscles honed in the boxing ring and by the rugged life of the camps. His mixed martial arts training had given him keen instincts. Any man on watch outside the Utamysh compound had a machine gun slung over his shoulder. They considered themselves soldiers of the caliphate and trained like any other military, always at the ready.

Like in Utamysh, Plotnikov was known as "the Canadian" in jihadi online chat rooms and portals where he began to post videos that showed the once clean-shaven and reserved young man displaying a scraggly beard and a sinister smile. In one of the videos, narrated by Plotnikov and shot in what appeared to be a well-stocked bunker, he offered up a prayer that he would have the opportunity to kill infidels, nonbelievers like his own parents.[5]

In one scene Plotnikov turned the camera on himself and in Russian espoused alarmingly violent views.

> We are not suffering, we are not in need. We need only Allah's help and he does not leave us, his servants. We have food, we have someone to make that food and there are other brothers who perform their duties and this will be rewarded.
>
> And therefore non-believers you will never see what you would like to see. We have food. Allah is with us; we have our guardian, Allah, but you do not have one. We will kill you. We are not superheroes, we are also in need of Allah's help and he is helping us and I am asking Allah that by next spring he gives us an opportunity to kill more non-believers, so the military trucks blow into pieces, fly around like rags. Allah is almighty and he will assist.

He could have just as easily said those words in English or French. In high school he went by the nickname "Willy" and talked about joining the Canadian army. Now he was living in the woods undergoing terrorism training. Chechen rebels have been found fighting alongside Al Qaeda insurgents all over the world. In fact, Nawaf Alhazmi — who boarded American Airlines Flight 11 on the morning of September 11, 2001, and with his younger brother, Salem Alhazmi, slit the throats of two flight attendants as the plane left Logan Airport and hurtled toward the World Trade Center towers with Mohamed Atta at the controls — trained in Chechnya according to the *9/11 Commission Report*.[6]

Plotnikov, and the others training in the woods, believed that anyone who did not embrace radical Islam or sharia was an infidel. Even moderate Muslims were the enemy. Plotnikov had not been raised Muslim. His father was an Armenian Christian, and his mother, a Ukrainian Tatar, practiced Russian Orthodox Christianity, unlike many of her fellow Tatars, who were Sunni Muslim. The couple had baptized their son as a Christian. When Plotnikov was nineteen, his parents became members of the Jehovah's Witnesses.

Back in Canada a friend of Willy's had alerted his parents to the videos, and his father would later describe the difficult decision he was forced to make. His son was clearly headed down a dangerous and disturbing path, and Vitaly Plotnikov knew that some members of the FSB were notoriously brutal to Muslim insurgents. Tracking down his son could put him in even more danger with the Russian antiterrorism forces, but it was a choice he felt he had to make. Investigators from the Royal Canadian Mounted Police took the Plotnikovs' missing persons report and shared it with the FSB in early 2011.

"The Canadian" would not be hard for the FSB to locate. Even after he shed his expensive clothing for camouflage, he stuck out among the Chechens in Dagestan. After his father had tipped them off through the Canadian Mounties, Russian antiterrorism agents picked up Plotnikov for interrogation. But there was not much else Russian investigators could do. Plotnikov had every right to be in the country. He was Russian by birth, and the missing persons report filed by his parents would not be enough to compel him to go home. Certainly his internet activity was a concern, but not a crime. The FSB demanded that Plotnikov give its agents the names of all his contacts in Canada and the United States who were English-speaking Russian natives and who, like him, identified with the beliefs of the Caucasus Emirate. Some of those contacts came from the online network World Assembly of Muslim Youth, whose website was riddled with propaganda from Al Qaeda sympathizers.

One of the people Plotnikov named was Tamerlan Tsarnaev.

Instead of being scared into coming home after the FSB interrogation as his parents had hoped, Plotnikov slipped back "into the forests." The last time his family heard from him was an exchange of messages on VK.[7] A year before his death and after he had been questioned by the FSB, he contacted his parents to ask for money. According to a published transcript of the conversation, he then chastised them for posting photos of his mother "half-naked on the beach" and added: "Praise to Allah, Lord of the Worlds."

"It has turned out that our understanding of life has diverged," Plotinikov wrote to his parents. "We have to accept this and that we don't understand each other. I understand you already. I hope that you understand me someday and accept me. Forgive me for disappointing you. My life changed so accept me as I am."

His father responded with gratitude: "Thank you for writing Willy." Then he added: "There's no need for fanaticism . . . If you want to devote your life to your faith, then join a religious school or preach in a mosque . . . Mom removed the photos . . . We miss you."

"Dad, my life isn't compatible with the people who live in sinful America," the son responded.

The elder Plotnikov logged onto the site repeatedly to message his son, with his last message reading, "Are you coming home?"

There was no answer, but he learned his son's fate from the site when some of Willy's friends sent condolence messages in the hours after he died.

———

As darkness descended over the Utamysh compound on a night in mid-July 2012, Plotnikov was likely exhausted. Camps like the one in which he lived were comparable to marine training sites like Combat Town at Camp Lejeune, in North Carolina. At the terrorist training camps in Dagestan and Chechnya, the focus was on building bombs and hitting civilian targets. On this night Plotnikov's fingertips may have ached from the tedious task of rewiring tiny toy car parts and remote controls until they became ignitions for pressure-cooker bombs, and his shoulders probably felt the weight of machine guns even after he put them down. He

Roseann Sdoia in the arms of a stranger, Northeastern University college student Shores Salter, who helped her after the blast. They remain friends to this day. Photo courtesy of US Attorney's Office. Trial exhibit.

Leo Woolfenden, three, is hurried to safety by Boston Police Officer Thomas Barrett. Photo courtesy of US Attorney's Office. Trial exhibit.

14:50:06:19

Detonation, from a surveillance photo inside the Forum restaurant. Photo courtesy of US Attorney's Office. Trial Exhibit.

Dzhokhar Tsarnaev tweet in the hours after he detonated a weapon of mass destruction on Boylston Street, April 15, 2013. Photo courtesy of US Attorney's Office. Trial exhibit.

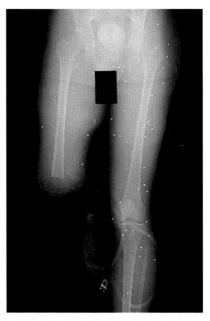

X-ray of Marc Fucarile with embedded projectiles from bomb. Photo courtesy of US Attorney's Office. Trial exhibit.

Krystal-Marie Campbell and her best friend, Karen Rand McWatters, in the moments before the blast that took Krystal's life and Karen's limb. Photo courtesy of US Attorney's Office. Trial exhibit.

Boston University student Lingzi Lu, one of the fatalities. Photo courtesy of US Attorney's Office. Trial exhibit.

BPD Unified Command Center during the hunt for the Boston Marathon bombers. Photo courtesy of Boston Police Department.

FBI Special Agent Vincent Lisi, then the agent in charge of the bureau's Boston field office (left), revisits the scene of the Boston Marathon attacks with ABC News Chief Investigative Correspondent Brian Ross, March 2016. Photo courtesy of the FBI's Boston field office.

FBI Special Agent Kieran Ramsey, then-assistant agent in charge of the bureau's Boston field office and now the legal attaché in Rome, talks about the victims of the blasts in March 2016. Photo courtesy of the FBI's Boston field office.

BPD Commissioner William Evans on Boylston Street with an ATF agent and a BPD captain, April 2013. Photo courtesy of Boston Police Department.

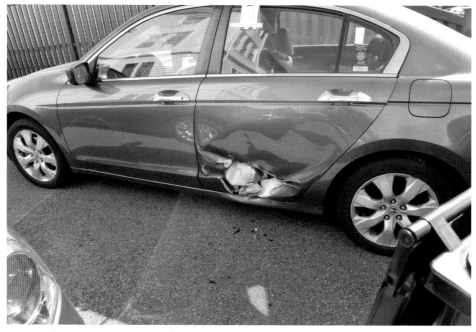

Aftermath of the gunfight in Watertown on April 19, 2013: a pressure cooker lodged in the side of a car. Photo courtesy of US Attorney's Office. Trial exhibit.

From left to right: Watertown Police Department Sergeant John C. MacLellan; Sergeant Jeffrey J. Pugliese; Officer Miguel A. Colon, Jr.; Officer Timothy B. Menton; and Officer Joseph B. Reynolds. Photo courtesy of Watertown Police Department.

MIT Police Officer Sean Collier. Photo courtesy of US Attorney's Office. Trial exhibit.

The spot where MIT Police Officer Sean Collier was assassinated, raising questions about the video footage shown in the Tsarnaev trial in which his killers were tiny dots on a screen. Photo courtesy of US Attorney's Office. Trial exhibit.

The *Slip Away II* dry-docked boat where Dzhokhar Tsarnaev hid, writing and carving anti-American screeds on the walls inside. Photo courtesy of US Attorney's Office. Trial exhibit.

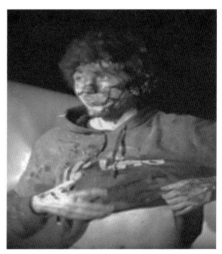

Note written by Dzhokhar Tsarnaev on the inside of the dry-docked boat *Slip Away II*, April 19, 2013. Photo courtesy of US Attorney's Office. Trial exhibit.

Blood-splattered bottom of the *Slip Away II* after Dzhokhar Tsarnaev was captured on April 19, 2013. Photo courtesy of Dzhokhar Tsarnaev's defense team. Trial exhibit.

Dzhokhar Tsarnaev pulled from the *Slip Away II* in Watertown, April 19, 2013. Photo courtesy of Massachusetts State Police. Trial exhibit.

Tamerlan (right) and Dzhokhar Tsarnaev outside of their Cambridge home. Photo courtesy of Dzhokhar Tsarnaev's defense team. Trial exhibit.

Tamerlan in front of an Islamic flag often associated with jihad that investigators discovered in executing a search warrant at his Norfolk Street home after the blasts. Photo courtesy of US Attorney's Office. Trial exhibit.

Zubeidat and Tamerlan Tsarnaev. Photo courtesy of Dzhokhar Tsarnaev's defense team. Trial exhibit.

Tamerlan in his American boxing helmet. Photo courtesy of Dzhokhar Tsarnaev's defense team. Trial exhibit.

The Tsarnaev family arrives in the United States (left to right): Dzhokhar, Tamerlan, Ailina, Anzor, and Bella. Photo courtesy of Dzhokhar Tsarnaev's defense team. Trial exhibit.

Tamerlan Tsarnaev and Katherine Russell at the start of their romance. Photo courtesy of Dzhokhar Tsarnaev's defense team. Trial exhibit.

State Department paperwork from Tamerlan Tsarnaev's A-file showing two different faces on nearly identical documents. To this day the State Department has not offered an explanation. Photo courtesy of US Attorney's Office. Trial exhibit.

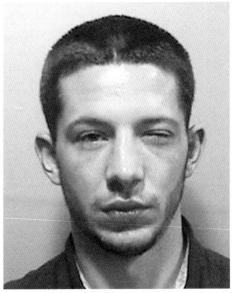

Brendan Mess, one of the three men killed in Waltham on September 11, 2011, after a 2012 arrest in Cambridge on assault charges. Photo courtesy of Cambridge Police Department.

Tamerlan Tsarnaev after being arrested for slapping his girlfriend in the face on July 10, 2009. Photo courtesy of Cambridge Police Department.

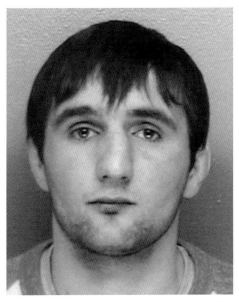

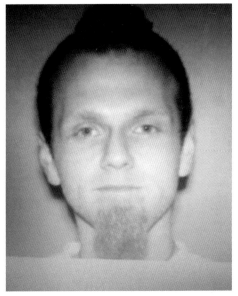

Ibragim Todashev after being arrested in connection with a violent road rage incident in Boston, February 11, 2010. Photo courtesy of Boston Police Department.

Daniel Morley after being arrested for threatening to kill his mother, June 9, 2013. Photo courtesy of Topsfield Police Department.

Tupperware bomb — for the possession of which no one was charged — recovered from the back of the Mercedes carjacked by Tamerlan and Dzhokhar Tsarnaev. Photo courtesy of US Attorney's Office. Trial exhibit.

Oath Ceremony Schedule for TAMERLAN TSARNAEV

Oath Ceremony Location Information

170 PORTLAND STREET

BOSTON

MA   021141706

Room Number: MAIN FINGERPRINT FACILITY

Gate Number: MAIN FINGERPRINT GATE

Date: 10/16/2012   Type: ADMINISTRATIVE

Gate Time: 08:00 AM   Start Time: 08:00 AM

Copy of Tamerlan Tsarnaev's invitation to take the oath of US citizenship — citizenship for which he was not eligible. State Department documents through a Freedom of Information Act request to USCIS.

Dzhokhar Tsarnaev in his bedroom in front of a black flag associated with jihad. Photo courtesy of US Attorney's Office. Trial exhibit.

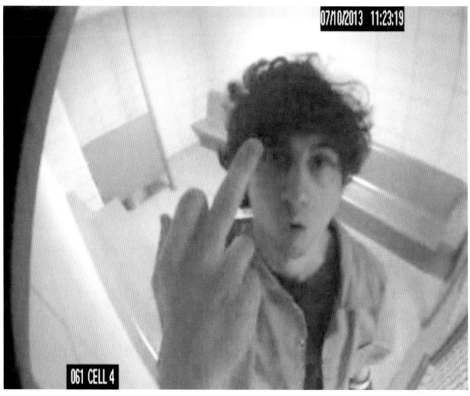

Dzhokhar Tsarnaev's one-finger salute to the camera as he awaited arraignment at the John Joseph Moakley Courthouse in South Boston, July 10, 2013. Photo courtesy of US Attorney's Office. Trial exhibit.

had slimmed down since leaving Canada, likely due to long training runs and the fact that hearty food was scarce in the forests.

International soldiers and Russian intelligence agents and police officers made their way to the carefully hidden compound in a convoy of five-ton troop carriers. They even brought a small light armored tank, knowing that the men inside were heavily armed. The raid had been well planned, and those in charge wanted to ensure that it was well executed.

Plotnikov's hideout, a small farmhouse, was home to seven other mujahideen, guerrilla fighters who had all vowed to bring sharia back to Russia's Northern Caucasus. They flew their own nationalist flag and consistently referred to Russian authorities as "invaders." Two of the men with whom Plotnikov had been training, Islam and Arsen Magomedov, were not just guerrilla insurgents. The men were notorious terrorists, commanders of the region's most brutal criminal gangs, and suspected in orchestrating dozens of murders and deadly bombings of police checkpoints, civilian-filled trains, and Russian Federation television stations.

Along with the Magomedovs were five other men who ranged in age from twenty-five to thirty-five, budding jihadists who had very few prospects when they left their families other than to go "into the forests." By comparison, Plotnikov had led a privileged life.

After a long day, the other seven men went to bed and left the Canadian standing guard, unaware that just outside the tiny village, under the cover of darkness, a raid was being prepared that would level their camp.

————

Russian Interior Ministry counterterrorism forces wanted to move in without being seen by the prying eyes of Utamysh villagers, so they had evacuated some women and children living near the camp. Not everyone in the Muslim village supported the continuing carnage in their region, but most distrusted Russian Federation law enforcement officials. Dressed in combat gear, the men moved as silently as possible as they carefully checked their guns and grenades, switched off the safeties of automatic weapons, and even loaded a small rocket-propelled grenade. Some of the most violent men in the Northern Caucasus, an area that has long been one of the most volatile and lawless places in the world, were inside the hideout. At that time it was not unusual for a Russian police officer to be assassinated every week.

The Russian Federation forces knew the jihadists would not likely surrender, not even when they heard dried dirt and rocks being crushed under the tracks of a tank and the wheels of the troop carriers, indicating that they were vastly outgunned and outmanned. When the first bullets were fired the mujahideen grabbed their own guns, prayed that Allah would give them strength in battle, and returned fire. A video later released by the Russian Interior Ministry showed the scene lit up with tracer rounds and bombs for hours.

When the sun rose over the mountains on July 14, 2012, all seven of the Islamic militants were dead. The Russians photographed their slain bodies lying in the scrubby grass as proof.

The camp was a smoldering shell. Cars belonging to the insurgents were still burning. The walls of the farmhouse were pitted with gunfire, and its windows had all been blown out. Russian Federation counterterrorism coalition forces also lost a man: an officer with the Russian Interior Ministry. Three other Russian agents were wounded.

Overall, however, the mission was considered a success.

The Russian Interior Ministry's National Antiterrorism Committee (NAC) released a statement that praised the Utamysh killings and hinted at how the terrorist enclave had been discovered: "We received information about their possible movements from an informant." The same news portal for the Caucasus Emirate — which at the time was run by the late Doku Umarov, the man known internationally as Russia's Osama bin Laden — also released a statement about the dead, but it celebrated their martyrdom: "May Allah reward all the brothers, who sincerely believed in the promise of their Creator, with gardens of Firdaws, and exchange this transitory world to the eternal Paradise."[8] These gardens, the mujahideen believed, were the highest form of paradise for the martyred.

The statement went on to reference the informant who had led Russian Federation soldiers to the training camp: "Invaders have announced that they identified the personalities of mujahedeen killed near the village of Utamysh. According to the Russian aggressors, mujahedeen got into an ambush because of a tip from an informant."

As the farmhouse smoldered the militants mourned, the Russian Interior Ministry prepared to bury its dead agent, and Tamerlan Tsarnaev left the region with a one-way Aeroflot ticket from Sheremetyevo International Airport in Moscow to JFK and then to Logan Airport on July 17, 2012. Investigators found a receipt for the ticket in Tamerlan's bedroom on Norfolk Street and photographed it as evidence. It remains unclear how the unemployed twenty-six-year-old on welfare paid for the flight.

CHAPTER ELEVEN

The Informants

High-level officials in the Pentagon and CIA likely exchanged classified intelligence regarding the successful Russian raid that killed seven Islamic militants in the Northern Caucasus. The region had become an international problem not just because of persistent internecine war between Chechens and the Russian Federation but also because of its geography. It is located at Europe's doorway into Asia and contains critical oil and gas pipelines.

If the informant was someone, as many believed, who had been flipped into cooperating by foreign counterintelligence agents from the CIA, DHS, Immigration and Customs Enforcement (ICE), NSA, or FBI, someone might be in line for a promotion or even a higher-paying private-sector job in the lucrative defense industry as a result.

It was also possible, ironically, that Plotnikov himself had helped recruit the informant when he gave the FBS a list of the men with whom he had exchanged jihadi ideals online. One of those men was Tamerlan Tsarnaev. Another was a notorious nineteen-year-old jihadi recruiter named Mahmud Mansur Nidal.[1]

The United States had had Nidal under surveillance for months.[2] And the Russians had marked him as one of their most wanted men after suspecting him of recruiting a brother and sister to serve as suicide bombers in one of the bloodiest attacks attributed to his ragtag group of insurgents. The bombers drove vehicles packed with explosives into a police checkpoint in Dagestan. The brother detonated the first blast. His sister followed, but only after emergency responders had arrived. Fourteen people were killed and dozens more wounded, according to Russia's National Antiterrorism Committee. After the blasts Nidal went underground. So Russian counterterrorism officials building the case against him were surprised when he showed up in May at the Al-Nadiriya Mosque on Kotrova Street in Makhachkala — the main Salafi mosque in Dagestan's capital — and chatted with Tamerlan. According to reports citing Russian officials, this was not an isolated incident. Nidal met with Tamerlan near the mosque multiple times. Then, on May 19, 2012, counterterrorism forces tracked Nidal to his hideout. When he launched a grenade at officers as they approached to arrest him, they cut him down in a blaze of gunfire. A video of the standoff posted on YouTube shows that a crowd of Nidal's supporters surrounded the counterterrorism forces and shouted "Allah Akbar" (God is great) at the masked commandos.[3]

At a congressional hearing after the Boston Marathon bombing, Congressman William Keating referred to Tamerlan's meeting with Nidal and the fact that one of the most wanted men in Russia surprisingly emerged from hiding to meet with the American at the mosque several times in May: "He [Tamerlan] was meeting with a known terrorist insurgent, Mahmoud Nidal; someone already on their radar screen in Russia . . . Now he came back to the US after the person he met with reportedly was killed, and the other person who was known to him was killed. So he sort of beat feet [made tracks] and went home."[4]

———

The purpose for placing anyone on the two primary terror watch lists — TECS and TIDE — is to create an alert any time he travels. But Tamerlan was on both lists, and when he landed in the United States after spending six months overseas in a terrorist hot spot, no alarms were raised. Then there was the question of his passport, which he had reported stolen — or at least that's what he told his wife. "He told Katherine (Karima) that he had been robbed, his papers had been robbed, and he needed a new passport," her landlord, Joanna Herlihy, said.[5]

Tamerlan's father, Anzor, would tell the *New York Times* an entirely different story following the marathon bombings: "His passport was about to expire in June or in July [actually, in August] and that is why I said, 'You have to get a Russian passport.' Because we left Kyrgyzstan for the States to seek political asylum in the States and Kyrgyzstan refused us citizenship," he said from his home in Dagestan, where he was living with his ex-wife.[6] The last valid passport that Tamerlan possessed came from the Kyrgyz Republic, where he had been born, and was slated to expire on August 11, 2012.

Tamerlan had indeed applied for a Russian passport to replace the one issued in Kyrgyzstan that he had used to gain entry into the United States as a political refugee when he was sixteen years old in 2002. But as congressional investigators would find, he left Russia without picking up the new passport.

"I was here at that time and went there [to an office to apply for the passport] together with him," Anzor said. "We gathered documents and he had to wait. It's not done instantly, some time passes, up to six months, maybe three or four months. He left Russia on a Kyrgyz passport because we came from Kyrgyzstan; we have Kyrgyz passport. We were in Kyrgyzstan. His Kyrgyz passport was about to expire, and he did not have time to get a Russian passport."

The *New York Times* reporter then asked Anzor why Tamerlan needed a Russian passport when he had a US green card. "He did not have American citizenship," Anzor said. "The Kyrgyz passport was about to expire, and if it expired then the man finds himself without citizenship, without anything. He would not be able to go anywhere, neither in Russia nor anywhere."

———

But when Tamerlan landed at Boston's Logan Airport on July 17, 2012, he breezed right through customs. An agent "scanned Tsarnaev's Alien Registration Card [green card] into the computer system . . . and admitted him into the country based on his LPR [legal permanent resident] status," according to the Office of the Inspector General of the Intelligence Community. This was the very loophole in immigration laws that the 9/11 Commission had said needed to be closed. Even more alarmingly, the report stated, the customs agent, Jim Bailey, told investigators that "he cannot recall" if he alerted the FBI regarding Tamerlan's return to the United States without a passport: Customs and Border Protection (CBP) officers, he explained to the inspectors, communicate with the FBI about potential terrorist watch-list suspects travel with "email, orally or via 'sticky note.'"

————

The DHS secretary at the time of the Boston Marathon blasts, Janet Napolitano, was grilled about lapses at a Senate Judiciary Committee hearing on immigration in April 2013. Reports in the media suggested that a misspelling of Tamerlan's name on the watch lists had led to his travel going undetected or at least unremarked. In her testimony before Congress, Napolitano said that despite the misspellings, redundancies in the DHS computer system allowed US authorities to be aware of his departure from the country in January 2012. But she said that by the time he came back six months later, an FBI alert on him had expired, so his reentry was not noted. "The system pinged when he was leaving the United States. By the time he returned all investigations had been closed," Napolitano testified.[7]

Senator Richard Blumenthal, a Democrat from Connecticut, pushed her for more answers and got this reply: "There's a lot of misinformation out there as to the two brothers. And of course this is an ongoing criminal investigation, so all threads are being followed." Napolitano mentioned a classified briefing scheduled for that very week and added: "Let's have that briefing and then see what, if any, questions arise at that point that may have any relevance at all to immigration legislation."

Senator Charles Grassley was not satisfied with the explanation that a man who remained on two terrorist watch lists traveled without being noted because an FBI alert had been lifted. The Implementing Recommendations of the 9/11 Commission Act of 2007 had amended certain sections of the Immigration and Nationality Act pertaining to the control of foreign nationals' travel. The 2007 law reiterated the need for exit data and required that such data be collected on all foreign nationals who entered the United States under the visa waiver program with the provision that air carriers are required to "collect and electronically transmit" passenger "arrival and departure" data to "the automated entry and exit control system" developed by the federal government. Clearly, according to Napolitano's testimony, that didn't happen. "It would be better," Napolitano told Grassley at the hearing, "if we could discuss those with you in a classified setting."

Whatever information was in Tamerlan's immigration records, the DHS secretary was not at liberty to talk about it publicly. That was a staggering admission, especially after the DHS had been forced to release Tamerlan's alien file pursuant to a Freedom of Information Act request filed by multiple news organizations, including *The Boston Globe*, in February 2016. The request had been made three years earlier and was steadfastly stalled by DHS until after Tamerlan's younger brother had been sentenced to death. Even with dozens of pages completely redacted, along with the redaction of the names of federal agencies that requested Tamerlan Tsarnaev receive citizenship (and waive any fees for the application process), the immigration file still contained troubling information.[8]

As noted already, Tamerlan had used multiple names and conflicting dates of birth. Then there were the startling discrepancies between two State Department Medical Examination for Immigration or Refugee Applicant forms. One had a photo of a blue-eyed man wearing a black-collared polo shirt attached to it and contained a passport number. The second had a photo of a teenage Tamerlan wearing an identical shirt, and the passport number was redacted. Finally, Tamerlan's notification of the time and place for taking the oath of citizenship raises questions by its very existence. He was told to report to 170 Portland Street in Boston on October 16, 2012, so he could finally become an American citizen. But thanks to his legal record, he was ineligible for US citizenship. It remains unclear if Tamerlan showed up at 170 Portland Street, but the document suggests, at a minimum, that someone was pulling strings to help him obtain the thing he had been craving since 2009.

Representative Michael McCaul noted the inconsistencies repeatedly as federal lawmakers tried to make sense of the Boston Marathon attack. That terrorism event would be the deadliest on American soil since 9/11 until an American, Syed Farook, and his Pakistani-born wife, Tashfeen Malik, murdered fourteen people at a Christmas party in San Bernardino, California, in 2015. Then in June 2016, another American terrorist and ISIS devotee, Omar Mateen, murdered forty-nine people at a gay nightclub in Orlando, Florida. In one of his 911 calls to authorities, Mateen "gave a shout-out to the Tsarnaev brothers," the FBI said. Mateen told an Orlando police hostage negotiator that the mass murder was sparked by the US bombing of an ISIS leader in Syria and that the "US is collaborating with Russia and they are killing innocent women and children," according to a transcript of that phone call, one of many Mateen had with the negotiator during the bloodbath. "My homeboy Tamerlan Tsarnaev did his thing on the Boston Marathon . . . okay, so now it's my turn."[9]

It remains unclear what Mateen's connection to the Chechens were, or whether he knew Ibragim Todashev, who told investigators that he and Tamerlan had murdered three men in Waltham, Massachusetts, on September 11, 2011 — the same day that Ibragim packed up and moved to Orlando. As with Tamerlan, the FBI had multiple interactions with Omar Mateen, and as with Tamerlan, the FBI closed a threat assessment investigation into Mateen not long before he violently erupted, despite a call from the owner of a gun shop alerting the FBI that Mateen attempted unsuccessfully to buy body armor but had succeeded in purchasing a large number of bullets.

Tamerlan Tsarnaev clearly did not become a citizen on that October day when he was summoned by USCIS to attend his oath ceremony. DHS will not explain whether that ceremony appointment ever took place or if something happened to disrupt the promise of citizenship. What is clear, however, is that in the weeks after that scheduled appearance the FBI continued to email immigration officials prodding them to approve Tamerlan's citizenship application, according to the Office of the Inspector General's report. And although Tamerlan's 2009 arrest for domestic violence made him ineligible for US citizenship for five years, his naturalization application was inexplicably reopened on August 28, 2012.[10] Moreover, he was told to report to take the oath of citizenship six weeks later, an impossibly short turnaround for a naturalization application

On October 22, 2012 — days after the initial oath ceremony was apparently scuttled for Tamerlan — a USCIS officer emailed David Cedearleaf, the FBI's special agent in the Boston field office's counterterrorism unit, saying that Tamerlan's name had popped up on the terrorist watch lists and asked if he "represented a national security concern." The next day, on October 23, 2012, Cedarleaf, who of course had investigated Tamerlan after the FSB warning in 2011, assured USCIS officials in writing that Tamerlan was deserving of full citizenship: "There is no national security concern related to [Tamerlan Tsarnaev] and nothing that I know of that should preclude issuance of whatever is being applied for." Cedarleaf would tell officials that he did not remember whether he searched Tamerlan's file or public sources before he replied to the USCIS official.[11]

The FBI insists to this day that Tamerlan's case file was closed after Cedarleaf's initial investigation in 2011 and was only reopened after the Boston Marathon attack.

On January 23, 2013, less than three months before the marathon bombings, Tamerlan made a second attempt to become a US citizen and had an interview with a USCIS officer to discuss the documentation related to his arrest for domestic violence. He fully expected to walk away from the interview with his citizenship. Instead the officer wrote, "The paperwork relating [to] the dismissal of charges in his domestic violence arrest did not arrive and his status was delayed."

Again.

Two weeks later, on February 6, 2013, an angry Tamerlan walked into Phantom Fireworks in Seabrook, New Hampshire, and asked for the "biggest and loudest" pyrotechnics in the store.[12] And David Cedarleaf was transferred away from terrorism duties and sent to work in the FBI's gang unit investigating the street gang MS-13.

CHAPTER TWELVE

Rats

The US Department of Justice began its practice of recruiting cooperating informants on March 14, 1961, when Attorney General Robert F. Kennedy instructed FBI Director J. Edgar Hoover to order every agent in every field office throughout the country to infiltrate organized crime groups. The FBI would need to reach down to the lower strata of the underworld and tempt bottom feeders up into the light. Working from the premise that most criminals would do almost anything for money, the FBI began its Top Echelon Criminal Informant Program.

Piling criminals from the bottom of the heap on top of one another with their courtroom testimony, wiretaps, and tip-offs paid off as the FBI began to topple underworld leaders, loosen the Mafia's stranglehold on the garbage industry, and level entire construction unions. The tactic worked for decades. The FBI similarly had informants in the KKK and biker gangs all over the country. After 9/11 the FBI mostly turned its informant recruitment efforts to Muslims who could be converted into mosque crawlers and rakers.

The arrests that resulted quickly from these efforts brought some FBI case agents unfettered discretion and authority. Just as they had let Mafia informants such as Sammy "the Bull" Gravano literally get away with murder, they were able to offer sweetheart deals to valuable cooperating informants, no matter how treacherous they were. Over the course of its fifty-year history, the Top Echelon Criminal Informant Program, the government's most effective tool against organized crime, hate groups, drug gangs, and terrorist organizations, had also become a scam that criminals, sometimes murderous criminals, could use to get paid by the FBI and, perhaps more important, gain its protection. Many unholy alliances between rats and sometimes rogue agents, such as that between Irish American mobster James "Whitey" Bulger and Boston-based agent John Connolly, have been documented in field offices all over the country.

The FBI tracks the productivity of its confidential informants, or CIs (also known as cooperating witnesses, or CWs), by aggregating their "statistical accomplishments" — that is, the number of indictments, convictions, search warrants, and other contributions to investigative objectives for which a CI gets credit. The FBI does not track the number of instances in which its agents let CIs run amok.

During the height of Hoover's COINTELPRO operations in the 1960s and 1970s, the FBI had roughly fifteen hundred informants. In the 1990s the drug wars brought that number up to about six thousand. Then, after 9/11, the FBI recruited so many new informants — including derelicts looking for leniency in their own legal problems or upcoming jail sentences, liars looking for immigration favors, Muslims looking for revenge on members of competing Islamic sects, and narcissistic egomaniacs who wanted to be revered as Jason Bourne–type figures — that it had to hire an outside software company to help agents track their secret spies. Today there are anywhere from fifteen thousand to twenty thousand snitches on the FBI's payroll, many of them "mosque crawling" to inform on fellow Muslims in the United States and overseas.

At the start of 2015 the House Homeland Security Committee unanimously voted to approve the Countering Violent Extremism Act of 2015, written by Republican Congressman Michael McCaul, which created an agency in the DHS dubbed Countering Violent Extremism (CVE). Congress earmarked $10 million in additional funding to counter what McCaul called "the long reach of international terrorists into our communities or the homegrown hate spread by domestic extremist groups."[1] In other words, the funding was largely for paid informants.

There is a valid argument for using informants to prevent terrorist attacks from occurring. For example, BPD Captain Robert

Ciccolo, a vaunted veteran commander who had been in Kenmore Square working the Red Sox game detail on April 15, 2013, when the bombs exploded at the finish line blocks away, received a disturbing text message from his son Alexander less than four months later, on September 11, 2013. In the message Alexander indicated that he sympathized with jihad. Captain Ciccolo called the FBI, which initiated an investigation that used an informant. The informant "befriended" Alexander and furnished the FBI with secretly wiretapped conversations that ultimately prevented a horrible bloodletting.

Alexander Ciccolo revealed to his new "friend" that he admired the Tsarnaev brothers and that he planned to "take a pressure cooker . . . Uhm [*sic*] fill it up with, ah, black powder . . . ball bearings, nails, glass, rocks . . . you know."[2] The pressure cookers would have built-in timers, he said, and he boasted that the "brothers in Boston paid four hundred dollars for the amount of fireworks they used." Ciccolo wanted his attack to be bigger than what the Tsarnaevs pulled off. He wanted to plant a bomb at a school and then shoot the students as they ran from the carnage. He told the informant he would be wearing a GoPro camera, like the one the San Bernardino attackers Syed Farook and Tashfeen Malik would wear nearly three years later when they killed fourteen people at a California office party.

On July 4, 2015, nearly two years after Captain Ciccolo alerted the FBI to his son's radical leanings, Alexander purchased a .223 Colt, an AR-15 rifle, a 556 Sig Arms SG550 rifle, and two powerful Glock handguns. Members of the JTTF arrested him minutes after he illegally bought the weapons — from the informant. Prosecutors said in an indictment that Ciccolo had planned to "kill innocent people in support of ISIL [ISIS]."[3] A day before his arrest, Ciccolo's mother, Shelley Reardon, had driven him to Walmart in Adams, Massachusetts, where he bought a pressure cooker. Alexander and the informant were members of a jihadist-sympathizer closed group, and Alexander went home and sent him the following message: "Allah Akbar! I got the pressure cookers today. Alhamdulillah."

Ciccolo also mentioned that he had built ten Molotov cocktails using Styrofoam soaked in motor oil. The Styrofoam "would cause the fire from the exploded devices to stick to people's skin and make it harder to put the fire out." Investigators also recovered two machetes and a long curved knife from Alexander's western Massachusetts apartment, the same style of weapons he had seen used in the ISIS videos he downloaded.

Captain Ciccolo has been lauded as a hero by BPD Commissioner William Evans, who called him a commander who made "the incredibly hard decision to turn in his own blood to save him from shedding the blood of innocent people."[4]

———

In February 2016 the DHS alerted twenty-nine "high target" cities, including Boston and New York, that their DHS funding would be slashed by 1.3 percent. Boston, which had received $18 million from the federal government earmarked for homeland security initiatives in fiscal year 2015, received $17.7 million in fiscal year 2016.[5] Rene Fielding, chief of Boston's Office of Emergency Management, explained that the cuts collected from the cities would be used to fund "nonprofits"— primarily to provide security to mosques and synagogues.[6]

Privately police officials complained that it was a way for DHS officials to pay imams at mosques for goodwill. Advocacy groups such as the Council on American-Islamic Relations (CAIR) may have noble missions, but they also attract angry activists. Better to be inside than outside the tent, the reasoning went, and grant money can go a long way with nonprofit organizations.

Federal judges had started to take a closer look at the use of Muslim informants after the case of the so-called Newburgh Four, four Muslim men arrested in 2009 for allegedly planning to shoot down military planes flying out of the Air National Guard base in Newburgh, New York, and allegedly participating in a separate plot to blow up two Bronx synagogues. There were allegations that the FBI had actually organized both plots and encouraged the four men to carry them out by plying them with food and money.

A report by the Human Rights Institute at Columbia University Law School found that roughly half of the federal prosecutions of Islamic terrorism cases relied on informants: "Indeed, in some cases the Federal Bureau of Investigation may have created terrorists out of law-abiding individuals by conducting sting operations that facilitated or invented the target's willingness to act. According to multiple studies, nearly 50 percent of the more than 500 federal counterterrorism convictions resulted from informant-based cases; almost 30 percent of those cases were sting operations in which the informant played an active role in the underlying plot."[7]

The American Civil Liberties Union (ACLU) was concerned that Muslims were being targeted and coerced into informing on their neighbors, especially given the NYPD Terrorist Interdiction Program started by NYPD Commissioner Ray Kelly and continued under his successor, Commissioner William Bratton. Both Kelly, a Harvard University graduate, and Bratton, a longtime commissioner of the BPD and the MBTA Transit Police, had seen Boston and New York attacked by extremists. The ACLU said that sending spies into mosques and hookah bars was illegal and the NYPD's "purported rationale for this unconstitutional surveillance" was nonsense.[8] The NYPD disagreed and released its own report in 2009, titled "Radicalization in the West: The Homegrown Threat." The report stated that some of the warning signs that someone was becoming radicalized were changes in appearance and behavior and cited "wearing traditional Islamic clothing [and] growing a beard," abstaining from alcohol, and "becoming involved in social activism."[9] These behaviors could also just be signs of a person choosing to be an observant Muslim.

Tamerlan Tsarnaev had stopped drinking and doing drugs. He had traded his designer clothes for traditional Muslim robes, wearing them to pizza parlors and Starbucks stores in his Cambridge neighborhood. According to Dzhokhar Tsarnaev's defense attorneys, these changes in behavior made him a perfect recruitment target. In a court filing they would write, "The FBI made more than one visit to talk with Anzor, Zubeidat and Tamerlan, questioned Tamerlan about his Internet searches, and asked him to be an informant."[10]

The US Attorney's Office and the FBI responded in a letter sent to the defense on March 14, 2014, that "the government has no evidence that Tamerlan Tsarnaev was solicited by the government to be an informant. As for information about any contacts between the government and other Tsarnaev family members, it appears from your letter [cited in a defense legal brief] that this information is already available to you through the family members themselves."

The government couldn't disprove the defense's claims that Tamerlan had been recruited as an asset in those FBI proffer reports, family interviews, and information they received from their client, Dzhokhar. But the defense team still wanted answers. They wanted details about Tamerlan's trip to Dagestan, for example. The defense wanted to know why the government refused to hand over any of the immigration records for any member of the Tsarnaev clan other than their client, writing, "While Dzhokhar's own A-file contains his father's claim that he had been arbitrarily arrested and tortured in the family's home country of Kyrgyzstan, and that he had a well-founded fear of further persecution justifying political asylum in the United States, the documents in Dzhokhar's file do not include any of the reasons why the United States government concluded that the father's asylum claim was valid."

More important, however, was the mystery swirling around the FBI's involvement with Tamerlan Tsarnaev and whether the pressure he felt to be an informant led to the attack on the Boston Marathon, questions Dzhokhar's attorneys asked in their defense brief:

The FBI made more than one visit to talk with Anzor, Zubeidat and Tamerlan, questioned Tamerlan about his Internet searches, and asked him to be an informant, reporting on the Chechen and Muslim community. We further have reason to believe that Tamerlan misinterpreted the visits and discussions with the FBI as pressure and that they amounted to a stressor that increased his paranoia and distress. We do not suggest that these contacts are to be blamed and have no evidence to suggest that they were improper, but rather view them as an important part of the story of Tamerlan's decline. Since Tamerlan is dead, the government is the source of corroboration that these visits did in fact occur and of what was said during them.[11]

Tamerlan had been desperate to become a citizen, as shown by his participation in the 2009 photo essay "Will Box for Passport." He wanted to box in the Olympic games on the US team, which only citizens were eligible to do. He also had connections in the drug world, as the murders on Harding Avenue in Waltham indicate.

The separate investigation into the drug trafficking crew of Eritrean immigrants, Operation Run This Town, would tie them to the Ruger P95 that Tamerlan used to assassinate MIT Police Officer Sean Collier. Confidential informants were at the center of that investigation. Dzhokhar had gotten the gun from his childhood friend from Cambridge, Stephen Silva, an Eritrean immigrant with ties to the leader of the crew operating out of Portland.

Other unanswered questions included: Why was Tamerlan allowed to travel to a terrorist hotbed while on two watch lists; why had he recorded his conversations with his mother's second cousin, a leader in an Islamist organization in the Caucasus; and why was his application for citizenship — for which he was ineligible because of his arrest for domestic violence — reopened after his return from Russia?

The Office of the Inspector General of the Intelligence Community examined those issues and the questions of whether Tamerlan was an asset (and if he wasn't, why not) in its heavily redacted report on information sharing among intelligence agencies in the wake of the marathon bombings. The IG posited the following additional questions:

1. Why did the CT [counterterrorism unit of the FBI] agent not visit Tamerlan's mosque [in Cambridge]?
2. Why did the CT agent not interview the woman Tamerlan was accused of assaulting?
3. Why did the CT agent not interview Tamerlan's wife, Katherine Russell, aka Karima Tsarnaeva?
4. Why was Tamerlan not asked about whether he sympathized with Chechen rebels?[12]

The report also lamented that the FBI had been less than cooperative with the IG's review, a complaint that Senator Charles Grassley would repeat: "The FBI has a pretty dismal record of responding to my questions. I wish I could say that all of those unanswered issues have been fully dealt with, but they have not. Ignoring my questions does not make them go away. They need to be answered fully and completely, and in good faith."[13]

Former Somerville Police Chief Tom Pasquarello heard Grassley's remarks. Pasquarello was a longtime DEA agent who had run his own informants and noticed the similarities in Tamerlan's case to his own use of CIs in multiple takedowns all over the world. As a longtime law enforcement official, he could not ignore the seeming coincidences. For Pasquarello it was personal. He had been close to Collier and had issued him a Somerville police badge to honor him after his death.

PART 3

Heaven Down the Barrel of a Gun

Countdown to Detonation

CHAPTER THIRTEEN

Maybe, Maybe Not

Khairullozhon Matanov couldn't keep quiet any longer. The Quincy cabdriver turned to his passenger, a businesswoman named Ann Munson whom he picked up most mornings to drive to the MBTA's station in Braintree so she could take the Red Line into town. "Those guys on TV," he said. "The bombers. I know them. I was just at their house. I was at their house that night. They are from Chechnya."[1] It was Friday morning, April 19. The news of the day was that Tamerlan had been killed and Dzhokhar was on the run.

In a series of later FBI interviews, Matanov would describe his visit to the Tsarnaevs' messy third-floor apartment at 410 Norfolk Street in Cambridge, on the evening of April 15, 2013, hours after the bombing. He knocked on the door and heard his friend Tamerlan Tsarnaev yell, "Open." The twenty-six-year-old Tamerlan was in the living room with his nineteen-year-old brother, Dzhokhar, watching the news on TV. Nearly every channel was running nonstop coverage of the chaos and carnage on Boylston Street: the smoke, the screaming, the scattered severed limbs, and blood everywhere. In the apartment a laptop streaming CNN also aired endless loops of the chaos and heroic rescue efforts: spectators using their belts, shirts, and shoelaces as tourniquets to tie off the mangled limbs of strangers; doctors who ran the marathon sprinting to operating rooms; and former New England Patriots offensive lineman Joe Andruzzi carrying an injured woman to safety.

Khairullozhon was twenty-three, a Russian-speaking immigrant with a scrawny frame and floppy black hair. He and Tamerlan had met and become friends a few years earlier at the

Prospect Street mosque in Cambridge, where they attended Friday prayers and observed holidays such as Eid al-Fitr, the highest of Muslim holy days, together. Khairullozhon's roommate at the time? Ibragim Todashev, the Chechen who would confess to the September 11, 2011, triple murder in Waltham. Tamerlan gave Khairullozhon boxing lessons, and they played weekly pickup soccer games in Cohasset. After Eid al-Fitr the year before, the two friends had climbed Mount Monadnock in New Hampshire. That was the first time Tamerlan talked about the mujahideen to Khairullozhon. "We didn't have secrets," Khairullozhon would tell the FBI.

He claimed to have never suspected that the Tsarnaevs were the bombers. How could he? Tamerlan had called him less than an hour after the blasts, at 3:31 PM — a call that cell phone records confirm. Tamerlan said that he was at the store buying milk. "During this conversation they discussed the bombings in Boston," an FBI report states. "Matanov suggested that maybe something blew up in a kitchen near the finish line, to which Tamerlan responded: 'Maybe, maybe not.'"[2]

The two made plans to have dinner together that night.

It was sundown by the time Khairullozhon walked into the Norfolk Street apartment, and Tamerlan seemed more like the old Tam he had known when he first arrived in the country. Tamerlan's face was freshly shaved, and he was wearing sweatpants and boxing shoes. Neither Tamerlan's wife, Karima, nor their toddler daughter, Zahira, was home.

After greeting the brothers, Khairullozhon commented that the bombing was very bad and voiced his concerns that the public might direct its outrage at Muslims. He plopped down on the couch next to Dzhokhar, who was stroking the family cat, a curious detail given that Dzhokhar had told the EMTs who treated him in the back of an ambulance after his capture that he was allergic to cats. Initially Khairullozhon told investigators that Karima was not at home, a statement he later revised. She was at home, he said, cooking chicken. Khairullozhon also expressed sympathy for eight-year-old Martin Richard, who had died in the second blast. Tamerlan turned on him and snapped, "Do you think the US drones that dropped bombs in Pakistan and Afghanistan did not kill any children?" Then he softened his tone: "So what if a kid dies? God will take care of him."[3]

Tamerlan smiled as he watched the coverage on TV. Every newscast replayed one image over and over: seventy-eight-year-old marathoner Bill Iffrig being hurled to the ground after the first bomb exploded, his bright-orange tank top juxtaposed against the gray, billowing smoke behind him. He lay prone on the ground, stunned, just yards from the finish line. Half a dozen Boston police officers sprang toward Iffrig and stood around him in a protective huddle as chaos erupted behind them. A blue-and-yellow-clad volunteer helped Iffrig to his feet. The sight of Iffrig falling as the smoke rose in the background made Tamerlan laugh.

Tamerlan disappeared into his brother's room, and Khairullozhon tried to engage Dzhokhar in conversation about what had happened. Dzhokhar responded by saying that for some people the bombing was a good thing, for others it was a bad thing.

Dzhokhar was always a quiet kid, Khairullozhon told the FBI, but that night his demeanor was particularly aloof. At 5:04 PM that day he had tweeted from his account @J_Tsar: "Ain't no love in the heart of the city. Stay safe people." He had also marked another tweet, from an account called "Death," @GMCoderGoddi. It read, "The ultimate sacrifice is within you, the battle within is defined by the word jihad."[4]

When they were finally ready for dinner, the Tsarnaev brothers climbed into Matanov's cab and they went for kebabs at a storefront eatery in Somerville called Man-O-Salwa a little more than a mile away. Khairullozhon saw Tamerlan again two nights later, along with his wife and baby. Nothing seemed out of the ordinary. "I didn't think they would do anything like this,"[5] he told Ann Munson, the passenger in his cab.

Munson insisted that they go together to the police. They drove directly to the Braintree police station and sat down with Detective Matt Heslam, who started the interview by saying, "Crazy set of events, huh?"

"I can't believe it. I can't believe that happened with them, like they — they were nice people, like the way they talk," Khairullozhon responded.

The detective continued, according to a transcript of the interview: "Everybody is kind of in shock. Everything that's going on. Do you guys mind if I record it? Just so I don't miss anything."

"Yeah, you can record it."

"Okay, awesome," Heslam answered. "You guys came here to share information, whatever you have with us, so we appreciate that, and uh, just fire away whatever you guys have. We'll probably pass it on to the feds and they'll take it from there."

"My name is Khairullozhon Matanov."

"Do you want to write that down for me? What's your nationality?"

"I am Uzbek."

The detective nodded. "Okay."

"So, I know this guy, uh, Tamerlan. Tamerlan Tsarnaev."

"He's the older brother, right?"

"Yeah," Khairullozhon answered. "The thing is, uh, two years ago I met him in the mosque, Cambridge mosque . . . I pray, and just like, you know."

Khairullozhon's phone rang in his pocket, and he answered it in Russian, telling the detective that it was his mother calling. Heslam looked at Ann Munson as Khairullozhon chatted on the phone. "Umm. Can you do me a favor? Can you just open up your purse for me real quick?"

She did, saying, "It's fine. Bless your heart. My father was a policeman. And I came in to verify that I know him. I call him Mike because I can't pronounce his name."

Heslam asked the woman if she knew the Tsarnaev brothers, which she did not. "Nope," she said. "Just him."

Khairullozhon hung up the phone and said, "My mom is like worried. So I know him since that time and we used to play sometimes soccer. I have their, like, you know the phone number and they call me sometimes."

"Okay," the detective answered. And waited.

"So then like I heard today in the morning that like it was him and actually I didn't see their photos last night and then they said like he got shot and he's dead and I can't imagine that he did it, that kind of stuff, and if anything, I can help, like to do, I am open to that."

The detective waited again.

"But only think I know that I used to call them and just like for the soccer reason, like you guys, you guys gonna come play with us today. We spoke in the Russian language."

Heslam asked for the younger brother's phone number. At that moment the only trace of Dzhokhar was the abandoned stolen SUV and bloody handprints on the hoods of cars on backstreets in Watertown. Khairullozhon had been calling Dzhokhar's phone all morning. He said, "It says it was blocked or something happened with it."

"Anything happen in their lives in the last year or so that you saw a change?" Heslam asked.

"No, they were like so, so nice people," Khairullozhon answered, stammering. "We talked about football. That's all. I don't know what they shared about family life. He told me about his life, he was a boxer, he won like the championship in the New England a couple of times I think."

"Older brother?"

"Yeah," Khairullozhon answered. "The only thing I know about the younger is he used to study. That's why I don't see him too many times, ya know, couple times I just saw him and like I took his phone number."

Heslam asked about the other Tsarnaevs: "Maybe something happened to their mother or their father or family member or anything?"

"Their father and mother were also nice people. I think they left this country."

"Have you ever met them?"

"Yeah. I met the father."

"And they left and went back to Russia?"

"I don't know, Russia or Kyrgyzstan or somewhere like that."

Heslam continued to press for more information: "Do you know if they left willingly or if the government had anything to do with it?"

"No, I think they like just wanted to like go there, see their relatives there, down there."

"Do you know if the younger brother has a girlfriend or anything somewhere?" Heslam asked.

"No. As I told you, I don't know the younger brother too much. But I know the older brother has a wife and a very sweetheart daughter. And I don't think they live together, but I'm not sure where they live right now."

"Anything else?"

Khairullozhon stammered again: "That's only I know, you know, like I was just like you know life is someone sees me, like anyways, like and I have a call to them so they will like definitely probably say like, hey, you call them, what you doing?" He explained that it had been Munson's idea to tell the police what he knew and that he hadn't called the FBI because he had really limited his friendship with Tamerlan to the mosque.

"Every Friday, we, we as a Muslim, we go at noontime to pray over there," he said. "We exchanged the contacts, like this and that. We went to play soccer. If you want to become the boxer, I can take you, like I know some coach that can train you to the boxing. And then there was like, this event we went together to the box last year I don't remember a lot. He took me there. He was a gold something. He said everyone knows me here because I, I become champion."

"Golden Gloves?" the detective interjected.

"Yeah. I think. In Lowell somewhere."

The detective asked for Khairullozhon's address and phone number and then rose to say good-bye.

"Should I contact the FBI?" Khairullozhon asked, and then nervously added: "I don't think it's like really big, my information because like I've studied the law, that's not gonna have anything cause I just saw him, like ya know?"

"It's what?"

"I studied the law. I didn't really graduate, but I almost am done there back home."

Heslam explained that any information could be helpful, especially as the younger brother still had not been captured. Khairullozhon agreed to cooperate as long as it was before the noontime prayer.

"I feel better already," Matanov told the detective as he stood up. He had not mentioned his Wednesday visit to the Norfolk Street home the day before Sean Collier, the MIT police officer, was murdered, or the sweets he had brought for Tamerlan's little girl. He didn't mention that he had called Dzhokhar's cell phone repeatedly that morning, nor did he tell Heslam that he had posed in front of a black flag of jihad with Tamerlan on a high Muslim holiday and that the photo was still on his laptop.

All of that information would be revealed later, after the FBI trailed Khairullozhon around the clock with a low-flying plane and eventually arrested him.

CHAPTER FOURTEEN

Vaseline, Fireworks, Backpack

Dias Kadyrbayev first noticed the red laser dots on his girlfriend Bayan's forehead. He then noticed that they appeared elsewhere on her body, and when he looked down, he saw that he was covered with them, too. Then came a man's voice over a bullhorn: "Jahar! Come outside! Come outside now! Come out with your hands up!"[1]

Dias pulled back the plastic shade. It was still daylight but raining. Three unmarked cars were parked outside his building. Six FBI agents from the elite military-like Hostage Rescue Team were outfitted in full SWAT gear with night-vision goggles on their helmets, and they were holding long guns with their scopes focused steadily on Dias and his girlfriend. FBI Special Agent John Walker, a tall, well-built man who wore a jacket emblazoned with his agency's initials, stood in the middle, holding the bullhorn. It was 5:00 PM on Friday, April 19, and Dzhokhar Tsarnaev was still missing. By then investigators knew that he had nonchalantly returned to the campus of UMass Dartmouth the day before. He had gone to the gym with Azamat Tazhayakov, and then he had partied with his boys in nearby New Bedford that night. On Thursday afternoon Dzhokhar went back to his Pine Dale dorm room and Skyped with his brother, Tamerlan, sometime before 4:02 PM, when his swipe card indicated that he left the UMass Dartmouth dormitory. He climbed into his battered green Honda Civic with its black replacement hood and drove to Cambridge: home. Hours later, one cop would be dead, another would be clinging to life, a young businessman would be traumatized, and a suburban neighborhood would be littered with bomb parts and bullet casings.

The next day, Friday, the campus had been evacuated. Agents were searching Dzhokhar's room in Pine Dale and interviewing his shy, nervous roommate, Andrew Dwinells.

Not only had Dzhokhar been in New Bedford the previous day, but on Friday morning the FBI got a hit on an iPhone registered to him. It pinged from a cell tower roughly 984 yards away from his buddies' off-campus apartment at 69A Carriage Drive. The cell phone ping made investigators believe they had found Dzhokhar in New Bedford, while the hunt for him was still under way in Watertown.

The call was made at 10:06 AM to Zubeidat in Russia, whose phone was being monitored by counterterrorism officials as her younger son continued to elude authorities. What the FBI didn't know was that a group of friends had shared a cell phone plan to save money. All of their calls were billed to Dzhokhar, the only American (through naturalization) among them. Dias had called Zubeidat, but FBI agents thought they had found their fugitive.

Walker believed that Dzhokhar was hiding inside and that the entire apartment might have been booby-trapped with bombs.

"Come out with your hands up!" Walker shouted.[2]

Dias and Bayan put their hands in the air. She was crying and saying, "They're going to shoot us. They're going to shoot us." Azamat came out of his bedroom to join them, his own arms aloft. Shaking, he exclaimed, "What the fuck!"

Together they walked outside. Azamat went first and began walking toward the man in the FBI windbreaker.

"Stop right there!" Walker ordered. "Take off your shirt."

He turned to Dias and said, "You, too." He ordered a female ICE agent to search Bayan.

"Do you have any bombs? Weapons?" Walker demanded. They all shook their heads, and Azamat yelled, "No!"

Dias threw his T-shirt on the ground and let his basketball shorts fall to his ankles. He stepped out of them and walked toward the FBI agent. He was forced to his knees, his hands bound by plastic handcuffs behind him. Then Azamat was told to get on his knees.

"Where the fuck is Jahar?" Walker demanded. "Who's in the house?"

"Nobody!" Dias answered. An agent in SWAT gear escorted Dias to an unmarked sedan. Dias was made to sit in the backseat where he couldn't see Azamat or Bayan. Then Walker climbed into the front seat of the car, reclined his seat, and turned around. He was a frightening man.

"He didn't look at me. He looked through me," Dias would later say.

"Listen to me. Where the fuck is Jahar? Don't fuck with me. Tell me where he is," Walker said.

Dias fought back tears. "I don't know. I don't know."

"This is the biggest thing to ever happen in Massachusetts. Jahar Tsarnaev is dead," Walker told Dias. "Whether he is still living or going away, his life is over. LOOK AT ME!" Dias did. "Repeat back what I said!"

"Jahar is dead."

There was another reason Walker thought that Dias knew exactly where the fugitive was. The night before (Thursday), after photographs of Suspect White Hat and Suspect Black Hat were released, Dias had exchanged text messages with Dzhokhar.

"Yo, bro. You saw the news?" Dias texted him at 8:43 PM.[3]

Shockingly, Dzhokhar answered. He and his brother were getting ready to kill a cop and go on the run, but he had time for his college pals, fellow Russian immigrants.

"Yeah, bro. I did."

"For real?"

"I saw the news," Dzhokhar answered. "Better not text me, my friend. LOL."

"You saw yourself in there? ahahaha . . . hahahaha," Dias responded.

"If you want," Tsarnaev texted, "you can go to my room and take what's there but ight [*sic*] bro Salam aliekum."

"What's wrong with u?" Dias texted, ending the conversation, "hahah."

———

The FBI was searching the apartment and Dias was still cuffed in the car when he heard the dispatcher say on the radio that the suspect had been found in Watertown: "Captured. The suspect is in custody." Still, Dias and his roommate were hardly in the clear. At that point the media had begun to swarm into the area. Walker repeated what he had told Dias about Dzhokhar's life.

"His life is over. He's dead. One way or the other he's dead. Your life does not have to be. You have to tell me the truth right now. Don't make a mistake," Walker told them. Dias simply nodded, agreeing to cooperate.

Walker ordered a uniformed New Bedford police officer to transport Dias to the nearby Dartmouth State Police barracks for questioning. They didn't have an arrest warrant, and the occupants of 69A Carriage Drive were not in custody. But Dias was all too happy to get away from the TV cameras and photographers that were outside his home. So was Azamat. When Walker's decision to detain the men without an arrest warrant was later questioned, he snapped, "This was a sophisticated crime, a sophisticated act of terrorism. The suspects were able to flee the scene. It was likely . . . [part of] a larger conspiracy."[4]

———

Azamat and Dias were questioned in separate rooms, both still shirtless. It was freezing. They were shivering and willing to talk.

Dias confirmed that he had sent Azamat a text — "Dzhokhar is on the news as the marathon bomber" — following the FBI's release of photos of Suspect White Hat and Suspect Black Hat just after 5:00 PM on Thursday. Dias didn't call the FBI. Neither did Azamat. Instead, they met each other in Dzhokhar's dorm room.

Dias later testified that Dzhokhar "told me to take whatever I want" and that he then told Azamat and a third friend, Robel Phillipos, to meet him there. The three were stunned. They had seen Dzhokhar nearly every day that week. They had gone to the gym, played video games, and watched news coverage together of the carnage left on Boylston Street. All three had exchanged texts with Dzhokhar on the day of the attack. Azamat had even discussed opening a Starbucks in Kyrgyzstan with Dzhokhar after graduation.

Then they started to recall other conversations, ones that had seemed like harmless rants about Islam at the time but in the context of the bombings were alarming. Weeks earlier they had been setting off fireworks along the banks of the Charles River in Boston when Dzhokhar began to brag: "I know how to build a bomb. I know all the ingredients to build a bomb."[5]

Another time he had confessed to Azamat that he thought "martyrdom would be a peaceful death."

As they moved around Dzhokhar's side of the dorm room just after 10:00 PM on Thursday, Azamat pointed out a backpack like the one used to conceal the pressure-cooker explosive devices days earlier, but he didn't want to touch it. Dias picked it up, pulled out a jar of Vaseline, and exclaimed, "He used this to make the bombs!" Then he pulled out firework casings, with the black gunpowder emptied out. "Take it," Azamat said.

Robel sat at the edge of Dzhokhar's bed, watching, Dias told the agents. Then they grabbed Dzhokhar's laptop and got ready to leave. It was 10:30 PM.

———

Roughly fifteen minutes earlier the Tsarnaev brothers had fired two rounds at MIT Police Officer Sean Collier's head and two bullets into his chest. "If they had contacted law enforcement with the identity of the marathon suspects it would have expedited their arrest," former Somerville Police Chief and longtime DEA agent Tom Pasquarello said. "MIT police officer Sean Collier would still be alive today living his dream as a Somerville Police officer."[6]

At a time when anyone with a smartphone, including the students, knew that Sean Collier was dead, the brothers had dumped the backpack in the apartment building's Dumpster, the contents of which were then picked up and brought to the massive Crapo landfill of the Greater New Bedford Regional Refuse Management District. Under questioning Dias asked about his girlfriend, Bayan, who had also been arrested. Dias and Azamat joked about smoking weed and complained about the cold. They asked for T-shirts, which the troopers gave them.

Dias and Azamat were driven back to their apartment around 4:00 AM, still free men and not charged with any crime. But the morning after that, federal agents arrested them on immigration violations. The charges would be upgraded in the coming months to obstructing a federal terrorism investigation. Robel was arrested at his mother's Cambridge apartment and charged with lying to federal investigators. Twenty-five federal investigators took five days to find the discarded backpack at the Crapo landfill. By then, investigators said, the "condition of the backpack and its contents had been altered," which federal prosecutors would say repeatedly during the trials of Dias Kadyrbayev and Robel Phillipos.

––––

Dzhokhar hadn't used his laptop much. He was well known for dealing weed, but he was hardly a good student. At the time of his arrest he had a cumulative GPA of 1.094. His transcript would show that his grades were abysmal the entire time he attended UMass Dartmouth. He earned seven F's over three semesters: two in the fall of 2011 for chemistry, two in the spring of 2012 for critical writing and reading and a math course, and three in the fall of 2012 for chemistry, American politics, and psychology. Those poor grades were going to lead to the loss of his financial aid, which would mean he would be kicked out of school. Around the same time, spring 2012, Dzhokhar began to express jihadi-inspired views online, using an identity that he mostly kept secret from his UMass classmates and weed customers.

FBI Special Agent Stephen Kimball would uncover a secret Twitter account — @Al_Firdausi — a profile Dzhokhar created in early 2012 that was full of tweets praising an American Islamic militant, Anwar al-Awlaki, and hoping for "victory over kfur [kaffirs]."

"Dua [calling out to God] is truly the weapon of the believer, pray for the oppressed it is your duty," read one tweet. Another read, "It's our responsibility my brothers & sisters to Allah to ease the hardships of the oppressed and give us victory over kufr [kaffirs]."[7]

Investigators were especially concerned about a tweet sent from that account on April 16, 2012, a year before the marathon bombing, which the FBI later said could be interpreted as a threat against the Boston Marathon runners. It read: "They will spend their money and they will regret it and then they will be defeated."

There was a second Twitter account under the name @Ghuraba — which can be loosely translated as the Arabic word for *strangers* — the profile image for which was a picture of Mecca.

Even if Dzhokhar was beginning to show more interest in Islamic extremism than in obtaining an American education, getting kicked out of school would cut into his drug-dealing proceeds. Students, many of whom would testify about buying weed from him, were his best customers. So he told a sob story about his homeland to university administrators and asked for help, Mark Preble, vice chancellor of administration and finance and the chief financial officer at UMass Dartmouth, would tell investigators. Dzhokhar filled out a Satisfactory Academic Progress Report, which allowed students to plead for forgiveness citing hardship. It was signed January 24, 2013 — the day after his brother met with immigration officials in Boston — and in it Dzhokhar blamed "terrorist accusations" made against relatives in Chechnya (a place he had never been) for his failing marks: "This year I lost too many of my loved relatives. I was unable to cope with the stress and maintain schoolwork. My relatives live in Chechnya, Russia, a republic that is occupied by Russian soldiers that falsely accuse and abduct innocent men under false pretenses and terrorist accusations. I am at a point where I can finally focus on my schoolwork. I wish to do well so one day I can help out those in need in my country, especially my family members."[8]

Dzhokhar's interest in Chechnya began apparently in 2011, when — as a seventeen-year-old high-school student — he wrote to an expert on Chechnya who just happened to be an associate professor of Islamic history at UMass Dartmouth, Brian Glyn Williams. The professor, as previously noted, was a former CIA agent who wrote material for the Jamestown Foundation and responded to Dzhokhar when he reached out to him looking for information on Chechnya: "I hope I didn't contribute to it [the brothers' radicalization, which led to the marathon attack]," Williams told the local *South Coast Today* newspaper. "That kid and his brother identified with the Chechen struggle." There was no mention in the article of Tamerlan's participation in the Jamestown-sponsored event in Georgia, Russia, which Russian intelligence officials later told investigative reporters he attended in the summer of 2012.

————

Not a single one of Dzhokhar's pot customers or classmates called 911 when they saw their friend "Jahar" on the news on Thursday, April 19, 2013. Elizabeth Zamparelli, who had been a friend of Dzhokhar since childhood, would later explain it this way in a Boston federal courtroom, with her friend at the defendant's table in front of her: "Just none of us thought it could be. It was like a joke."[9]

That prompted Assistant United States Attorney Nadine Pellegrini, one of the prosecutors, to explode: "You thought the marathon bombing was a joke?" Zamparelli giggled nervously and then answered, "No, not at all. Because it just was very much not who I knew my friend to be."

CHAPTER FIFTEEN

Better to Be a Dog than the Youngest Son

Seven days after the deadly blasts on Boylston Street, US Attorney General for Massachusetts Carmen Ortiz drafted a sealed criminal complaint against Dzhokhar Tsarnaev, who was still hospitalized in critical condition, and filed it in South Boston US District Court at the John Joseph Moakley United States Courthouse. The charges contained in the thirty-count indictment were long and complicated. They included use of a weapon of mass destruction and conspiracy, bombing of a place of public use and conspiracy, malicious destruction of property and conspiracy, use of a firearm during and in relation to a crime of violence, use of a firearm during and in relation to a crime of violence causing death, carjacking resulting in serious bodily injury, interference with commerce by threats or violence, and aiding and abetting others in criminal acts.

Dzhokhar had already confessed to being involved in the marathon attack via his note written in Number 2 pencil on the side panels of the *Slip Away II* and the carvings he had made in the wood and highlighted with fire extinguisher concentrate:

"The US Government is killing our innocent civilians."

"I can't stand to see such evil go unpunished."

"We Muslims are one body, you hurt one, you hurt us all."

"Now I don't like killing innocent people it is forbidden in Islam."

"Stop killing our innocent people and we will stop."

When he was brought to Beth Israel Deaconess Medical Center, he was questioned without having been read his *Miranda* rights after the US Attorney's Office dubbed him a public safety exception. FBI Agents Gregory Hughes and Matthew Dowd questioned him for sixteen hours without a lawyer. The government feared that the sophistication of the bombs recovered in Watertown and at the marathon finish line indicated a likelihood of more suspects on the loose.

"Immediately we had apprehension that a coordinated attack of this nature was a sophisticated crime, a sophisticated act of terrorism. They were able to flee the scene. It was likely not one person, likely two or more people or a larger conspiracy," explained FBI Special Agent John Walker.[1]

Dzhokhar cooperated, more or less. He told the agents that he had driven his battered green Honda to Boston with Tamerlan around 2:30 PM on Monday and that the brothers each had a "backpack containing an explosive device." Dzhokhar's backpack was brown; his brother's was black. Together they cost $99.98.[2] Tamerlan had bought them a day earlier at a Target store in Watertown, just blocks from the scene of the firefight that would leave Transit Police Officer Dic Donohue clinging to life. Prosecutors asserted in court filings that the brothers "each . . . decided on their own where they would stop near the finish line."[3] They picked their targets intentionally. Tamerlan stood behind a swarm of people not far from an area for dignitaries — including survivors of the Sandy Hook massacre in Newtown, Connecticut — who sat in metal stands near a media riser, and dropped his backpack bomb on the sidewalk. Dzhokhar dipped his right shoulder and slid his concealed explosive to the ground behind a row of children standing on a metal barricade closer to the marathon route.

"Jahar could not remember whether he or his brother was closer to the finish line," the agents wrote. "Just before detonating the device, Jahar placed a call to his brother with the other device to try and synchronize the two detonations. He used a trigger mechanism built according to the instructions in the *Inspire* Magazine article.

"Jahar stated that there were no other attacks planned, there were no unaccounted devices, and the only two individuals involved in the attack planning and execution were Jahar and Tamerlan," the report, filed as part of the indictment, stated.

————

At a hearing held inside his heavily guarded room at Beth Israel, Dzhokhar would meet his death penalty defense team for the first time. Two FBI agents had grilled him again that morning before federal public defenders Miriam Conrad, William Fick, and Timothy Watkins came to his room to protect their client's rights. Only then was he read his *Miranda* rights. Assistant US Attorneys William Weinreb and Aloke Chakravarty represented the government in the crowded room. Judge Marianne B. Bowler, a US magistrate, oversaw the proceedings: "Today is Monday, April 22, 2013. The case of *U.S. v. Tsarnaev* will now be heard. Will counsel please identify themselves for the record?"[4]

After introductions were made all around, she continued: "For the benefit of counsel and for the physician, I have called this conference because I want to establish before we conduct the initial appearance the mental state of the defendant." Bowler turned to Stephen Odom, one of Dzhokhar's surgeons. After establishing the physician's credentials as a trauma surgeon, Bowler asked for a summary of Dzhokar's condition.

> He has multiple gunshot wounds, the most severe of which appears to have entered through the left side, inside of his mouth and exited the left face, lower face. This was a high-powered injury that has resulted in skull-base fracture, with injuries to the middle ear, the skull base, the lateral portion of his C1 vertebrae with a significant soft-tissue injury, as well as injury to the pharynx, the mouth, and a small vascular injury that's been treated. He has, in addition to this, some ophthalmologic injuries that have been treated. He

has multiple gunshot wounds to the extremities that have been treated with dressings to the lower extremities; and in the case of his left hand, he had multiple bony injuries as well that were treated with fixation and soft-tissue coverage, as well as tendon repair and vascular ligation.

Following more details, including the pain medication he was on, she asked Odom, "Does he know where he is, and does he know what has happened since arriving at the hospital in terms of procedures?"

"He definitely knows where he is. He knows that he has had multiple procedures, but I'm not sure how aware he is of the specifics. He knows that he has an injury to the neck and to the hand."

"In your professional opinion, based on your training and experience, is he lucid enough to understand and respond to basic questions, if not vocally, using hand signals?"

"He is able to respond vocally," Odom answered.

The judge then summed up: "All right. At this time, I find Dr. Odom to be a very credible witness and fully informed about the medical and mental state of the defendant, and on this information I will proceed with an initial appearance forthwith."

The public was already clamoring for information about the surviving Boston Marathon bomber, so Dzhokhar's lawyer, William Fick, made a request: "Your Honor, may I ask that the record be sealed?"

"It will be sealed."

Weinreb immediately objected. Police had worked around the clock since 2:49 PM on the 15th to bring Dzhokhar to justice. The public had a right to know exactly what charges he would face and what kind of shape he was in.

"In conjunction with the initial appearance, we will make an oral motion to unseal the complaint," he told the court.

"That will be granted once we commence the initial appearance," answered the judge. The arraignment was short and sweet.

Dzhokhar had followed Tamerlan down Boylston Street, and now his older brother was with Allah and he was handcuffed to a hospital bed with a shattered jaw and broken bones, facing the death penalty. As he lay alone in his room, his thoughts may have turned to a Chechen expression he had joked about in the past: "It is better to be a dog than the younger son."

CHAPTER SIXTEEN

Dead Men Tell No Tales

On September 11, 2011, Khairullozhon Matanov, the cabdriver who would have dinner with the bomber brothers on the night of the Boston Marathon attack a year and a half later, came home just after 10:30 PM to find the door to his Brighton apartment open and unlocked. He was perplexed, but not panicked. He was letting his friend Ibragim Todashev crash at his place, and Ibragim had already proven irresponsible about things, like locking the door behind him. He dialed his roommate's phone and heard it ring in the bathroom. The shower was running. Khairullozhon went into his garage, where he could steal his neighbor's wireless signal and download some videos on his laptop. Ibragim came in a few minutes later and said, "I'm leaving town." He had three duffel bags packed in his room, and his laptop under his arm. A car was waiting outside. Khairullozhon helped him carry the bags out. As they hugged good-bye, Ibragim gave his EBT card to Khairullozhon, scribbling the PIN on the top so his friend could withdraw the cash still available on it, and returned the spare key to the apartment. Khairullozhon went back inside and threw away the towel that Ibragim had used after his shower.

Khairullozhon didn't remember later whether the towel was bloody. He couldn't explain why he had thrown it away. He wouldn't talk to Ibragim again until April 16, 2013, the day after the bombings in Boston. Then he called Ibragim on his cell phone at home in Orlando, Florida, and they talked for twenty-two minutes. Khairullozhon insists that the subject of their mutual friends, the Tsarnaev brothers, never came up, and neither did the bombing. The date of the call was just a coincidence.

"I got my green card," Ibragim says he told Khairullozhon. "I'm going back to Russia."

———

This was the first of the many suspect stories that Khairullozhon would tell the FBI. If he thought his cooperation with the Braintree police on the Friday morning when the manhunt for Dzhokhar was under way would leave him in the clear, he was wrong. The FBI would interview him more than a dozen times and surveil him using a technique meant to be psychologically stressful, what Special Agent Tim McElroy would describe as "bumper lock surveillance." The FBI wanted Matanov to be "certainly aware of people following him, cars following him, things of that nature. It was not covert in any manner."[1]

The surveillance was kept up around the clock from the time he left the Braintree police station on April 19, 2013, until he was arrested on May 26 on charges that he had destroyed evidence connecting him to Dzhokhar and Tamerlan Tsarnaev and had lied to the FBI about his contacts with the brothers after the marathon bombing, including dinner on the night of the attack. While under bumper lock surveillance, Matanov tried to lose his tail several times by using "evasive driving styles. He was making sharp turns, traveling in an erratic manner on the expressway, going through different lanes of traffic quickly, things that were obviously a sign of concern to the surveillance personnel at the time for public safety and other reasons," according to McElroy. Twice he even confronted FBI agents demanding to know why he was being followed. The FBI also used a drone to follow the Tsarnaev brothers' pal, officials confirmed during Matanov's arraignment, prompting 911 calls to the Quincy Police Department more than once.[2]

There was a reason the FBI was keen on Khairullozhon Matanov in connection with the bombing. Was the dinner he treated the Tsarnaev brothers to at a Somerville kebab restaurant some sort of a celebration? Moreover, following the marathon bombing, Tamerlan came under fresh suspicion for the unsolved triple murder in Waltham a year and a half before. The gruesome event on the tenth anniversary of 9/11 had all the hallmarks of a ritualistic killing, and authorities had reason to believe that Matanov had useful information about that atrocity, too.[3]

Khairullozhon was reluctant to discuss events of that night. "I am worried about the date. I don't want to make a problem for myself or something else,"[4] he explained in an interview with the FBI.

Matanov's roommate Ibragim Todashev had fled Boston on September 11, 2011, and headed south in a hurry, Khairullozhon told the FBI agents. The FBI already knew that Tamerlan had left the country four months later for his motherland — where the Russian FSB had warned the FBI and the CIA in March 2011 that he would go to join the jihad.

After the marathon attacks, friends of the three victims in Waltham — Brendan Mess, Rafi Teken, and Erik Weissman — told investigators about Tamerlan's connection to the dead men, but he never became a suspect. Now the case was reopened with a vengeance, especially after relatives publicly complained that they pointed the finger at Tamerlan as the most likely killer only to be ignored by investigators.

A review of court records related to Operation Run This Town, the DEA/DHS investigation into Eritrean drug dealers in Portland, Maine, allegedly sending money to overseas terrorists, suggests that Tamerlan could have been a CW repeatedly cited by prosecutors. In wiretapped conversations a CW makes plans to meet up in Boston-area locations with Tamerlan's old friend and former Cambridge Rindge and Latin classmate Hamadi Hassan, who was a primary target of the investigation. The Boston-area locations were ones to which Tamerlan had connections — such as a parking lot near Wai Kru and a 7-Eleven near the Cambridge mosque.

It is plausible that the killings of three drug dealers in a Boston suburb — most of whose relatives had disowned them — was not a big enough case to lose a CW in Operation Run This Town. Many of the records in the case inexplicably remain under seal, including transcripts of the sentencing for the gang's leader, Icy, and Hamadi Hassan, Tamerlan's former classmate.

Gerry Leone, the Middlesex district attorney in whose jurisdiction the triple murder had occurred and who first mentioned the "two men" who left the Waltham apartment alive on September 11, 2011, quit his job four days after the Boston Marathon attack, on the same day that the world learned that the bombers also had killed a police officer, carjacked a young businessman, and engaged investigators in a wild firefight that had left another police officer in critical condition and one of the Tsarnaev brothers dead. As the governor of Massachusetts issued a shelter-in-place order for a large swath of the commonwealth, Leone quietly resigned and announced that he would join Nixon Peabody, a prestigious 150-year-old law firm that counted many former prosecutors, judges, and political advisers among its attorneys. Nixon Peabody boasted of its new hire: "As the Department of Justice's first ever Anti-Terrorism Task Force Coordinator for Massachusetts, Leone initiated nationally recognized and unprecedented cooperation among federal, state and local authorities to protect the Commonwealth from terrorist threats following September 11."[5]

The announcement stunned law enforcement circles. Leone was not only a storied prosecutor respected by rank-and-file police officers and the young district attorneys who worked for him; he was also viewed as a political star with a bright future. No one could imagine him taking a quiet desk job in the private sector, no matter how much that move increased his income. His resignation came in the midst of a huge Middlesex County case — Sean Collier's murder — and while the office was embroiled in a controversial shaken-baby murder case that had wrongly imprisoned an Irish nanny. It was a very odd time to bow out, especially for a prosecutor with expertise in terror cases.

It remains unclear whether Leone ever alerted the FBI to the bizarrely savage triple murder on Harding Avenue in Waltham on September 11, 2011, which would have been a local case, not a federal one, or about Tamerlan's connections to the victims. There was also an odd, coincidental personal connection between Leone and Tamerlan. Leone had a second job as a Golden Gloves referee at Lowell Stadium, where Tamerlan won championships for Team New England in the National Golden Gloves in 2009 and 2010.[6]

When the three men were murdered on Harding Avenue, Leone was an executive board member of the Massachusetts Anti-Terrorism Advisory Council, a perfect fit for the former federal prosecutor who had successfully sent failed shoe bomber Richard Reid to the federal Supermax facility in Florence, Colorado, where he would spend the rest of his life in solitary confinement. He was also a consultant to the FBI's Joint Terrorism Task Force. Certainly Leone knew that the date of the murders and the manner in which the men had been nearly beheaded and the two Jewish victims sexually mutilated were indications that Islamic terrorists should have been suspected as the perpetrators. All of which had led to questions among his peers about whether he had been pressured to put the Harding Avenue investigation on the back burner at the behest of the feds.

Whatever his reasons for resigning, Leone was no longer a prosecutor in May 2013 when an FBI agent and local Massachusetts State Police investigators who used to work under him flew to Orlando to talk to Ibragim Todashev. The interview was videotaped but, for still inexplicable reasons, the video remains under court-ordered seal to this day.

———

Khairullozhon told the FBI that he got to know Ibragim and the Tsarnaev brothers through the Prospect Street mosque in Cambridge. All of them were Russian Muslims with their own distinctive personalities. Khairullozhon was the floppy-haired goofball who liked fedora hats and American women. Ibragim was the fighter with cauliflower ears, sinewy muscles, and a nose smashed flat as if he had fallen on his face too many times. Dzhokhar was the quiet one, garrulous with his own friends but painfully shy in the presence of his older brother. Tamerlan was the most devout Muslim among them. The former party boy had given up drinking, drugs, and all other forms of debauchery. Instead he liked to lecture endlessly about Islam, Anwar al-Awlaki videos, and US government conspiracies. Ibragim hated the change in his onetime hard-partying friend.

"This guy, Tamerlan, he smoked more marijuana than anybody. Anybody," Ibragim complained to his roommate, Matanov would tell the FBI. "We were always at the clubs. He changed."[7]

That change was even more noticeable when Tamerlan came back from Russia. He had a six-inch beard and had replaced his designer jeans and button-down shirts with a long white robe. For Ramadan, Tamerlan wanted Khairullozhon to hike up Mount Monadnock with him because "Islam teaches people to be brothers." All the way up the mountain Tamerlan talked about his plans to join the jihad, Matanov told the FBI.

In August 2012, a few weeks after his return from Russia, Tamerlan met Khairullozhon at the Prospect Street mosque for a service on Eid al-Adha, the festival of sacrifice that is celebrated at the end of the period for the Hajj, the annual pilgrimage to Mecca. Sometime during the day someone snapped a photo of Tamerlan and Khairullozhon "seated in front of a black flag with a sword and a shahada phrase," the statement of faith in Islam that the FBI would find on Matanov's laptop despite his efforts to delete it.[8] That flag is often dubbed the black flag of jihad and is flown by members of ISIS and other extremist groups linked to Al Qaeda. Khairullozhon told the FBI that all Tamerlan wanted to talk about anymore was jihad. He showed his friends videos of insurgent attacks on Americans in Afghanistan and ranted about Syria: "Everybody there is dying and no one cares in this country."[9] He boasted that he was going to be a mujahideen.

"Did you see the bombing in Chechnya?" Khairullozhon said he asked Tamerlan at one point. "Government people died."

"I hope it was Ramzan Kadyrov," Tamerlan answered. Khairullozhon knew that was the Chechen president. Another Muslim friend overheard the remark and defended Kadyrov. Tamerlan quickly grew heated. Khairullozhon stepped in: "*Brats* [brothers], it is Eid, a time for celebration. Let's go to the beach."

Tamerlan, who was unemployed, drove a white Mercedes. He drove it to the beach that day, while Khairullozhon got behind the wheel of his taxi. They posed for more pictures, which he deleted from his laptop after leaving the Braintree police station the Friday morning after the bombing. That night Khairullozhon went to Norfolk Street for Eid dinner with Tamerlan's family. Zubeidat was there, covered, making chicken and salad for the family. Then they sat down in front of the TV and watched a jihadist video, Khairullozhon remembered, and Tamerlan asked him about Ibragim.

"He's in Florida with his wife," Khairullozhon answered. Tamerlan nodded. He hadn't seen Ibragim in a while, not since September 2011. Ibragim had been lying low, and Tamerlan had been busy planning a terrorist attack.

———

On April 21, 2013, an FBI agent called Ibragim's cell phone. They wanted to talk to him about Tamerlan, the Prospect Street mosque, and the calls and texts he had exchanged with Tamerlan on September 11, 2011, evidence that put them both in Waltham at the time of the triple killings.

Since leaving Boston in 2011, Ibragim had remained in Orlando and wasn't willing to go back. He told the agents he would only cooperate if he would be allowed to go back to Russia right afterward. The FBI informed him that he had been put on a no-fly list, and his only way off it was to answer their questions. Ibragim agreed.

On May 22, 2013, three investigators arrived at Ibragim's apartment. Massachusetts State Troopers Curt Cinelli and Joel Gagne were assigned to the specialized CPAC Unit within the Middlesex County District Attorney's Office investigating the unsolved triple murder in Waltham. FBI Special Agent Aaron McFarlane was assigned to the bureau's Boston field office. In anticipation of being allowed to leave the country, Ibragim had purchased a ticket on a May 24 flight to Russia, telling his family back home that he was sick and tired of what he called "the harassment of Chechens in America."[10]

The investigators arrived at Ibragim's apartment at 6022 Peregrine Avenue in Orlando at 7:30 PM. They would have preferred to conduct the interview at the police station, but Ibragim refused: "If you want to meet you come to me."[11]

The investigators had their guard up. They knew Ibragim was a violent man with a long rap sheet full of minor brawls and fights that had escalated to bloodshed within minutes.

In 2010 he had gotten into a fender bender in downtown Boston that turned ugly fast. BPD officers arrived on the scene to find him red-faced and screaming, "You say something about my mother? I will kill you!"[12] He might have been short, but he was strong. It took three officers to pin him to the ground and handcuff him. Cinelli had talked to one of the arresting officers. "He was an animal," the cop told the trooper. "It was like fighting a refrigerator."

And on May 4, 2013, just weeks before the Massachusetts investigators' arrival in Florida, FBI agents from the Tampa field office had been surveilling Ibragim's movements with low-flying planes and around-the-clock teams when they saw him get into an argument over a parking spot with a father and his son. Ibragim tried to pull his white Mercedes into the spot at an outlet mall for which the other two men had been waiting. The father yelled, "No way, I was here first. My blinker was on."[13] The argument turned into a fistfight, and all hell broke loose. Ibragim knocked out the son, who lost several teeth. The father was badly bloodied. The FBI observed the entire event but could not intervene. It was their job to watch a possible terrorist, not stop a felonious assault. Off-duty Orange County Deputy Sheriff Larry Clifton responded to a 911 call placed by a passerby and arrested Ibragim for aggravated battery. Clifton wrote in his report: "I immediately recognized the marks on his ears as [those of] a cage fighter/jujitsu fighter. I know from training, experience, and watching a lot of sanctioned fights how dangerous these men can be. I told this suspect that if he tried to fight with us I would shoot him."[14] With that warning Ibragim quieted down and was taken into custody.

———

Ibragim greeted the three men with: "You can't come into my house with your shoes on. I'm Muslim." The investigators slipped off their shoes and entered the sweltering apartment through a door emblazoned with the image of an AK-47. The floor was sticky under their socks, and the room was dark. McFarlane noticed a samurai sword hanging on the wall in the living room, exactly the type of weapon that could have delivered the fatal blows to the Waltham victims. He kept an eye on it as Ibragim sat on the edge of a mattress on the floor. Cinelli sat on a folding chair across from the witness and quietly switched on a small tape recorder concealed in the pocket of his suit jacket. McFarlane sat on a step in a nearby staircase, and Gagne stood next to him.

The conversation started off friendly. The investigators tried to make Ibragim comfortable by paying him compliments about his accomplishments in the cage and commented on some of the bouts they had watched. (Investigators had studied some of his professional fights on YouTube before showing up to interrogate him.) They told him they were going to audio- and videotape the conversation, and Ibragim nodded. But when the conversation turned to the night of September 11, 2011, Ibragim became agitated. He twitched and stammered and denied knowing anything about the murders, despite the cell phone calls that put him in Waltham with Tamerlan that night. McFarlane also told him what the investigators knew about the phone calls he had exchanged with Tamerlan.

"I didn't kill nobody and I need your help," Ibragim told them. He repeatedly changed his story. The investigators waited. They gave him water, watched him smoke one cigarette after another. After nearly three hours of idle chitchat combined with repeated questions about his whereabouts on the night of the murders, Ibragim asked them to turn off the video camera. They did.

"If I tell you my involvement is there any chance . . . you need me to testify?"[15]

McFarlane didn't respond immediately, and Ibragim then blurted out a confession: "Okay. I was involved in it, okay. I, I had no idea Tam was gonna kill anyone. Will you guys help me?"

Cinelli immediately read him his *Miranda* rights and prepared a document from the FBI called an Advice of Rights form. Ibragim became more anxious: "After I tell you, are you going to take me to jail right away?"

He then dropped his chin to his chest and mumbled, "How much time will I get?" Cinelli recited his *Miranda* rights again and had him sign the form. It was 10:25 PM. "I need more butts," Ibrahim said.

Gagne volunteered to go get more cigarettes and took the opportunity to step outside and text the prosecutor who was overseeing the Waltham investigation about their progress: "He signed *Miranda*. He's about to tell us his involvement. Standby."[16]

"Amazing," the prosecutor texted back.

"He will be in custody after interviews."

"Don't put him in custody until we get a warrant," the prosecutor texted both troopers (the arrest warrant was still being sworn out back in Massachusetts). Cinelli — who was eager to put cuffs on Ibragim after his confession of nearly beheading three men and sexually mutilating two of them, or at least being in the room when it happened — showed the text to McFarlane.

With Middlesex District Attorney Gerry Leone gone, the Democratic governor had put a political appointee in his place. Her name was Marian Ryan, and she had a reputation for cautiousness. This was a big case potentially involving international radical Islamic terrorism. She told the prosecutor overseeing the case that she wanted the troopers to wait until they had hard evidence or a confession in writing before taking Ibragim into custody.

"Okay he's writing a statement now in his apartment," Gagne texted the prosecutor. Excited that the unsolved triple murders could be near a conclusion, he added, "Who's your daddy?"

Cinelli handed Ibragim a white legal pad and a pen. He sat on the mattress, pulled over a small white coffee table to use as a desk, and started to write:

> My name is IBRAGIM TODASHEV
> I wanna tell the story about the robbery
> me and Tam did in Waltham in September
> of 2011. That was [illegible] by Tamerlan.
> He offered me to rob
> the drug dealers. We went to their
> house we got in there and Tam had
> a gun he pointed it with the guy that
> opened the door for us [illegible]
> we went upstairs into the house
> with 3 guys in there. [word crossed out] we put them
> on the ground and then we [word crossed out]
> taped their hands up.[17]

When Ibragim was almost finished, Gagne stepped outside to call a Middlesex County prosecutor. Then Ibragim asked to go to the bathroom, for the third or fourth time, and was given permission. Cinelli had a bad feeling. The energy in the room had changed. He whispered to McFarlane: "This is going to go bad." Then he grabbed the samurai sword that was hanging on the wall next to a black Islamic flag and stashed it behind a shoe rack in the kitchen, to be on the safe side. At 12:03 AM Cinelli sent a text to Gagne: "You better get back here." The suspect was jumpy.

"He is in vulnerable position to do something bad," Cinelli then began to text to McFarlane, not wanting to speak out loud within earshot of the rattled suspect, who was still in the bathroom. He couldn't finish the text. Ibragim came out of the bathroom, noticed the empty spot on the wall where his sword had hung, and his manner shifted. He sat back down on the mattress with the coffee table in front of him. Cinelli sat on a stair to continue his text. McFarlane moved the folding chair to sit in front of Ibragim as he picked up the pen to write. McFarlane was looking down at his own notes when he heard a loud noise and felt a blow to the back of his head that knocked him off the chair.

Ibragim had "propelled" the white coffee table "into the air," opening a gash in McFarlane's head that would take nine staples to close. Ibragim raced past the stunned FBI agent into the kitchen and frantically rummaged through cabinets and drawers. Cinelli was right behind him. McFarlane drew his gun and followed.

"Show me your hands!" McFarlane shouted at Ibragim.

Ibragim had found what he was looking for: a red broom that he could use as a karate stick. He raised it over his head and charged — "incredibly quickly," Cinelli remembered — toward McFarlane, whose head was gushing blood.

"Stop right there! Stop right there!" McFarlane yelled. Ibragim kept coming. The agent fired. The bullets knocked Ibragim back for a matter of seconds, but he sprang up again and lunged headlong at the investigators. McFarlane fired again. "There was no doubt in my mind that Todashev intended to kill both of us," he would explain to other FBI officials. "In order to stop this threat I shot Todashev three to four times. Todashev fell backwards but did not go to the ground. He then reestablished his footing and suddenly lunged again toward us. I then shot him three or four more times in order to stop his continuing deadly threat. This time Todashev fell to the ground face first and I believed this threat had been eliminated."

Gagne drew his weapon and came through the front door with an agent from the FBI's Tampa field office.

The twenty-seven-year-old Chechen immigrant was facedown on the floor. Shot seven times, once in the head and six times in the body, he was pronounced dead at the scene. Gagne called

911 from his cell phone. McFarlane was "bleeding profusely," he remembered.

Cinelli was grateful to be alive. "I am certain Agent McFarlane's actions saved me from serious physical injury or death," he told his superiors. He also turned over the recording device hidden in his pocket. It had captured most of the chaos inside the hot, crowded apartment.

When he collapsed, Ibragim fell on Cinelli's feet, and the trooper had to wear hospital booties at the crime scene so the blood on his soaked socks could be preserved as evidence. His shoes were still at the door.

———

Ibragim's death became an international incident. His father, Abdul-Baki Todashev, held a press conference in Moscow in which he called the FBI agents "bandits" who had tortured and executed his son. "I want justice and an investigation in accordance with American laws to punish those who are guilty," Abdul-Baki Todashev said. "They were not FBI employees, but bandits."[18] He held pictures of his dead son's bullet-riddled body over his head and described the carnage as a scene out of a movie.

Ibragim was not a US citizen. He was instead, like Tamerlan, a lawful permanent resident. His earlier brushes with the law should have led to deportation hearings, but that never happened. Tatiana Gruzdeva, his girlfriend, who had been arrested as leverage against him, would not be so lucky: She was deported.

Ibragim's father would not let up the pressure on US officials. With the help of his boss, Chechnya's President Ramzan Kadyrov, the senior Todashev wrote a letter to US President Barack Obama that he shared with the international press corps.

> Did my son know that he had the right to remain silent or did he have rights at all, including the right to live? Being a citizen of another country he might not be aware of the laws as he was only 27 years old and

wanted to live so much. No, they left no chances for him inflicting 13 gunshot wounds and multiple hematomas on his body. After what FBI agents have done to him whatever excuses they come up with nobody would believe them because my son is dead and cannot talk for himself. They did it deliberately so that he can never speak and never take part in court hearings. They put pressure on my son's friends to prevent them from coming to the court and speaking the truth. I rely on you, Mr. President, and hope that the prosecutor's office and the court do not let the agencies conducting internal investigation on this case prevent the truth from coming to light so that at least some part of our grief, caused by the murder of our son, is relieved, and that the murderers stand trial instead of sit in their desk chairs.[19]

The FBI imposed a gag order on its agents about the case, and Ibragim's death certificate was sealed. But the less the FBI said, the more suspicious his death looked. To make matters worse, *The Boston Globe* uncovered McFarlane's sketchy past as an Oakland, California, police officer. By the time he was thirty-one he had been investigated by Oakland Police Department's internal affairs staff multiple times and retired under a cloud of suspicion with a disability pension, saying that he had been hurt on the job, but apparently not hurt enough to prevent him from pursuing a career in the FBI, which he managed to do without giving up his $52,000 annual disability pension.[20]

The Council on American-Islamic Relations immediately got involved, providing legal advice and, when Ibragim's dad obtained a tourist visa to travel to the United States, providing a driver. CAIR said that the FBI had been trying to bully Ibragim into becoming an informant and had used similar tactics to intimidate his Muslim friends. "FBI agents have threatened to wrongfully arrest them [the Muslim friends] unless they became informants and spied on local mosques, Muslim restaurants and hookah lounges. The DOJ [Department of Justice] must rein in the atrocious abuse of ethics and the rule of law by overzealous agents who have apparently disregarded the protections enshrined in our Constitution, which are essential to maintaining liberty and justice in our legal system. We also urge community members never to be intimidated by abusive law enforcement tactics and to maintain their right to remain silent and their right to an attorney when approached by FBI agents,"[21] Hassan Shibly, the executive director for CAIR in Tampa, said in a press release after Ibragim's death.

The FBI would not confirm or deny the allegations.

As the chorus of critics grew louder, Florida Attorney General Jeff Ashton ordered an independent investigation into Ibragim's shooting. Ashton met with CAIR representatives and Ibragim's father to try to assuage their anger. In the end Ashton's office released a 161-page report that exonerated the three Massachusetts investigators of any wrongdoing.

"Mr. Todashev, a trained Mixed Martial Arts fighter, struck the FBI agent in the head with a coffee table and then armed himself near the front door of the address. As he then re-engaged [McFarlane] and [Cinelli] they both perceived Mr. Todashev's movements towards them as being potentially life threatening," according to the report, written by the attorney general's chief of investigations, Eric Edwards. "The use of deadly force by [McFarlane] on May 22, 2013, was reasonable and justified, and therefore, lawful."[22]

The cops were cleared, and to this day the Waltham triple homicide case remains open. Dead men tell no tales. But their friends do.

CHAPTER SEVENTEEN

Allah Sent Him Money

Hiba Eltilib, Brendan Mess's girlfriend, told investigators there was a gun stashed "for protection" at the Harding Avenue apartment. The murderers left behind $5,000 in cash and thousands of dollars' worth of hydroponic marijuana, but took the gun. Ibragim Todashev did not get to answer investigators' questions about the gun before he attacked them and Special Agent McFarlane killed him.

The missing gun, investigators believed, might explain the two muzzle flashes observed by multiple witnesses during the Watertown firefight, after which only one gun, the Ruger P95 carried by Tamerlan Tsarnaev, was recovered. A BB gun that had been discarded on a resident's lawn was also recovered. The muzzle flashes suggested that another shooter might have been on the scene, possibly a resident of the house at 89 Dexter Street from which Dzhokhar Tsarnaev had emerged, or even the man whom Tamerlan had called right after the murder of MIT Police Officer Sean Collier: a native of the Caucasus named Viskhan Vakhabov. He and Tamerlan prayed together at the Cambridge mosque. Their brothers were friends and classmates at UMass Dartmouth, and, prosecutors said, Viskhan was a liar who refused to testify in front of a grand jury on the grounds that "he could incriminate himself in the Boston Marathon bombings," a statement that should have made him a person of interest in connection with the bombing plot. But for some inexplicable reason, the federal government did not consider him a suspect and fought hard to keep his interviews with the FBI a secret, calling him an unreliable witness — albeit a witness who had spent a lot of time with both Tsarnaev brothers. The three had even been together in the days immediately before, and then again after, the Boston Marathon attack, working out at Wai Kru.

There was immediate speculation among local law enforcement officials that the FBI was shielding Viskhan from scrutiny because he was another of the bureau's many Muslim informants. Considering the spy planes and around-the-clock JTTF teams of investigators used to monitor other friends of the Tsarnaev brothers like Ibragim and Matanov, the FBI's lack of interest in Vakhabov seemed especially strange.

Speculation that he was an informant increased after a team from the FBI's own Cellular Analysis Survey Team, or CAST, studied the calls made on two prepaid T-Mobile "burner cells" purchased by Dzhokhar on April 14, 2013, the day before the Boston Marathon attack, using the name Jahar Tsarni. He gave Tamerlan one phone and kept the other. The next day Dzhokhar called Tamerlan at 2:49 PM, the exact time the pressure-cooker bomb detonated in front of Marathon Sports. Twelve seconds later Dzhokhar exploded the second bomb in front of the Forum restaurant. At 2:51, Tamerlan called Dzhokhar's phone, a call that lasted for thirty seconds. They connected somehow — to this day no one knows how they got out of Boylston Street in the mayhem — and made their way toward Dzhokhar's green Honda, which apparently had been parked close enough for them to jog to after the bombs were detonated and then drive, in the chaos, to a supermarket in Cambridge in under an hour. The burner phones gave investigators another lead: Tamerlan called his friend Khairullozhon, the cabdriver, at 3:15 PM.

With that call the burner phone's signal pinged off towers near the Whole Foods supermarket in Cambridge, leading investigators to request the store's surveillance video between 3:00 and 5:00 PM. Bingo: The video showed Dzhokhar as he casually strolled into the Prospect Street store at 3:12. He lingered in front of the dairy section, picked up half a gallon of milk, and then slowly walked to the register where he paid $3.49 for the milk and got change from a $20 bill. The video showed him as he left the store. Less than a minute later he hustled back in to exchange the skim milk for regular. He left the store again, hustling back in seconds later to inexplicably exchange his second purchase for another half gallon before he climbed into the passenger seat. With Tamerlan behind the wheel, the brothers headed home to Norfolk Street a few blocks away. Assistant US Attorney Aloke Chakravarty was astonished at the video, saying that the brothers "killed two young women that day. They killed a little boy. They maimed and permanently disfigured dozens of people. At least 17 amputees. At least 240 were injured. And after they did it, he coolly, not 20 minutes later, went to the Whole Foods to make sure he got the half-gallon of milk that he wanted." How could people be so "capable of such hate, such callousness that you could murder and maim nearly 20 people and then drive to Whole Foods and buy milk?" he wondered.[1]

The phones were used again the next day, putting both brothers in Boston until that night, when Dzhokhar's phone was tracked to New Bedford and then shut off. At that point he partied with his boys. They smoked weed and went to the UMass Dartmouth gym, where they stayed, until his brother called him on another number to tell him to get his ass home: The FBI had released photos of them on the news, and their faces were everywhere. Dzhokhar turned the burner phone back on during the long ride from New Bedford to Cambridge. The phone put him back in Cambridge at 8:17 PM.[2] Two hours later the brothers were on the campus of MIT, where they sneaked up behind Sean Collier's cruiser and ambushed him. As they fled the crime scene in the Honda, Tamerlan made an eighty-eight-second phone call from the burner phone. This call was to Viskhan.

"It's undisputed that Tamerlan Tsarnaev contacted him on April 18th, I believe, between the time that Officer Collier was murdered and the time that Dun Meng was carjacked," Assistant US Attorney William Weinreb said.[3] "He has given quite inconsistent statements about what that conversation was about and what Tamerlan Tsarnaev may have asked him or said to him."

The inconsistencies Weinreb referred to were in reference to the April 20, 2013, visit an FBI agent made to Viskhan's house in Allston, about a five-minute walk from the spot where Dun Meng was carjacked. The agent's interview of Viskhan didn't last long. Viskhan told the agent about his childhood in Russia and his family's move to the United States with the help of the United Nations in 2004. The Tsarnaev brothers were his first friends in the United States, and the two families were friendly with each other. In fact, Dzhokhar was so close to Viskhan's younger brother that they decided to attend the same college. When he first met Tamerlan, Viskhan told the agent, he and Tamerlan "would smoke, drink, and go to clubs."[4] Tamerlan even "introduced him to some of his weed smoking friends." Then in 2011, right around the time the FSB notified the FBI about Tamerlan's and his mother's radicalization, there was a dramatic change. He didn't want to go out anymore and even lectured Viskhan: "Just because you say you are a Muslim, it does not mean that you really are. A true Muslim would not go out and smoke and chill out." Viskhan refused to tell the agent what he and Tamerlan talked about in the phone call on the night of April 18. All he would say was that Tamerlan was clearly inspired by the jihad during his trip to Russia and would repeatedly say that being a mujahideen was the only "proper path" for Muslims. Tamerlan had even called him from Russia during his six months in the motherland, talking about jihad.

None of that was enough to lead the FBI to make Viskhan the subject of surveillance, or a witness in Dzhokar's trial. In fact, the feds would later say they couldn't find him.

Vishkan didn't take the stand, but another man who hung around with "the Russians," as federal prosecutors called them, took the stand to talk about Tamerlan's metamorphosis from a guy who smoked a lot of weed with them to one who chastised them for being infidels. His name was Rogerio Franca. His friends called him Roger. In the spring of 2012, not long after Tamerlan returned from Russia, Roger, a limo driver, had just dropped off a client on Boylston when a man in a long robe caught his eye. It was Tamerlan and his wife, Karima, who was completely covered.

"Roger," Tamerlan said with a smile. "Are you a Muslim yet?

When Roger said no, Tamerlan and his wife turned their backs and walked away.

———

Another man of interest to investigators was Magomed Dolakov. In his interviews with the FBI, cabdriver Khairullozhon Matanov had identified Dolakov as one of the men with whom he had socialized and discussed jihad at the Tsarnaev apartment. He also fit the description of the mysterious man that Watertown Sergeant Pugliese had seen acting suspiciously during the firefight, hopping a fence and running away. A white male in his twenties, Magomed had a degree in physics from the National Research Nuclear University in Moscow. He had moved to Cambridge from Houston, Texas, in July 2012, a month before Tamerlan returned from his trip overseas. Magomed spent most of his time in the library at MIT, where he had been accepted into a master's program and was waiting for classes to begin. That is where the FBI found him. They asked him to meet at a nearby Starbucks for a chat, and Magomed complied.

The talk turned fairly quickly to politics in Russia, with Magomed claiming that his family had been targeted by the FSB, whose agents "would go around and just kill people."[5] He told the FBI he had attended services at the mosque on Kotrova Street in Makhachkala, Dagestan, where the FSB had taken surveillance photographs of Tamerlan during his time in the area. "Yeah, I know Tamerlan," Magomed told the FBI agents. He met him at the mosque on Prospect Street in Cambridge during the celebration of Eid in 2012. He remembered that Tamerlan was wearing the traditional all-white robe worn by Muslims during holy days. "I could tell he was radical," Magomed said. "He was not open to any other beliefs."

The next day Tamerlan picked him up so they could meet friends, including Khairullozhon, at the beach in Quincy and then invited him for dinner at his home. "Tamerlan's wife was there," the FBI noted. "They continued to talk about Islam, and Tamerlan continued to express his radical views on Islam." Karima did not seem to mind the conversation; in fact, she seemed to support it. She was there when Tamerlan began to describe the mujahideen as "brave" and say that he planned to become one.

"What about your wife, your daughter, your responsibilities?" Magomed said he asked. "Your daughter would grow up without a father."

Tamerlan scoffed. Karima said nothing. Magomed claimed that he didn't see Tamerlan again for months, not until he started to attend services more regularly himself at the Prospect Street mosque.

"I asked him if he was working," Magomed recalled. "He said Allah sent him money."

The last time Magomed saw Tamerlan and Dzhokhar was on April 12, 2013. It was Friday, and he had gone to the mosque to pray around noon. The two brothers were also there to pray. Dzhokhar had a runny nose and kept wiping at his face with a tissue, Magomed told the FBI.

"Are you still training?" Magomed reported asking Tamerlan. "I need to get into shape before the summer comes. Can I go with you one time and train?"

"How about right now?" Tamerlan answered.

Magomed claimed that he hesitated, that he hadn't meant that very minute, but that Tamerlan wouldn't take no for an answer. He insisted they go to the Norfolk Street apartment to pick up workout clothes for Magomed. As they climbed into a Honda CR-V registered to the Tsarnaev family patriarch, Anzor, Tamerlan grabbed a large box that was on the backseat and moved it to the rear of the SUV. A white sheet covered the contents. Tamerlan stared at Magomed and then said forcefully: "I am sending clothes to my mother in Russia." Then the three of them headed to Brighton to work out at Wai Kru, a two-hour workout that began at roughly 3:00 PM. "Dzhokhar was doing his own thing. He was very quiet, as usual," Magomed said. That interview was the last the FBI conducted with Magomed, who disappeared days later. Dzhokhar's defense attorneys were eager to talk to Magomed about the radicalization of their client's older brother, but his whereabouts were unknown. "We can't find him," defense attorney Miriam Conrad would tell the court, adding, "neither can the government."[6] Conrad's implication seemed to be that perhaps the government didn't want Magomed talking so they let him flee.

———

The FBI, multiple sources told me, wanted to present evidence to a grand jury about what Tamerlan's widow, Karima/Katherine, knew about the plan to attack innocent civilians at the marathon. She lived in a house festooned with jihadi flags and where Tamerlan was engaging in living room target practice with a BB gun, shooting at a target hung on the wall. The FBI believed that Karima knew more than she was saying and that they could charge her with obstruction of a federal terrorism investigation. However, the US Attorney's Office denied the FBI's recommendation that she be charged, which subsequently caused tension between federal prosecutors and FBI agents.

Investigators at the state and federal level doubted that the Tsarnaev brothers had acted alone in bombing the Boston Marathon, but occupants of 89 Dexter Avenue had mysteriously vanished from Watertown, Chechens known to be friendly with Tamerlan were missing, and federal prosecutors were focused on the case against Dzhokhar. They had their man, and publicly suggesting that accomplices could still be at large might provoke panic.

But then the arrest of a man named Daniel Morley for attacking his mother led to the discovery of a massive cache of bomb-making materials, including a giant pressure cooker concealed in a duffel bag along with blue surgical gloves, a machete, Russian assault rifles, and the top to a box matching the exact size and brand of pressure cooker — a six-quart Fagor — used in the bombs that had exploded at the Boston Marathon's finish line. Daniel had a direct personal connection to Tamerlan.

CHAPTER EIGHTEEN

Have to Answer to God For

Glenda Duckworth was terrified. Her son Daniel Morley was a genius, but sometimes he just wasn't right in the head. Sunday, June 9, 2013, was one of those times. As soon as she returned to her Topsfield, Massachusetts, home after dinner with her live-in boyfriend she could feel Daniel's distress, even before she saw him. That's how long she had been dealing with his dramatic mood swings. She made him an egg salad sandwich and carried it into the living room where he was trying, without success, to get an old VCR to play a videotape he had pulled from storage. She could see he was frustrated, but she never anticipated what happened next.

"He became madder and grabbed my glasses off my face and put them on the electric stove and switched the ring on high. He ripped [from my neck] a chain and heart pendant my son Matthew bought me for Mother's Day. He dragged me to the living room by the arm and pushed me into a chair and drew a cat face on me while yelling, 'Bitch, burn in hell,'" Glenda explained to police after she had flagged them down in the street, crying and in her bathrobe. She had escaped the rampage by crawling out a bathroom window. Daniel had attacked her boyfriend, too, but he managed to climb out the bedroom window, leaving the twenty-seven-year-old alone inside. "My son is out of control!" she told officers. "He said he is going to burn down the house."[1]

Topsfield Police Detective Sergeant Gary Hayward had expected that he would be responding to another run-of-the-mill domestic call about some whacko off his meds who had barricaded himself in a bedroom. When he pulled up in front of the gate that surrounded the large suburban house on a picturesque street, the distraught woman and her boyfriend, David Bloss, were sitting on a bench across the street from their home. Still crying, she said, "I've never seen him this bad; Daniel is very dark, unstable, but this is by far the worst I have ever seen him."

Other responding police officers quickly joined Hayward, including the MSP STOP (Special Tactical Operations) team in full tactical gear. Daniel would eventually emerge from the house with his hands up. Without incident, the police would bundle him into an ambulance and to take him to Beverly Hospital for a psychological evaluation. Then everyone went inside the house, where the police could take the shaken older couple's statements.

Topsfield Police Officer Gary Wildes followed the ambulance closely in his cruiser, and en route to the hospital he received an alarming message from his colleagues back at the house. In the young man's bedroom closet they had discovered a twenty-four-quart pressure cooker next to a brand-new duffel bag that was an exact fit for it. A giant bag of fertilizer, the kind often used by bomb builders, was also on the closet floor, and bundles of blue surgical gloves were inside the duffel. When the ambulance pulled to a stop in the hospital's emergency room bay, Wildes lit it up with emergency lights, put the cruiser in park, got out, and pulled the ambulance door open to stare directly at Morley.

"Is that pressure cooker bomb active?" Wildes asked.

"Yes, sir. I'm sorry, sir. It is," Morley replied.

"It is an active bomb," Wildes dispatched over his radio. "Repeat. Suspect says it is an active bomb."

———

It is standard practice to search for weapons after what is known as an EDP (emotionally disturbed person) call, and it was during such a search that police opened the closet and discovered the explosives gear. Bloss signed a consent order for police to search the rest of the room, and what they found was terrifying.

There was a fully loaded Mosin-Nagant M44 rifle, the standard rifle of Soviet troops during World War II, in an unlocked wooden box near Daniel's bed — which was a violation of

Massachusetts gun laws. There was an unloaded .22-caliber hand-gun with two fully loaded clips nearby. There was an assortment of "plasticuffs" (plastic handcuffs) stored alongside hundreds of rounds of ammunition, including rounds created for the Russian military. Knives and swords, like the one Ibragim Todashev had on his wall in Orlando, were arranged on a bookshelf in what the police described as a "makeshift temple." A painting of a man next to what appeared to be the Boston skyline as an airplane hovered over him was displayed at the center of the swords. There were computer parts, wires, and ball bearings that were eerily similar to the projectiles that had sprayed Boylston Street with the detonation of the two pressure-cooker bombs at the Boston Marathon. Dismantled phones were scattered in boxes all over the room, and there was a bucket with aluminum foil, along with brown rice flour and an Ignite-O fire starter log. There was a jug containing calcium, and a coffee grinder with metal shavings next to commercial-grade aluminum and steel wool. What appeared to be emptied whipped cream containers that narcotics officers recognized as high-tech "hides" for paraphernalia such as explosives were found in a closet next to a T-shirt with an MSP emblem, the kind usually issued to troopers. Also in the closet was a shoebox containing dead bird parts. Airholes had been cut into the top of the box. A green stuffed animal had been set ablaze and left in a bucket in a screened-in porch.

Perhaps the most chilling item founds in the room, however, was the top for a box that had once contained a six-quart Fagor pressure cooker, the size and model detonated at the marathon. A chemical recipe for thermite — a combination of metal powder fuel and metal oxide that, when ignited by heat, can act as an accelerant and is often used for bomb fuses to create a more powerful explosion — appeared on the back of the box top. The recipe was scribbled in pen like a laboratory formula, much like the ones Daniel used as a veterinarian technician in MIT's Division of Comparative Medicine, a lab located inside the Stata building, outside of which MIT Police Officer Sean Collier had been killed. Daniel's employment with MIT had been terminated in July 2012. Morley told his mother that he didn't want to conduct tests on animals any longer, but it was more likely that he had been fired.

The police officers on the scene had all studied the pictures from the marathon bombing enough to know that they were looking at basically every component needed to build the kind of bombs that had been detonated there. Besides, the FBI had repeatedly indicated that its agents had not "definitively determined where the bombs were built."

The houses around 18 Washington Street were quickly evacuated, and traffic was diverted away from Topsfield's town square. National Grid, the local utility, was called to turn off the gas in case of an explosion. Law enforcement officials set up a command center at a nearby building where cops, firefighters, paramedics, state police hostage negotiators, the bomb squad, and the STOP team strategized about how to proceed inside the house. The Boston Marathon attack had happened just two months earlier; no one was taking any chances.

Later court filings would confirm that the FBI had interrogated Dzhokhar Tsarnaev repeatedly in the hospital in an effort to identify bomb-making accomplices. One of their briefs would state:

> The Tsarnaevs had access to a small arsenal of bombs. They used two of them at the Marathon and several days later used four more in Watertown. They also indicated to the man they carjacked that they planned to travel to New York to explode additional bombs. These facts suggested the existence of a larger plot to wage a multi-pronged attack on different cities, as well as the possible existence of yet more unused bombs and other bombers waiting to pick up where the Tsarnaevs had left off.[2]

There was also the startling assertion made by the government in that same brief that the Tsarnaev brothers lacked the sophistication to build the bombs, raising the possibility that they had worked with accomplices: "The Marathon bombs were constructed using improvised fuses made from Christmas lights and improvised, remote-control detonators fashioned from model car parts. These relatively sophisticated devices would have been difficult for the Tsarnaevs to fabricate successfully without training or assistance from others." The government would even argue that the evidence suggested that others had built the marathon bombs for the Tsarnaevs or at the very least assisted them and provided a place to do it.

> The Tsarnaevs also appeared to have crushed and emptied hundreds of individual fireworks containing black powder in order to obtain explosive fuel for the bombs. The black powder used in fireworks is extremely fine; it was therefore reasonable to expect that if the Tsarnaevs had crushed the fireworks and built the bombs all by themselves, traces of black powder would be found wherever they had done the work. Yet searches of the Tsarnaevs' residences, three vehicles, and other locations associated with them yielded virtually no traces of black powder, again strongly suggesting that others had built, or at least helped the Tsarnaevs build, the bombs, and thus might have built more.[3]

Before long, FBI agents from the Boston field office showed up at the house Daniel Morley shared with his mother and her boyfriend, which struck the cops on the scene as strange. No one had called the FBI yet. One bomb squad technician would later say, "It was very surprising to us that the FBI responded immediately to a scene for a crackpot." The commanding officers from the

MSP and the Topsfield Police Department looked at each other with raised eyebrows. *Did you call them?* the questioning looks said. Both shook their heads.

The MSP bomb squad technicians geared up to go inside. They examined the pressure cooker and discovered it was empty. But "the place is full of bomb components that could be used to build a device," the bomb squad sergeant radioed to Topsfield police officers. "We need a further check."

A notebook on a table was opened to show bizarre drawings, such as a Star of David with a swastika scrawled inside. To make matters worse, David Bloss told police that on the day of the marathon attack he had looked at Glenda and demanded, "Where is your son?" He had been doing yard work that morning when he noticed that Daniel had slipped away. Daniel came home two days later and told his mother he had gone fishing with his friend Marc Pascuito. Bloss didn't believe him and suspected that Daniel was somehow involved in the bombing.

When Glenda told her son she had been worried about his safety when the news broke and they didn't know where he was, Daniel's response deepened Bloss's suspicions.

"What's the big deal?" Daniel answered. "People are dying all over the place."

Several weeks later on June 8, the evening before Daniel would attack his mother, the two of them were sitting at the kitchen table, and she asked about his friend Marc, with whom he said he'd been fishing at the time of the bombing. She hadn't seen him in a while, and the two had been inseparable.

"I'm not hanging around with him anymore. Marc wanted me to do something really bad. I didn't want to do it. I need to get away from my friends, get a fresh start," Daniel answered. After a pause he continued in a shaky voice, near tears. "I'm sorry for what I've done with Marc and I will have to answer only to God."[4]

Glenda repeated the conversation to Detective Sergeant Hayward and urged him to investigate Marc, who had always struck her as a strange duck. Once he had looked out her living room's picture window and remarked: "This is great. You can see people coming and have time to grab your gun."[5]

"It was like he was looking around at the house as a fortress, not a home," David Bloss told Hayward. "Marc told us that he knew Tamerlan Tsarnaev. He said he had boxed with him, or against him or something. But the kid is not truthful all the time."

Police found rather disturbing letters that Marc, an army wash-out who lived with his parents in Medford, had written Daniel. The letters were full of grandiose references to obscure gods and video games.

> What words capture the gravity of our friendship and its vast import to me? If such verbiage exists, it eludes me. I can only say that you are an individual whom I am glad to call my confidant, and that I am proud and honored that you may refer to me as the same. May Quetzalcoatl smile upon you.
>
> Yours in the glory of the Triumvirate, Marc Pascuito.

In another he wrote:

> In the hopes that you never stop seeking the truth, never back down, and eternally remain skeptical of wizzids. Your homie, Marc Pascuito.

The Triumvirate, Glenda explained, referred to Daniel, Marc, and their friend Vladimir Zaitsev, a UMass Amherst student who lived in western Massachusetts. All of them, Glenda reluctantly told police, had expressed some "anti-government and anti-Semitic views," Hayward wrote in a search warrant affidavit, "and [were] very unfavorable towards Israel."

Hayward also sent a report to the FBI and JTTF stating the following:

Daniel Morley had items consistent with bomb
   making materials.

Daniel Morley stated to his mother that he and
   his friend Marc Pascuito had done things that
   he could only answer to God for.

Daniel Morley stated to his mother that Marc
   Pascuito was trying to get Daniel to do something real bad.

Daniel Morley told both Mr. Bloss and Ms.
   Duckworth that Marc Pascuito stated he
   had boxed with or boxed against Tamerlan
   Tsarnaev, the suspect in the Boston Marathon
   bombing.

Daniel Morley had a Russian friend only
   known as "Vlad."

The pressure cooker and other items were
   purchased prior to the Boston Marathon
   bombing.

Daniel Morley had strong anti-government
   beliefs as well as anti-Semitic beliefs.

Dr. Breen, a terrorism expert, analyzed a painting located on a temple made by Daniel
   Morley and stated it was possibly containing
   a skyline in Boston and a plane that may be a
   potential target area.

An agent from the JTTF came to the Topsfield Police
Department headquarters to collect Morley's laptop, which was
sent to Quantico where it could be analyzed and the findings
listed in what is known as an FBI Forensic Toolkit report.

In the meantime Hayward started to dig into Daniel's past.
His father, Peter, was an Englishman who moved to the United
States to take a job at MIT. University officials say that he was
employed there from October 1994 until December 2010 as a

sponsored research technical supervisor in the Laboratory for Nuclear Science. After that he took over the MIT machine shop, from which the aluminum found in Daniel's room had allegedly been taken. Peter is now employed by MIT's Lincoln Lab, which describes itself as a place that "researches and develops advanced technologies to meet critical national security needs." Daniel also worked at MIT in various jobs between October 2005 until July 2012.

Hayward found other connections, all coincidental, linking Daniel to Tamerlan Tsarnaev. Both men had taken classes at Bunker Hill Community College in 2008 and were involved in mixed martial arts and attended boxing gyms in the area, such as the Somerville Boxing Club, at that same time. Both were students of anarchist literature. Tamerlan subscribed to the *Sovereign* newspaper, which published stories exploring conspiracy theories such as those suggesting that 9/11 was an inside job. The examination of Daniel's laptop would show that he had a heavy interest in the group Anonymous. His arrest record also raised eyebrows.

The NYPD had arrested Daniel in 2011 as he led an Occupy Wall Street march in New York City. A photographer captured the moment when he was thrown to the ground and handcuffed by a captain. After a search warrant had been approved, investigators also found among his belongings a card naming him as a member of the New Hampshire Liberty Forum, a libertarian group based in Keene. The chief of the Keene Police Department was so worried about anarchist groups in the area that he applied for a grant from the federal government to obtain an armored BearCat, like the one used in the effort to extract Dzhokhar from the boat in Watertown. The police chief wrote that "groups such as the Sovereign Citizens, Free Staters and Occupy New Hampshire are active and present daily challenges."[6] The chief also wrote that police were concerned about "several homegrown clusters that are anti-government and pose problems for law enforcement agencies." The membership emblem for Liberty Forum reads: "Free State Project. Liberty in Our Lifetime" next to the slogan "Many Paths to Liberty!"[7]

At Beverly Hospital, Daniel was charged with two counts of assault and battery, possessing a hoax device (the empty pressure cooker that he had said was an active bomb), and making a bomb threat. His father had to post $20,000 in cash for Daniel's bail, an indication of how serious the charges against him were, and the state sent him to Bridgewater State Hospital for a psychological evaluation.

Bloss's suspicions that his girlfriend's son was involved in the Boston Marathon bombing were bolstered by flyers that started to arrive in the mail at 18 Washington Street from Phantom Fireworks, the store in Seabrook, New Hampshire, where Tamerlan had purchased two "lock and load mortar kits"[8] that prosecutors said were likely used to build at least the pipe bombs hurled at police in Watertown. Before the marathon attack, David said, he had never gotten such a flyer, which were addressed to his home without a named recipient.

"I never purchased a firework in my life and I didn't know why I was suddenly getting these flyers," David explained.[9] He was puzzled that authorities were not looking at Daniel more closely, especially given the government's fears that the Tsarnaev brothers had not acted alone in the marathon bombing plot, a fact that the media had reported repeatedly.

———

For some inexplicable reason the FBI insisted, and continues to insist to this day, that Daniel had nothing to do with the marathon bombings — despite the ball bearings in his bedroom alongside a giant pressure cooker, the top of a box for a six-quart Fagor pressure cooker, the fireworks flyers, and the connections to Tamerlan.

"Can the FBI hide someone in a hospital?" David wondered. He had dealt with Daniel's mental illness for more than a decade, and every previous hospitalization had lasted for five days. Without any charges being brought, Daniel would be kept in a psychiatric ward at Tewksbury Hospital for nearly two years.

———

Months after Daniel had been arrested and confined to a psychiatric ward, Topsfield police officials were stunned to learn that he would not be indicted for possession of the explosive materials and weapons stashed in his room. He would not be held accountable for the chaos on his block or the massive police response after he attacked his mother. The Office of Essex County Prosecutor Jonathan Blodgett referred all questions regarding Daniel's case to the FBI. And the FBI wasn't talking.

Carrie Kimball-Monahan, spokesperson for the Essex County District Attorney's Office, explained that all of the evidence in the case had been turned over to the FBI. "We *nolle prosequied* the bomb threat charge," Kimball-Monahan said, meaning that the case against Morley would be dropped without even being heard in superior court, unusual for such serious charges. "Mr. Morley must comply with [the] Department of Mental Health, including medications, and not abuse his family. If he complies with these conditions and stays out of trouble, the case will be dismissed."[10]

Kimball-Monahan then referred all questions about Daniel to the FBI with no real explanation as to why she was doing so, and the FBI would not answer any of them. No one in the federal government has publicly addressed whether Daniel may have been responsible, however unwittingly, for building the bombs used at the Boston Marathon. But a friend of Daniel who asked not to be identified said he told the FBI that Daniel had repeatedly boasted of building bombs that would target "corporate America" and be detonated under billboards for giant companies, like banks. Marc Pascuito said something similar: "I don't think Danny bombed the marathon, but he had a lot of anger at corporate America."[11]

In an affidavit filed on April 21, 2013, regarding the devices deployed at the marathon, Special Agent Daniel R. Genck of the counterterrorism squad of the FBI's Boston field office wrote that "many of the BBs were contained within an adhesive material" and "contained green-colored hobby fuse."[12] Green-colored hobby wire was one of the items recovered in Morley's bedroom.

In what is referred to as a superseding federal indictment, a follow-up indictment with additional charges in the arrest of Dzhokhar Tsarnaev, reference is made to a machete that was never recovered at the crime scene on Boylston Street or near the Watertown firefight. No machete was found at the Tsarnaev apartment at 410 Norfolk Street or in Dzhokhar's green Honda. There was none in the stolen Mercedes SUV. No machete was ever entered into evidence or mentioned at trial in the case against Dzhokhar.

However, Tewksbury police recovered a machete at Daniel's house. A photo of it was entered into evidence and recorded on Hayward's report.

The superseding indictment, filed June 23, 2013 — two weeks after Daniel's arrest on June 9 — stated: "DZHOKHAR A. TSARNAEV and Tamerlan Tsarnaev armed themselves with five IEDs, a Ruger P95 9mm semiautomatic handgun, ammunition for the Ruger, a machete, and a hunting knife, and drove in their Honda Civic to the Massachusetts Institute of Technology ('MIT') in Cambridge, Massachusetts."[13]

The machete is part of another mystery that continues to swirl around Daniel: the unsolved 7-Eleven robbery that took place at 10:20 PM on Thursday, April 18 — at the same time Collier was murdered. A video of the robbery shows a man talking on a cell phone while he robbed the clerk of less than $29 in cash. Initially police officials, including MSP Colonel Tim Alben, blamed the bombers for the 7-Eleven robbery. The following day that statement was retracted, and police officials said the bombers were not responsible. But multiple sources — including David Bloss — have said the robber was Daniel.

In 2014, I showed David a copy of the Cambridge Police Department screen shot of the tape of the robbery, and he gasped, saying, "Oh my God. That's Danny."[14]

The photo prompted David to open up about the fears he had harbored since April 15, 2013, the day "Danny disappeared" for two days, claiming upon his return that he had gone fishing with his friend Marc. When Hayward first asked Glenda where her son Daniel had been on Patriots' Day, she told him that Daniel "was sleeping all day," clearly a lie to protect her son. The night he came back and his mother talked with him about the marathon bombing, Bloss said, "It was surprising. He was cold about it, used the term *collateral damage*."

No one has been charged with the 7-Eleven robbery that police initially announced the Tsarnaev brothers had committed. Friends of Daniel have also viewed the screen shot I showed David and have had reactions similar to his. "No question," said one, who has been questioned by the FBI, "that's Danny." A Cambridge police official referred questions about the 7-Eleven robbery, a crime with local jurisdiction, to the FBI. The FBI had no comment.

FBI officials claim that Tamerlan and Dzhokhar Tsarnaev built the bombs they used at the marathon by following a recipe in *Inspire*, an Al Qaeda magazine. But the FBI's analysis of the bombs debunked the bureau heads' insistence that the Tsarnaev brothers had constructed them. FBI technicians at the Terrorist Explosive Device Analytical Center in Quantico determined by late April 2013 that the bombs had a much more sophisticated design than that shown in the online magazine, including differences in the initiators, power source, and switch or trigger. For example, the Boston bombs used a toy car remote control for the switch or trigger, while *Inspire*'s recipe called for a motorcycle remote starter to be used.

The FBI electronics forensics report also cited circumstantial evidence of Daniel's involvement. On February 19, 2013, he searched the internet for the term "learning Russian for beginners." Then on March 10 he searched for the address of a Manchester, New Hampshire, gun range called Firing Line. Exactly ten days later the Tsarnaev brothers visited that range, where they rented 9mm handguns and engaged in target practice for about an hour. Daniel had posted pictures of himself on social media websites shooting guns at Firing Line around the same time.

After spending nearly two years in a hospital, Daniel is a free man. All of the charges he potentially faced in connection with abusing his mother, the bomb materials in his room, and even the guns (for which he had a license) were dismissed without prejudice.

Following his release in June 2015, Daniel was asked if he had robbed the 7-Eleven to distract cops while the Tsarnaev brothers broke into the lab where he had previously been employed, the one where he could have been making thermite, the bomb accelerant for which a recipe had been scrawled on the back of the top to a Fagor pressure-cooker box. He smiled and refused to answer.

There has never been any explanation as to why the Tsarnaev brothers were on the MIT campus. The theory that they went to steal Collier's gun is debunked by video evidence played at Dzhokhar's trial. In the grainy video Collier is shot and Dzhokhar and Tamerlan flee the shooting. Then, as an afterthought, Dzhokhar goes back to try to get the gun, leaving his fingerprints in the cruiser and on the gun handle. Morley wasn't going to talk about the bombs, or the Tsarnaevs, or whether he helped them. He answered with just two words and a shrug: "Wasn't me."

PART 4

Justice Seekers

CHAPTER NINETEEN

One-Finger Salute

It was the second bomb blast that ripped thirty-three-year-old Joseph "JP" Norden's right leg from his body, severely burned him, and peppered him with shrapnel. Boston firefighters wrapped a tourniquet tight around his severed leg and raced him to Brigham and Women's Hospital. He would undergo dozens of surgeries and nearly die several times. When doctors finally removed his breathing tube, his first question to his mother, asked with tear-filled eyes, was, "Where's Paul?"[1]

His mother, Liz, fought back her own tears, gently squeezed her oldest son's raw, bruised hand, and told him: "Paul's okay. He's worried about you."

Paul, JP's thirty-one-year-old brother, was alive but not at all okay. He had also lost his right leg and suffered serious burns. Flying ball bearings left his face swollen with bruises and seared scars into his skin. The brothers had been waiting near the finish line to cheer on their friend, Somerville firefighter Mike Jefferson, who was running in the marathon. After the first bomb exploded, the Norden brothers and their friend Marc Fucarile used their own bodies to shield Mike's mother, daughter, and aunt from harm just in case the attack wasn't over. The second blast came twelve seconds later, and the men took the brunt of the explosion. Marc lost both legs, his right leg gone from the hip down, his left from the knee down. Liz didn't know her sons' fate that bright Patriots' Day afternoon until she got a call from Paul, who was in the back of a van with other people who had lost limbs and were desperately fighting to stay alive.

"Mom, I'm hurt real bad and I can't find JP," he told her. Bleeding and burned, all he cared about was finding his brother.

"I was in shock," Liz remembered. "The ambulance driver told me he was in critical condition, and we had to get to the hospital right away. All he kept asking about is his brother. And we couldn't find him. I didn't know if I lost both my boys."

That same day at Beth Israel Deaconess Medical Center, Paul reached for his mother's hand, his knuckles burned and raw. His mother knew the question on his mind and comforted him before he went into surgery.

"Don't worry," Liz told Paul. "JP's okay. Jackie's okay. I love you. I love you so much."

It didn't surprise anyone who knows the Norden family that the two brothers were so worried about each other, or that they had used their bodies as human shields to help protect the people around them. They are a close-knit clan, and Liz is a tough woman — a cancer survivor and a longtime single mom who raised her five children in Stoneham, Massachusetts, keeping a watchful eye on them. Everyone but JP still lived with her. She didn't know what would happen now that two of her sons had lost legs: "All my kids are real tight. This is absolutely devastating to everyone. I am glad they are alive but so sorry about what is happening to them. My poor boys. I want to see this cowardly piece of shit burn in hell."

The day finally came on July 10 when she could see the man who had maimed her sons. Dzhokhar was to be transported from Fort Devens — where he was being treated for his injuries in a federal prison hospital — to the John Joseph Moakley United States Courthouse in South Boston to face the charges contained in the thirty-count indictment against him. Transported under heavily armed guard, he was whisked into an underground garage and held in a cell until the court proceedings.

Ailina and Bella Tsarnaeva appeared for their brother's arraignment. Ailina was cradling an infant — her baby with her new boyfriend. Court officials had designated two distinct sections for the spectators, almost like a wedding. Tsarnaev supporters sat in the rows to the right of the courtroom, behind the defense table. The victims and their families filled the rows on the left, behind the lawyers from the federal government who would represent them and the entire country. Liz was in the front of this section. Reporters selected to be in the courtroom sat in the middle rows, along with law enforcement personnel who had worked the case, including MIT Police Chief John DiFava; BPD Commissioner Ed Davis; Watertown Police Chief Ed Deveau; FBI Special Agent Vincent Lisi, the new agent in charge of the bureau's FBI field office; and Kieran Ramsey, the assistant special agent in charge. Behind these top officials sat first responders, still traumatized by what they had seen on Patriots' Day.

As Dzhokhar's sisters sobbed and wiped tears from their faces with the ends of the hijabs wrapped around their heads, their brother was led into the courtroom in an orange jumpsuit, his legs shackled and chained to his hands, one of which was wrapped in a cast to set the bones shattered by gunfire in Watertown. His face was distorted and bruised from the bullet that had smashed through it, his floppy black hair was disheveled, and a scraggly attempt at a beard clung to his chin. But he was smiling. He even swaggered a little.

"I would like to acknowledge and note for the record that there are 30 victims and family members here in the courtroom today, and they have the statutory right to be present at this proceeding pursuant to 18 United States Code, Section 3771," began US District Court Magistrate Justice Marianne Bowler, who had presided over Dhokhar's hospital room arraignment. She would not be the judge at his trial, but she was a well-respected court magistrate, known as a no-nonsense woman.[2]

"We're here at this time for the purposes of arraignment. Ms. Clarke, Ms. Conrad, have you reviewed the indictment with your client?"

Defense attorney Judy Clarke put a comforting hand on Dzhokhar's shoulder as she answered. It was one of her signature moves, an attempt to make her client seem sympathetic, worthy of intimacy. She hoped it sent a message to jurors that the teenager in front of her was not an evil barbarian. Dzhokhar's own mannerisms, however, undermined her efforts. He looked around, yawned, and smiled crookedly. He almost appeared bored by the proceedings.

"We have."

"And have you explained the nature of it to him today?"

"We have."

"And does he understand it?"

"Yes," Clarke answered.

"And is he prepared to be arraigned here?"

"He is."

"And does he waive the reading of the indictment in its entirety?"

"He does."

"And what are the maximum penalties?"

Assistant US Attorney William Weinreb would take the lead for the government side. It was a death penalty case. Only one capital punishment case had been tried in his time at the US Attorney's Office, and that defendant, Gary Lee Sampson, who had grown up in Massachusetts, was sentenced to death in 2003 on federal carjacking and murder charges stemming from a weeklong crime spree that had left three people dead. That trial had taken place in the same South Boston federal courthouse where Dzhokhar now stood. After his conviction Sampson had become a celebrity of sorts, whose commissary account is filled with donations from strangers. Dzhokhar had already gained his own bizarre notoriety: A growing group of women and teenage girls found him to be a dashing figure whom they insisted was the victim of a government plot to frame an innocent man. Some of them had gathered outside the courthouse wearing T-shirts emblazoned with his face and the word INNOCENT, or holding provocative signs like GOT PROOF? Some had even gotten tattoos of what had become his avatar, a roaring lion — a symbol adopted by many young jihadists radicalized primarily on the internet — and they called themselves the Jaharians.

Weinreb had walked by them and others in the crowd on his way into court that morning. He had also shared the hallway with the wounded and loved ones of the dead. It was a cathartic day for the city of Boston, and he was ready.

"Your Honor, on Counts 1, 2, 4, 6, 7, 9, 13 and 15 of the indictment, the maximum penalty is up to life imprisonment or the death penalty, five years of supervised release, and a $250,000 fine. On Counts 3, 5, 8, 10, 12 and 14, there is a maximum penalty of life imprisonment or the death penalty, and a minimum mandatory term of imprisonment of life, except on Count 3, on which there is a minimum mandatory term of imprisonment of 30 years. The defendant would also be subject to a fine of up to $250,000 and five years of supervised release.

"On Count 11, the maximum term of imprisonment is life, followed by five years of supervised release and a $250,000 fine. On Counts 16, 17 and 18, there is a maximum term of life imprisonment or the death penalty, a minimum mandatory term of imprisonment of 25 years, up to five years of supervised release, and a $250,000 fine.

"On Count 19, a maximum term of imprisonment of 25 years followed by five years of supervised release and a $250,000 fine . . .

"On Count 21, a maximum term of imprisonment of up to 20 years, followed by three years of supervised release and a $250,000 fine . . .

"On Counts 23, 25, 27 and 29, a maximum term of imprisonment of life followed by five years of supervised release and a $250,000 fine. And finally, on Counts 24, 26, 28 and 30, there's a maximum term of life imprisonment, a minimum mandatory term of life imprisonment, a five-year term of supervised release, and up to a $250,000 fine."

Bowler turned toward the defense table. "Are you ready to proceed?"

Clarke answered, "Yes."

"Will the defendant please stand?"

Dzhokhar rose, and Bowler's clerk, Brendan Garvin, began to read.

"Mr. Tsarnaev, as to Counts 1, 2, 4, 23, 25, 27, 29 of the indictment, charging you with use of a weapon of mass destruction resulting in death and conspiracy to use a weapon of mass destruction resulting in death, a violation of Title 18, United States Code, Section 2332A, how do you plead, guilty or not guilty?"

Clarke interjected. "Your Honor, as to all counts we've advised Mr. Tsarnaev that today it's appropriate to enter not guilty pleas, and we would ask the court to enter not guilty pleas."

The judge wanted to hear the words from Dzhokhar, not his death penalty defense lawyers. "Well, I would ask him to answer."

"Thank you, Your Honor," Clarke answered, patting Tsarnaev on the arm.

"Not guilty," he said, his voice heavily accented.

The clerk continued: "Counts 6, 7, and 9 charging death and conspiracy to bomb a place resulting in death in violation of Title 18, United States Code, Section 2332F, charging you with bombing of a place. How do you plead?"

"Not guilty."

And so on, five more pleas of "not guilty" as the remainder of the charges were articulated.

Bowler thanked Dzhokhar. "You may be seated."

Then she turned back to the prosecution. "How many witnesses does the government intend to call and what's the probable length of trial?"

"Your Honor, we anticipate the government would call 80 to 100 witnesses and that the trial would last approximately three to four months," Weinreb answered.

"And, Mr. Garvin, do we have a date for an initial status conference?"

"We do. It will be Monday, the 23rd of September, at 10:00 AM."

"So noted by counsel?" Bowler asked the defense.

"That's a good date," Clarke answered. "Yes, thank you."

"Mindful of the potential cost of these proceedings, I direct counsel for the defendant at this time to consider sooner rather than later preparing a proposed litigation budget for the trial judge. And I note that the provisions of the Guide to Judiciary Policies and Procedure, Volume 7, Part A, Chapter 6, Section 640, encourages the budget to be filed as early as possible. Ms. Clarke, I know you have experience with this. So I would suggest, particularly in this time of sequester, the sooner you can get to this, the better."

Taxpayers would pick up the tab for both the prosecution and the defense. More often than not, the US government paid more for the cost of the defense than for the cost of the prosecution, and the "proposed litigation budgets" did not factor in costs such as police overtime for security outside the courthouse — which in this case was on an unprecedented scale. Taxpayers would also have to cover additional costs for the Coast Guard and BPD marine units that patrolled the South Boston waterfront, the federal agents from the DHS who ringed the courthouse, the US marshals who surrounded Dzhokhar, and the undercover BPD detectives who were nonetheless recognized in the crowd, monitoring the people who lined up at six each morning during the trial for a spot in the seats set aside for spectators. With victims, police, media, and the public, the demand for seats was so overwhelming that two additional courtrooms had to be set up by the office of court administration, where streaming video from the main courtroom could be viewed on televisions provided for the overflow of journalists from all over the world.

"Thank you, Your Honor," Clarke answered.

Bowler continued: "All right, I'd also like to remind counsel of the presumption of public access to judicial documents and that this court frowns upon the sealing of judicial documents unless it's absolutely necessary. To date, many of the filings in this case have been sealed, and the court will look carefully in the future because the public has a right to know about the nature of the proceedings."

At least Bowler called for transparency, but as the trial progressed, hundreds of files would remain sealed, and an inexplicable shroud of secrecy would envelop the entire prosecution long after the trial ended.

"Are there other matters that counsel wish to bring to my attention at this time?"

Weinreb answered first. "None from the government, Your Honor."

"No, Your Honor. Thank you," Clarke then responded.

"All right." The judge got ready to stand up and concluded: "In which case the defendant is now in the custody of the United States marshals."

The hearing lasted exactly eight minutes. Two US marshals flanked Dzhokhar, each taking an arm to guide him. Before reaching the door, he turned his face toward his sisters, smirked, and blew them a kiss. The victims gasped at the gesture, which struck them as arrogant.

Ed Fucarile, whose son Marc had been with the Norden brothers in front of the Forum restaurant, was aghast. "He came out and he smirked at the families," he told reporters who had set up a bank of microphones outside, visibly angry. "The lawyers put their hands on his shoulders like it was going to be all right. My son is not all right."[3]

Marc was still hospitalized. An X-ray showed that his entire body was studded with BBs, and a nail was still lodged precariously close to his heart.

MIT Police Chief John DiFava didn't step up to the microphones but stormed away from the courthouse in a rage, saying, "I'm disgusted. I'd like to grab him by the throat. I didn't see a lot of remorse. That arrogant little piece of garbage didn't even look at the victims and was blowing kisses."[4] He had come to court to set eyes on the man who had robbed his officer, Sean Collier, of his future. "I wanted to see the person that so coldly and callously killed four people, one of whom being an officer of mine. He deserves to die."

One by one the victims expressed to reporters how astonished they were at the cold-blooded arrogance displayed by Dzhokhar in court. But they had no idea what he had done earlier in the day in the federal court's holding cell, a place he would become so familiar with that he would spend his time there playing "toilet roll basketball" — tossing pieces of wadded-up paper into the middle of a toilet paper roll — and reading the Quran.

Kevin Roche was the US marshal assigned to monitor Dzhokhar's activities in the cell that day. He was a seventeen-year veteran of the federal force and had seen almost everything in the cellblock. There had been attempted suicides and inmate-on-inmate attacks. Some accused criminals flooded their own cell with toilet water and sat in the resulting rancid mess. Roche had been called names he hadn't known existed. He had seen feces thrown at marshals by inmates who had scooped it up with their bare hands. Nothing could surprise him. Roche was also familiar with Dzhokhar. He had stood guard over the Boston Marathon bomber after his arrest at Beth Israel hospital, was there for his initial bedside arraignment, and had seen him roughly six other times while working the hospital detail. Roche had transported Dzhokhar to Fort Devens and to follow-up appointments at Beth Israel after the transfer. He had noted the prisoner's scowls, tears, and whining.

On the morning of July 10, 2013, Dzhokhar, in his orange jumpsuit, hopped onto a bench in his holding cell and preened his hair in the reflection of the camera. He raised his middle finger at the security camera, his face twisted into a sinister smile, and then flashed two fingers sideways into the camera, another international symbol that had the same meaning as the middle-finger salute: Fuck you.

The deputy who was monitoring the feed from the camera alerted Roche, who went to Dzhokhar's cell.

"We saw what you did. That is not going to be tolerated in this house," Roche admonished Dzhokhar. "This behavior will be dealt with."[5]

The teen's bravado disappeared. He slumped and apologized: "Sorry."

"Are you going to be a problem for the rest of the day?" Roche demanded.

"No, I'm done. I'm sorry."

The one-finger salute was caught on a surveillance video inside his cell, and word of the obscene gesture spread. An infuriated guard confided in me, quietly, at the courthouse. Without a picture, ABC News, for whom I covered the trial at the time, declined to run the story, even with the multiple law enforcement sources who insisted it had happened. Ultimately the prosecution would introduce the incident at trial as an indication of Dzhokhar's lack of remorse and defiance. "This is Dzhokhar Tsarnaev," Assistant US Attorney Nadine Pellegrini would tell the jury, adding that the one-finger salute had been followed by another offensive hand signal more commonly used in Europe. But it meant the same thing. The prisoner was "unconcerned, unrepentant and unchanged."[6]

Dzhokhar's defense attorneys countered to the jury that the hand signals were in fact viewed as a "peace sign" in Russia.[7] Roche scoffed. "I'm purebred Irish, and all four of my grandparents emigrated here from Ireland so . . . I perceived it as defiance. The way that I understood it growing up around my family and circle of people, that was it. It was a disrespectful sign. To me," he added, the middle finger and the sideways two fingers into the camera "were one in [and] the same. They meant the same thing to me."[8]

The jury got the message.

CHAPTER TWENTY

Food for the Dog

In the weeks after the man he considered his best friend, Dzhokhar Tsarnaev, was arrested for the murders of two young women and a little boy with a weapon of mass destruction designed to cause maximum harm and the later murder of a police officer, Stephen Silva had a message he wanted to share on Twitter: "tryna live life feds free," he tweeted on April 29, 2013. He would not be so lucky.

Stephen had grown up in Cambridge along with his twin brother, Steven. Steven was the "good brother," the one who didn't get into trouble, at least not as often as Stephen, who had taken to spending much of his time dealing drugs and smoking weed with Dzhokhar and other Cambridge Rindge and Latin classmates, including Robel Phillipos, who partied with Dzhokhar the week of the marathon attacks and would face trial, along with Azamat Tazhayakov and Dias Kadyrbayev, for obstructing the investigation into the Boston Marathon bombers.

Stephen's friends didn't invite him to Dzhokhar's dorm room on the night of April 18, 2013. So he was not involved in the effort to scrub it of evidence. Stephen also did not try to delete electronic fingerprints of his connection to Dzhokhar, as had another pal, Khairullozhon Matanov. Stephen bragged to reporters, in public tweets, and even to the cops about his friendship with the younger bomber. In November 2013, when transit police pinched him for selling bags of weed at the JFK stop on the MBTA's Red Line, he told the cops as they handcuffed him that he did drugs to cope with his close link to the deadly Boston Marathon explosions. "I smoke a lot of weed every day because my best friend was the bomber," Stephen volunteered.

Stephen was already on federal investigators' radar before he started calling attention so publicly to his close association with Dzhokhar. The FBI had the report about the two of them tossing beer cans out the window of Dzhokhar's car outside the Fourth of July house party in Arlington the summer before the bombing. They knew he had told reporters — while falsely claiming to be his brother Steven — that Dzhokhar was one of "the realest and coolest kids" he knew.[1] They knew Stephen had family ties to the Eritrean drug gang in Portland, Maine, targeted by Operation Run This Town. Just as they had done as part of that investigation, they set up a sting using an informant to monitor Stephen. For months Mario Millet, then a sergeant for the Massachusetts State Police with a lot of undercover experience on the FBI's North Shore Gang Task Force, and a CW, captured Stephen on audio- and videotape selling drugs and boasting about how close he had been to Dzhokhar. Stephen Silva was so full of bloated bravado that he even asked Millet to kill someone for him, on tape, according to court records.

A federal court filing described the sting this way:

> After Dzhokhar was charged in connection with the marathon bombing, the government identified Stephen and Steven Silva, two high school classmates of Dzhokhar who were well known Cambridge marijuana dealers, as individuals with potential information about the Ruger handgun that was used to kill MIT Police Officer Sean Collier. The Silva brothers refused to cooperate and both invoked their 5th Amendment rights. The government subsequently commenced this investigation of Stephen Silva with the goal of developing information about the gun that was used to kill Officer Collier.[2]

The undercover sting began in June 2014, right around the time Dzhokhar's friends began to cooperate with authorities one by one. A month earlier Stephen had sent out yet another tweet: "I seen a lot a niggas tell on their man."

Before long Stephen would join the chorus of voices "telling on their man." He would testify against Dzhokhar in federal court about the Ruger P95 he had lent him, the gun that the ATF had painstakingly identified despite its obliterated serial number and the convoluted route it had taken to reach the marathon bomber's hands.

In November 2011, Los Angeles native Danny Sun, Jr., had purchased the 9mm Ruger P95 at a Cabela's hunting and fishing store in South Portland, Maine, as part of a multi-gun purchase. Sun later told police that at some point over the next year, he paid off a drug debt by giving the gun to his dealer, Biniam "Icy" Tsegai, the main target in the Operation Run This Town case. Sometime in 2012, Icy handed off the gun to twenty-one-year-old Merhawi "Howie" Berhe, a fellow Eritrean, who then gave it to Stephen. Stephen said the gun came to him after Berhe's mother had found it in her son's sock drawer and ordered him to get rid of it.

Stephen made use of the gun himself when he ripped off buyers in a drug deal in Cambridge later that year. He also liked to show it off at parties, as he did on New Year's Eve in 2013, where Dzhokhar allegedly first saw it.

"Man, I need to borrow that gun," Dzhokhar told him. "I want to rip [off] some URI [University of Rhode Island] kids." Stephen agreed to lend it to him, and Dzhokhar picked it up roughly two months before the marathon bombings. Stephen gave it to him wrapped in a tube sock, along with bullets — which Dzhokhar had referred to as "food for the dog." Stephen then became annoyed with his friend, who kept "coming up with excuses" for not returning the gun. Howie wanted it back, and Stephen was in a bad spot.

He told this story over and over during drug deals with the FBI undercover agent and the CW.

> During the controlled buys, Silva repeatedly discussed, in detail, and on audio/video tape, with both the UC

[undercover agent] and CW-1 [first CW], the fact that, in February 2013, he provided the Ruger handgun to Dzhokhar Tsarnaev that was subsequently used to kill MIT Police Officer Sean Collier on April 18, 2013. Silva told the UC that Dzhokhar wanted the gun to rob a drug dealer in Rhode Island, and that Silva did not know anything about Dzhokhar's plans to bomb the Boston Marathon.[3]

Stephen would be arrested and charged with federal counts of drug dealing and firearms possession.

The gun became a key piece of evidence in the case against Dzhokhar. Defense attorneys had repeatedly argued that he was a gullible teen who had come under the sway of his intimidating older brother. The gun proved that Dzhokhar was an integral part of the deadly plot to bomb the Boston Marathon, and Stephen's testimony would bolster the government's case.

In May 2018, Silva was arrested again. He had been released from prison in December, 2015 but was still under a court-mandated period of supervised release. A state trooper pulled him over and found that he had swallowed three grams of powdered cocaine. The terms of his federal probation were modified to include a curfew requiring he stay home from 11:00 PM to 6:00 AM. By December, mail sent to that address was returned as undeliverable. It's unclear where Silva is now.

CHAPTER TWENTY-ONE

Kill to Be an American

Federal lawmakers, including Congressman William Keating, were furious that the FBI's top officials repeatedly refused to testify at congressional hearings looking into the Boston Marathon bombing. So the lawmakers decided to take matters into their own hands. They turned to actor Steven Seagal — the swarthy action hero who has long been rumored to be a CIA operative and who counts Vladimir Putin among his pals and has connections to politicians in Chechnya — to lead them into a war-torn country with roadblocks and cop killings where people vanished without warning. Their adventure sounded like a movie plot, but they were serious and their journey was very real.

The FBI had been stonewalling Congress for months — FBI Director Robert Mueller had rebuffed a request to brief the Homeland Security Committee in a closed-door classified session. Congressman Dana Rohrabacher suggested that lawmakers use Seagal and his connections to open doors in Russia, and in June 2013 that's what a six-member delegation of representatives — four Republicans and two Democrats — did.

Before they left, Rohrabacher explained to reporters that he had known Seagal for a number of years and that the two had often discussed thwarting radical Islamic terrorism. He repeatedly praised the actor for going out of his way to set up meetings for the delegation in Russia. Rohrabacher had been a speechwriter for President Ronald Reagan and was familiar with the way things had gotten done during the Cold War.

Seagal offered to set up a meeting with Chechen President Ramzan Kadyrov, but the lawmakers decided that a photo op with a man criticized by the State Department for heavy-handed tactics and human rights violations, such as burning down the houses of the families of suspected terrorists, might not go over well with constituents. So instead Seagal set up a meeting with Deputy Prime Minister Dmitry Rogozin and members of the FSB to review information the Russian agency had sent to the FBI's Boston field office about Tamerlan Tsarnaev and his mother, Zubeidat, back in 2011 — information the FBI refused to hand over to congressional investigators. The delegation also wanted a detailed explanation about a communication between the FSB and the FBI on April 22, 2013, regarding another Russian native, Ibragim Todashev, who had been living for a time in Massachusetts. Keating said the FSB's letter to the FBI had described Ibragim as among the "matters of significance" — another issue the FBI refused to explain. There was now an ongoing investigation into the circumstances under which an FBI agent shot and killed Ibragim during an interview at the Russian's Florida home exactly one month after the FSB sent its letter to the FBI, and the lawmakers wanted answers. "What information about Mr. Todashev did the FBI and CIA share with local law enforcement?" Keating wanted to know.[1]

"The Russians challenged us about the FBI's claim that it requested more information about Tsarnaev, information that the Russians told us they never received," Keating said. "We asked the FBI for specific dates and who that request was sent to and we never got an answer. The Russians were more cooperative than the FBI."

Following the marathon bombings, numerous officials connected to the case would resign, including the heads of the FBI and DHS appointed by President Barack Obama. DHS Secretary Janet Napolitano would do so less than five months after her congressional testimony on April 23, 2013, in which she testified that a "spelling error" had allowed Tamerlan to pass through US customs when he returned from Russia despite being on two terrorist watch lists. She knew the DHS USCIS file on Tamerlan contained multiple spellings of his name, aliases, and two different dates of birth.

The file also contained the letter that suggested government officials had set him up — telling him to show up to take the oath of citizenship when he wasn't eligible to become a citizen — and disappointed him in the end.

She announced her resignation on July 12, 2013. The next day would be the last day on the job for Richard DesLauriers, the special agent in charge of the FBI's Boston field office. DesLauriers had announced his resignation — four years before he was eligible for full retirement benefits — just ten days before his boss, FBI Director Robert Mueller III, did the same thing. Massachusetts law enforcement officials had always viewed Mueller with skepticism. The crooked FBI agents who ran James "Whitey" Bulger as an informant had reported to the criminal division of the US Attorney's Office in Boston, where for a time Mueller had been acting US attorney. Every time local cops got close to making a move against Bulger, their case would be blown. And they blamed Mueller and the FBI.

The fallout also affected David Cedarleaf, the special agent who corresponded with USCIS to help Tamerlan get his citizenship. He was transferred away from the Boston field office, and in 2016 US Attorney Carmen Ortiz celebrated the conviction of Dzhokhar Tsarnaev by awarding citations to everyone from that office who had worked on the case, with one exception — Cedarleaf.

The FBI could not produce officials who had resigned for congressional testimony. To this day no one from the FBI with direct knowledge about Tamerlan's relationship to the bureau has testified.

———

When James Comey was appointed the FBI's new director in June 2013, Representative Keating sent him a letter within weeks demanding answers.

> As a former District Attorney for twelve years, I share a great appreciation for the integrity of our judicial

processes and understand the challenges faced by the Federal Bureau of Investigations (FBI). For this reason, I would like to start out by of course congratulating you on your recent confirmation and thanking the men and women of the FBI for their exceptional work and commitment to protecting our country. I have been particularly engaged on the developments surrounding the Boston Marathon bombings in my home state and look forward to working with you on this matter further.

The dedication of the FBI's agents was made apparent in meetings I had in Boston (June 21, 2013) and Moscow (May 29, 2013). These official meetings were designed to investigate procedural and resource-related shortcomings leading up to and during the Boston Marathon bombings. The obvious intent of which is to help prevent future tragedies. Unfortunately, nearly all of these inquiries have gone unanswered. Further, the continued reluctance of the FBI to address Members of Congress on the Committee on Homeland Security (most recently on July 10, 2013) impairs Congress' responsibility to conduct proper oversight. It is not, as the FBI has described, an issue of who can provide testimony jurisdictionally, rather whether an agency that investigates homeland security issues is willing to share information critical to improving the security of our Nation. For example, we have no "jurisdictional" authority over the City of Boston, yet Boston's Police Commissioner has testified before Congress on improvements that can be made in our current homeland security processes and procedures.

Open questions remain, particularly in regard to inadequate information sharing, restrictive investigative guidelines/protocols, and an inability to follow up on suspicious activities/travel of individuals residing in the US. Finally, I would like to note that while in Moscow on May 30, 2013, I was able to obtain a read-out of the March 4, 2011, and April 22, 2013, communications from the Federal Security Service of Russia (FSB) to the FBI and Central Intelligence Agency (CIA). Despite numerous requests to obtain a copy of and discuss this information, I have not heard anything back from the FBI.

For these reasons, I am detailing some of my unanswered inquiries in this letter in order to illustrate that I am not in fact asking for any "materials related to active, ongoing law enforcement investigations," but am rather seeking information that will help Congress better address the homeland security concerns of my constituents, particularly following the Boston bombings. Perhaps, when viewed on paper, the procedural nature of these questions will become apparent, and the FBI will agree to assist in closing loopholes that may hinder the future identification or capture of dangerous individuals before lives are lost.

1. As mentioned earlier, I was relayed the information contained in both warnings about Tamerlan Tsarnaev while I was in Moscow. The March 4, 2011, message, in particular, was quite detailed. The FBI has admitted to receiving communications from the Russians and has reportedly tried to follow up on the March warning twice. (According to former Director Mueller's recent testimony before the Senate, the FBI followed up in August and October of 2012.) When I asked the FSB why they didn't respond to the FBI's follow-up inquiries, the

senior, deputy-level FSB officials in the room vehemently denied that any follow-up from the FBI occurred and asked me to provide them with concrete dates and names associated with such requests. I would ask that the FBI provide the exact dates of any follow-up communications stemming from the US and detail where they were sent. This information can aid in illustrating a lapse within the Russians' own internal communications and provide the opportunity to correct this in the future.

2. Your predecessor testified before the Senate Judiciary Committee on May 16, 2013, and stated that information in regard to Tsarnaev's travel to Russia was not adequately shared within the Joint Terrorism Task Force in Boston. He followed this statement by saying that the FBI has been doing better and improving its procedures since then. Please clarify what information in particular was not shared and how the system has been improved since the Boston Marathon bombings.

3. Further, Tamerlan Tsarnaev was flagged after his return from Russia and again when he applied for US citizenship. USCIS officials in Boston confirmed on June 21, 2013, that his name was flagged, but when they contacted the FBI they were told that his case was closed and that they could move forward with his naturalization process. Tamerlan Tsarnaev was subsequently granted a citizenship interview. Is the FBI required to conduct a second background check on a previously investigated individual if this individual is applying for citizenship?

4. The March 2011 communication from the Russians also contained information pertaining to aliases that Tsarnaev may have used and indicated the possibility of him altering his name. Is there a mechanism that can override the algorithms in place that proved inadequate in flagging Tsarnaev's travel to Russia in January 2012? Is there any way to incorporate outside tips on name changes into the consolidated terror watch lists?

5. Two Homeland Security Committee witnesses, namely former Mayor Rudolph Giuliani and former Senator Joe Lieberman, cited existing "laws" and "guidelines" that constrained the Tsarnaev investigation early on. Even Russian security officials stated that the FBI had told them that "legislation" had obstructed their ability to investigate. Are there such constraints to FBI investigations? If so, how can Congress assist in easing them?

6. Police Commissioner Ed Davis of Boston has testified to the fact that information about Tamerlan Tsarnaev was not adequately shared with local officers until the aftermath of the tragedy in Boston. While the FBI has indicated that information about Tamerlan Tsarnaev was in a database that local members of the Joint Terrorism Task Force (JTTF) had access to, these local officials could not search the database for something that they did not know existed. Further, police chiefs throughout the country have expressed concern over the fact that officers assigned to JTTF cannot share critical information with other officials, including their superiors

within the police department. Would you please explain why information about the Boston Marathon bombing suspects was not shared with the local police department in Boston? Further, would you detail current protocol in regard to information sharing between officers on the JTTF and their Department Heads?

7. The second communication from the Russian FSB on April 22, 2013, detailed Ibragim Todashev under "matters of significance." Did this communication initiate the FBI's investigation into Todashev? Since his name appeared in a mode of communication considered to be foreign intelligence, was it permitted to be shared with local authorities?

If need be, I would gladly discuss the sensitive nature of these requests in a secure environment. I thank you for your time and look forward to the FBI's response. Further, I look forward to working with you in your new position. My office remains open to your agency, and I hope that we can work together to facilitate greater communication between the FBI and Congress as we work together on matters of security and foreign emerging threats that affect homeland defense.

———

Lawmakers were not the only ones with questions about Tamerlan's immigration status. The Office of the Inspector General of the Intelligence Community would examine Tamerlan's citizenship application as part of a sweeping probe into information sharing among federal agencies. The IG's office released its findings in April 2014. Much of the information remains classified to this day and is redacted in the report. Still, it noted that Tamerlan had reported as stolen the passport he had been issued as a teenager in Kyrgyzstan and that he had applied for a Russian passport during his trip. But he abruptly left Russia without it on July 17, 2012 — two days after the raid that left William Plotnikov and others dead in the forests of Utamysh. When Tamerlan landed at Boston's Logan Airport, he breezed through US customs with just his legal permanent resident identification. The *9/11 Commission Report* had recommended that the practice of allowing political refugees, like Tamerlan, to travel to terrorist hotbeds and return to the United States using such documents be stopped.[2] The IG's report found that the customs agent "scanned Tsarnaev's Alien Registration Card into the computer system . . . and admitted him into the country based on his LPR [legal permanent resident] status."[3]

The FBI pointed the finger back at customs, telling the Office of the Inspector General that "there is a very good chance" that the FBI would have interviewed Tamerlan again upon his return from Russia had it known about the travel but that this would have "depended on what was learned from the Russians and from any secondary inspection during Tsarnaev's travel."

The reopening of Tamerlan's naturalization application by congressional investigators provided evidence for those who believe he was a federal asset.

————

People like Tamerlan Tsarnaev — unemployed, with a criminal record, and Muslim — were not exactly at the front of the line for citizenship. In fact, the lack of naturalization applications being processed by USCIS for Muslim immigrants who were far more qualified for citizenship consideration than Tamerlan led the ACLU to study the denials of citizenship for employed, college-educated applicants. Its ensuing report, called "Muslims Need Not Apply," argued that millions of Muslim applicants apply for asylum and citizenship every year and accused officials in the DHS's USCIS of "secretly excluding many aspiring Americans from Arab, Middle Eastern, Muslim, and South Asian communities from the promises of citizenship, legal residency, asylum, and other benefits by delaying and denying their applications without legal authority." It went on:

> For years, and without notice to applicants, their lawyers, or the public at large, USCIS has been blacklisting law-abiding applicants as "national security concerns" based on lawful religious activity, national origin, and innocuous associations. Once blacklisted, these aspiring Americans are barred from obtaining immigration benefits to which they are legally entitled. As a result, by putting their applications on indefinite hold or rejecting them for unfounded reasons, thousands of law-abiding immigrants have had their dreams of citizenship and other immigration status dashed, without ever being told why their applications were treated differently than others.[4]

———

Tamerlan had been identified as a threat to national security. He had spent his entire time in the United States collecting public assistance, and when he died, his death certificate stated, "Never worked."[5] But months after his trip to a terrorist hotbed where he had met with Islamic militants and prayed at a mosque that displayed the black flag of jihad outside, he sat for his citizenship test.

All that stood between him and US citizenship was a supervisor's approval, which was required, and a final swearing-in ceremony. Tamerlan fully expected the USCIS agent to check the box that read, "Congratulations! Your application has been recommended for approval." Instead the agent checked the next box, which read, "A decision cannot yet be made about your application," as noted in the 2014 report from the Office of the Inspector General.

"A USCIS officer interviewed Tsarnaev on January 23, 2013, but did not adjudicate his naturalization after the interview because USCIS had not received the court records relating to his 2009 arrest," the report stated. Tamerlan's arrest for slapping his girlfriend in the face had triggered the disqualifying "moral turpitude" clause.

Tamerlan's request to become a citizen was not being denied. It was being delayed — again. And he was furious. He demanded a name-change application and filled it out, requesting that his name be legally changed to Muaz, the name he had used in Russia, honoring a slain Chechen rebel. In the section where the form asked for an explanation for the name-change request, Tamerlan wrote, "The Russian people have been terrorizing my home country for all these years."[6]

After angrily scribbling his new name, Muaz Tsarnaev stormed out of the John F. Kennedy Federal Building in Boston's Government Center and headed back to Cambridge.

Days later, on February 6, 2013, he drove to Phantom Fireworks, in Seabrook, New Hampshire, where he asked the clerk to help him find the "biggest and loudest" pyrotechnics in the emporium. He spent $200 on two "lock and load mortar kits."[7] That same month, on February 23, he went to Macy's in Downtown Crossing, according to an FBI search warrant affidavit, where — with his wife, investigators believe — he bought "five kitchen appliances." As noted above, Macy's was the only department store in the country that sold Fagor-brand pressure cookers. The FBI also recovered seven issues of Al Qaeda's *Inspire* magazine on Tamerlan's computer, including one that contained the article "How to Build a Bomb in the Kitchen of Your Mom."

On March 6, 2013, Tamerlan drove around New Hampshire to buy bomb parts. Investigators analyzed the GPS in the Tsarnaevs' car and learned that it had been at the Walmart in Manchester, where he purchased two boxes of BB ammunition, containing a total of six thousand copper-head BBs. Two hours later investigators placed Tamerlan at the Walmart in Amherst, where two more boxes of BB ammunition were purchased. Next, there was a stop at the Walmart in Hudson, where more BBs were purchased. Then, on April 11, just four days before the bombing, prosecutors said the brothers visited Stateline Guns, Ammo & Archery in Plaistow, where they purchased $40 worth of ammunition.

Investigators also found a stack of anarchist newspapers, including the *Sovereign*, whose headlines blared "New Muslim Group Takes on Islamophobia in Tea Party" and "Senator Slams Department of Homeland Security for Wasteful, Frivolous Spending."[8]

What the FBI didn't find, however, was the location where the bombs were built.

CHAPTER TWENTY-TWO

It Was Him

It was March 4, 2015, the first day of Dzhokhar Tsarnaev's trial, and the swagger with which he had walked into the same court-house for his July 10, 2013, arraignment was gone. So were the cast on his hand and his youthful appearance. Being held in a soli-tary cell had aged him. He wore a black blazer and dress pants. The beard he had seemingly been trying to grow on that day in July when he showed his middle finger to the security camera in his holding cell was fuller, and his hair was cut shorter. Before the proceedings began he joked with his attorneys.

An eerie silence filled the courtroom as the clerk announced, "All rise," and US District Court Justice George O'Toole took his seat on the bench. Assistant US Attorney William Weinreb stood. His hair was freshly cut, and he wore a suit that was well tailored but not flashy. He turned to face the jury, seven women and five men from all over Massachusetts who had been painstakingly selected. Only one lived in Boston; the rest were from suburban towns scattered across the commonwealth: Dartmouth, Franklin, Ipswich, Malden, Marlborough, New Bedford, Osterville, Peabody (the home of two jurors), Scituate, and Woburn. Six alternates sat nearby.

Weinreb took a breath and proceeded to deliver his opening statement, using Dzhokhar's nickname, "Jahar," as he laid out the details of the crime, the suffering of its victims, and the govern-ment's case against the defendant as a coconspirator alongside his brother, Tamerlan, in the Boston Marathon bombings, the murder of MIT Police Officer Sean Collier, and their many and various other crimes.

When it was her turn to rise and address the court, Judy Clarke, as usual, first put a comforting hand on her client's shoulder. Then she stood up to begin her attempt to save his life. Her opening statement included a startling admission: "It was him."

She began: "We meet in the most tragic of circumstances, tragedy in the lives of the victims of the bombings, lives that were lost and torn and shattered: the loss of a precious eight-year-old boy, whose smile captured all of our hearts; a young woman who — with an infectious laugh, who was always there for her friends and her family; a young graduate student whose passion for music was so clear, and she embraced Boston as her home away from home; and a very fine young police officer whose lifelong dream was to protect and serve. The circumstances that bring us here today still are difficult to grasp. They're incomprehensible. They're inexcusable. You just heard about the devastation, the loss, and the unbearable grief, and we're going to see it, feel it, and agonize with every witness who comes to talk about what they saw, they felt, and they experienced and what happened to them and to those that they love.

"For the next several weeks, we're all going to come face-to-face with unbearable grief, loss, and pain caused by a series of senseless, horribly misguided acts carried out by two brothers: 26-year-old Tamerlan Tsarnaev and his younger brother, 19-year-old Jahar. The government and the defense will agree about many things that happened during the week of April 15th, 2013."

After detailing at length many facts of the case that were not in dispute, Clarke then made a pivot. "But," she said, "the essence of the charges are four sets of criminal acts: the bombings at the marathon that killed three people and injured many others, the murder of Officer Collier, the carjacking, and the shootout in Watertown. We do not and will not at any point in this case want to attempt to sidestep Jahar's responsibility for his actions, but the indictment alleges, and the prosecutor talked with you about why, and we think the question of why is important, and this is where we disagree.

"We have a different answer to this question: What took Jahar Tsarnaev from this" — she turned and pointed to a picture of

Dzhokhar and his brother — "to this" — and she pointed at an image of Dzhokhar and Tamerlan on Boylston Street, backpacks slung over their shoulders.

"The government has told you their answer to the question of why, and we ask you to look further. Clearly, Tamerlan Tsarnaev became obsessed with violent Islamic extremism. He became increasingly religious in a radical way. He traveled to Russia in — for six months in 2012 and explored violent jihad with people over there. He became aggressively obsessed with talking about Islam because of his radical views and his insistence that people accept them and agree with them. He disrupted services at the mosques here in Boston where he once fit in. It was Tamerlan Tsarnaev who self-radicalized. It was Jahar who followed him."

Clarke then laid out all the defense was able to get the prosecution to share or discover on its own about Tamerlan's radicalization, trip to Russia, online research, and purchases of bomb-making materials. After Clarke concluded her statement and sat down, it was finally the victims' turn to take the witness stand to confront the man who had set out to inflict maximum harm and to talk about their suffering.

———

Jessica Kensky ran for the last time in the morning of the day she lost her legs participating in a short road race in a nearby town before coming into the city to meet up with her husband, Patrick Downes, and partake of the Boston Marathon excitement: "I remember being happy. I remember feeling sunlight on my face. I remember feeling really free. I remember holding each other." Then came the booms. "I didn't see anything. I didn't feel anything. I just felt like I was on a rocket, shot straight into the air."[1]

When she hit the ground she saw that her husband's foot and part of his leg were completely detached: "I went into my nurse mode. I remember shifting myself to block his leg. This was a war zone." She tried to use her purse straps to tie a tourniquet around Patrick's mangled leg. Then she heard a man tell her, "'Ma'am, you're on fire.' He cut my clothes off. It feels really bizarre to be on a city street and have people removing your clothing. I wasn't even aware that I was on fire. I released control at that point."

Behind her in Marathon Sports, Shane O'Hara, the store's manager, heard what sounded like "a big cannon blast" and saw smoke engulfing the store. Then came the smell of gunpowder, burned hair, and sulfur — followed by bloodcurdling screams for help. He opened the door of the store and ushered people inside. Someone fell to the floor bleeding, a lower limb ruined. O'Hara was captured on his store's video camera as he tore a pair of shorts from a display to use as a tourniquet. Other customers inside the store followed suit, tearing apart clothes to tie off the gushing, wounded limbs of victims outside. O'Hara's voice shook with anger as he described on the stand how he is still haunted about the terrible decisions he was forced to make that afternoon, decisions ordinarily made by soldiers on the front lines in a combat zone, not store managers on a busy urban street. The entire scene was like something out of *Saving Private Ryan*, O'Hara remembered. "The things that haunt me the most is making those decisions . . . who needed help first, who needed more." He would try to comfort one injured victim and see someone in worse shape. As he tried to move where he was needed most, what he heard most were endless pleas of, "Stay with me. Stay with me."[2] He said that he could still hear those urgent, desperate cries in his sleep.

Those same agonizing memories nag at BPD Officer Frank Chiola, a former marine who had seen combat in Iraq. He heard the explosion and then was overcome by white smoke. "People were running, screaming, crying. You couldn't tell who was alive, who was dead." One woman was in terrible shape. For some reason he remembered that she was wearing blue eye shadow and had pretty eyes. "I later found out her name was Krystle. She had a friend near her calling out her name."

He tried to stem the bleeding, applying compression to her chest. When he did, "smoke came out of her mouth." His voice shook as the memory came back: "I helped her best I could. She was suffering. She was in pain. She was in shock. From the waist down it's really tough to describe, complete mutilation. That's as far as I want to say."

Roseann Sdoia remembered "two flashes of white light exploding at my feet." Then came nothing but excruciating pain. "I looked down and fortunately my leg was tucked under me. All I could see is blood pouring out of me, sort of where my knee should be. I looked on the ground and saw a foot and [it] had a little sock on it. In my mind I had to ask, did I have a sock on my foot? My answer was no. It was somebody else's foot in front of me." She tried to get up but failed — her other leg had been torn off below the knee. "I couldn't get up. I didn't have a leg. I knew it was bad. I knew I was bleeding out. I need[ed] to stay calm and stay conscious because if I didn't, I would die. I told myself I didn't want to live as an amputee . . . but then I thought I couldn't die."[3]

Lynn firefighter Matt Patterson said the bomb released an energy that felt like someone was "punching you square in the chest." He had been enjoying lunch at a steak house, Abe & Louie's, but the windows had been blown out. He climbed through the glass, hopped over a barricade, and raced to help a little girl whose hair was on fire. Her leg was gone. He would learn later that her name was Jane Richard. Her little brother was dying behind her, and she was losing a lot of blood. Patterson's own belt was too big to use as a tourniquet, so he yelled at a smaller man to take off his belt, and he tightened that around what was left of Jane's leg to stop the gushing blood. He picked her up and carried her to an ambulance, with the stranger whose belt he used running alongside him to hold it tight around her ruined leg. It was a horrifying memory even for a first responder used to gore. "It was open. It was charred," Patterson said. Her flesh looked like "meat through a grinder."[4]

During all of this heart-wrenching testimony, Dzhokhar Tsarnaev showed no emotion. He didn't flinch as videos were played of the bombing's bloody aftermath and anguished screams from the twisting faces of innocent victims. He didn't respond when BPD Superintendent Willie Gross, who had been on Boylston Street when the bombs detonated, mumbled "maggot" under his breath as he passed the defense table. One after another, victims took the stand to talk about the burns and the trauma and the surgeries and the lost wages and the apartments that had to be abandoned because of the staircases.

Evidence was presented of Dzhokhar running over and dragging his own brother, and of how his friends had turned on him. Girls he dated took the stand. His old teachers talked about what a loving little boy he had been, his wrestling coach testified about his athletic prowess, and a representative of a charity praised him for his patience. No evidence — whether against him or in his favor — registered a reaction. He doodled on a legal pad and stroked his beard and giggled with his attorneys. Rebekah Gregory took the stand on a prosthetic leg made to fit a high heel, all glamour and fiery temper as she stared down the man who forever altered her life and health. When she implored, "Look at me," he didn't raise his eyes. It wasn't until his mother's sister and other Russian relatives took the stand in a last effort to save Dzhokhar's life that he reached for a box of tissues and dabbed at tears.

His Aunt Patimat Suleimanova had to be removed from the witness stand after she began weeping uncontrollably, her chest heaving, her sobs echoing through the courtroom. One after another, his aunts and cousins took the stand, crying. They had come to the country under "hotel arrest" and were wearing electronic bracelets that were monitored by the FBI around the clock. It wasn't a vacation. They wanted Dzhokhar's life to be spared.

Until that day none of Zubeidat's relatives had seen Dzhokhar since his family left Russia for the United States in 2002, when he was eight years old — the same age as the marathon attack's youngest victim, Martin Richard. All of the relatives cried as they looked at him from the stand. His female cousins called him "brother."

"I am seeing my brother for the first time in so many years and it is not easy," Nadia Suleimanova, an ICU nurse at a hospital outside Moscow, said through tears.[5] Her mother is one of Zubeidat Tsarnaev's seven siblings.

Defense attorneys used the relatives' testimony as an opportunity to show the jury a series of Tsarnaev family photos taken in Dagestan. There were pictures of Dzhokhar as a baby in a cousin's arms, as a boy smiling as he finished his homework, and smiling as he washed dishes. Nadia said there was "never an occasion when there wasn't a smile on his face."

When Dzhokhar's gray-haired Aunt Shakhurzat Suleimanova took the stand, she rocked back and forth with a handkerchief clutched to her face, stealing glances at her nephew. "He was a good boy," she said, "a very quiet boy" — so shy that if someone asked him a question he would turn his face away.[6] Another cousin, Raisat Suleimanova, said Dzhokhar "was a sunny child . . . If you looked at him, you would want to smile, even if you didn't feel good at that time. I could only say good things about Dzhokhar." She also cried, remembering that Dzhokhar was a sensitive child who wept watching "Simba's father die" in the movie *The Lion King*. "One would want to hug him and not let him go. He was an unusual child."[7]

Defense attorneys used the women's testimony in an attempt to portray a child raised by a matriarch — Zubeidat, whose grip on sanity appeared to be slipping — and whose care had been left largely to his older brother, Tamerlan, who appeared to be radicalized during his last trip to Dagestan in 2012. During that trip Tamerlan argued with a relative — a tape of the conversation was played in court — and said in Russian, "I have this rage of hatred inside me."[8]

The relatives testified that Zubeidat went from being a fashionable, fun-loving woman with a penchant for fancy fur-trimmed coats and hats to wearing black hijabs and dark clothing that covered her entire body. "When she came like that, we were in shock," Shakhurzat said, referring to her sister's suddenly taking up the practice of covering. Their family, she said, was Muslim but not in any way radical. "We prayed. We fasted. No people like that."[9]

For all the tears, a spurt of terse words came from Assistant US Attorney William Weinreb as he cross-examined Raisat, who recalled Dzhokhar crying at *The Lion King* and said that "his kindness made everyone around him kind."

Weinreb asked her: "You would agree that the bombing of innocent people is not an act of kindness?"

The question led to an objection from Dzhokhar's defense attorneys, which was sustained by the judge.

Weinreb rephrased the question: "You would agree that a person who cries at the death of a cartoon character but was indifferent to the suffering and deaths of hundreds of people —"

Before he could finish the sentence he was cut off with another objection, which was also sustained.

———

For an entire summer Dzhokhar Tsarnaev had sat through his trial looking bored and impassive, even after he was found guilty in the first phase of his trial and even after he was sentenced to death, a sentence that shook the city that he had torn apart. Now, after he had received six death sentences, twenty sentences of life in prison, and four more sentences of seven to twenty-five years, he stood up and began to speak, the first time since the trial began that anyone had heard his voice, other than his lawyers and his spiritual adviser — the nun Sister Helen Prejean, inspiration for the movie *Dead Man Walking*. He mumbled softly in his heavy accent:

> Thank you, your Honor, for giving me an opportunity to speak. I would like to begin in the name of Allah, the exalted and glorious, the most gracious, the most merciful, "Allah" among the most beautiful names. Any act that does not begin in the name of God is separate from goodness. This is the blessed month of Ramadan,

and it is the month of mercy from Allah to his creation, a month to ask forgiveness of Allah and of his creation, a month to express gratitude to Allah and to his creation. It's the month of reconciliation, a month of patience, a month during which hearts change. Indeed, a month of many blessings. The Prophet Muhammad, peace and blessings be upon him, said if you have not thanked the people, you have not thanked God.

So I would like to first thank my attorneys, those who sit at this table, the table behind me, and many more behind the scenes. They have done much good for me, for my family. They made my life the last two years very easy. I cherish their company. They're lovely companions. I thank you. I would like to thank those who took time out of their daily lives to come and testify on my behalf despite the pressure. I'd like to thank the jury for their service, and the Court. The Prophet Muhammad, peace and blessings be upon him, said that if you do not — if you are not merciful to Allah's creation, Allah will not be merciful to you, so I'd like to now apologize to the victims, to the survivors.

Immediately after the bombing, which I am guilty of — if there's any lingering doubt about that, let there be no more. I did do it along with my brother — I learned of some of the victims. I learned their names, their faces, their age. And throughout this trial more of those victims were given names, more of those victims had faces, and they had burdened souls.

Now, all those who got up on that witness stand and that podium related to us, to me — I was listening — the suffering that was and the hardship that still is, with strength and with patience and with dignity. Now, Allah says in the Qur'an that no soul is burdened with more than it can bear, and you told us just how unbearable it was, how horrendous it was, this thing I put you through. And I know that you kept that much. I know that there isn't enough time in the day for you to have related to us everything. I also wish that far more people had a chance to get up there, but I took them from you.

Now, I am sorry for the lives that I've taken, for the suffering that I've caused you, for the damage that I've done. Irreparable damage. Now, I am a Muslim. My religion is Islam. The God I worship, besides whom there is no other God, is Allah. And I prayed for Allah to bestow his mercy upon the deceased, those affected in the bombing and their families. Allah says in the Qur'an that with every hardship there is relief. I pray for your relief, for your healing, for your well being, for your strength.

I ask Allah to have mercy upon me and my brother and my family. I ask Allah to bestow his mercy upon those present here today. And Allah knows best those deserving of his mercy. And I ask Allah to have mercy upon the ummah of Prophet Muhammad, peace and blessings be upon him. Amin. Praise be to Allah, the Lord of the Worlds. Thank you.[10]

It was a four-minute speech, and those in the courtroom strained to make out his words. The stunning apology came on the same day the judge affirmed, with a quote from Shakespeare, that Dzhokhar's capital punishment would go forward.

"The evil that men do lives after them," US District Court Justice George O'Toole said. "The good is oft interred with their bones. So it will be for Dzhokhar Tsarnaev."[11]

However, the verdict and sentencing hardly meant that the ordeal for the Boston Marathon victims was over. Appeals could take years, if not decades, to make their way through the courts, which is why some victims did not want the death penalty imposed.

Epilogue

An eerie quiet settled over the federal courthouse in Boston when the jurors, seven women and five men, stood facing Dzhokhar Tsarnaev as the jury foreman read the verdict slip. Dzhokhar stood as well, but never faced the jurors, even as one male juror removed his eyeglasses, wiped his eyes with a tissue, and leaned his body into the rail of the jury box as if to prop himself up. Two female jurors, their cheeks flushed red, sipped from water bottles. Another woman had her arms crossed in front of her. It took more than thirty minutes to read through the various factors the jury legally had to consider before it became clear that Dzhokhar would be sentenced to death. The jury found death an "appropriate" punishment for six of the seventeen capital counts he was facing following his conviction the previous month. One of Dzhokhar's defense attorneys, Miriam Conrad, covered her mouth with her hand. Once the verdict reading had been completed, police officers in the courtroom, including Watertown Police Chief Ed Deveau and Boston Police Commissioner Bill Evans, who is personal friends with the Richard family, exchanged pleased glances.

Throughout the proceeding the mood in the courtroom remained heavy and subdued. The judge's clerk, Paul Lyness, had admonished those assembled that "any outbursts" would be treated as contempt of court. There were none. Boston bombing survivor Karen Brassard, who was injured near the finish line, put a comforting hand on Liz Norden's shoulder as they filed outside after the verdict. Assistant US Attorney Steve Mellin, who had delivered closing arguments about the "river of blood" that the Tsarnaev brothers had left on Boylston Street on April 15, 2013, hugged a victim to his chest as they bumped into each other on their way out of the chamber. Tsarnaev watched as the jurors left the room. Then, wringing his handcuffed fingers in front of him, he was escorted through a side door. A court officer, who cannot be named because he is still employed in US District Court, described what happened next with utter contempt. "Everyone was crying and hugging each other. Hugging him. It was despicable," he remembered. "I'll tell you who wasn't crying. That piece of shit Jahar."

He might be crying now in his eighty-seven-square-foot cell in what is referred to as the "Alcatraz of the Rockies," Administrative Maximum Facility, or ADX Supermax, in Florence, Colorado, which has solitary cells for 490 male prisoners. Among Tsarnaev's fellow prisoners are shoe bomber Richard Reid — convicted in the same building where jurors sentenced the marathon bomber to death, by former Middlesex County District Attorney Gerry Leone — Unabomber Ted Kaczynski, and 9/11 plotter Zacarias Moussaoui. Judy Clarke successfully saved the lives of those three men. In fact, Tsarnaev was the first man or woman ever represented by Clarke to be sentenced to death, her first loss in a sense.

––––

The death penalty ruling, especially in a state like Massachusetts, remains controversial. An entirely new team of defense attorneys continue to argue that Dzhokhar was the victim of jurors, among them some who may have held Islamophobic views, who were too emotional when they imposed the death penalty. The cost of defending Dzhokhar during his two trials in 2015 — and the ongoing price of taxpayer lawyers who are still working to save his life — remains sealed under court order. "The fact that he is financially unable to pay for counsel on appeal should not be allowed to result in any potentially distracting public discussion about the travel and funding authorization," the lawyers — Gail Johnson, a federal defender in Colorado, and David Patton, a New York death penalty attorney — wrote in a brief submitted in a federal appeals court. Clarke also signed it. She is working as a consultant on the case. The death penalty was not a comforting sentence for the parents of Martin Richard. In an editorial the family, who are still strongly entrenched community activists in their Dorchester neighborhood, argued for the government to drop the death penalty and give Tsarnaev life in prison "to end the anguish" for their family. "As long as the defendant is in the spotlight, we have no choice but to live a story told on his terms, not ours," Bill and Denise Richard wrote. "The minute the defendant fades from our newspapers and TV screens is the minute we begin the process of rebuilding our lives and our family."

Others involved in the marathon case have started the process of rebuilding their lives. Many have started their own charitable organizations, like the Martin Richard Foundation, which raises money to carry on his message of "no more hurting people," by investing in education, athletics, and community. Boston Police Commissioner Bill Evans ran one of his many races wearing MR8 — Martin's Little League number — on his back to raise funds.

Tsarnaev's parents never returned from Russia. The last time anyone saw his sisters, Bella and Ailina, they were living with Katherine Russell, Tamerlan's widow, in an apartment in New Jersey.

Dzhokhar's friend Stephen Silva, the convicted drug dealer who boasted to cops, "My best friend is the bomber," and who lent the gun used to execute Sean Collier and in the gun battle in Watertown to the Tsarnaev brothers, was released in 2015 and vowed not to get in trouble again. He lied. He was arrested again on December 22, 2015, by a state trooper who pulled him over for a defective taillight and spotted white powder on his leg. "Mr. Silva was also chewing something and drooling all over his shirt," according to a court filing. The trooper asked him to open his mouth and found he had swallowed a plastic baggie of cocaine. As a result his parole conditions changed, but the court docket notes that officials have not been able to find him since, and mail to his address is returned. Silva, who also has ties to a dangerous inter-national drug crew, is apparently in the wind. Azamat Tazhayakov,

Dzhokhar's college pal, was released from a federal prison in May 2016 and deported back to Kazakhstan. Dias Kadyrbayev was deported, too, after being held at a low-security prison in northern Texas for roughly three years. Robel Phillipos, despite testimony from former Massachusetts Governor and Democratic candidate Michael Dukakis, was sent to a minimum-security prison in Pennsylvania and is living in Massachusetts. Quincy cabdriver Khairullozhon Matanov was harangued by a federal judge, who sentenced him to thirty months. "This record says you're a taxi driver. It is common lore that taxi drivers understand people. You don't understand us. Americans have a common sense of decency, and what's more they have a sense of duty that is virtually unparalleled. I'm not talking about a duty to country, I'm talking about a duty to humanity here. You failed in that duty." Matanov was deported in October, 2016.

Daniel Morley was released after nearly two years in a mental institution — an amount of time that is nearly unheard of in a state where psychiatric hospital beds are in short supply. It is unknown who paid for the extended stay. As of this writing, Daniel lives in Woburn, Massachusetts, and drives for The Ride — a state-sponsored transportation service for the elderly. The man who was accused of beating up his own elderly mother and her elderly boyfriend drives the elderly. I staked him out at his new house in Woburn, which is carefully monitored by local cops, with another investigative journalist, Bruce Gellerman from WBUR-Boston. Morley spotted us and led us on a slow-speed chase while behind the wheel of a state-owned vehicle. He refused to answer questions but to this day has not denied a single detail in this book.

Wounded Transit Police Officer Dic Donohue returned to work but retired in early 2016. A memorial to Sean Collier was erected at MIT. It took nearly six years for Boston to officially memorialize the victims of Boylston Street. One victim, however, was remembered shortly after the bombing. When fresh cement was poured near Marathon Sports, someone left a hand-scrawled message for one of the dead before it dried. It reads: I LOVE YOU KRYSTLE.

Tsarnaev's defense team has consistently said, "The story of Dzhokhar cannot be told without knowing the story of Tamerlan." They're right. Of course Tamerlan's story does not abolish his younger brother's guilt, but it certainly offers an alternative view of what went wrong — especially as it pertains to the Waltham triple murder investigation.

After years of pressure from Dzhokhar's taxpayer-funded lawyers, who argued that proof of "Tamerlan Tsarnaev's involvement in the Waltham triple homicide" being kept out of their client's trials violated the Federal Death Penalty Act, a federal judge partially unsealed a key document, albeit heavily redacted, in November 2019. The twenty-seven-page search warrant application for Tamerlan's second car, a Honda CR-V, which was found parked in Cambridge after the blasts, contained startling new details about the murders, even if eleven of the twenty-seven pages were completely blacked out. Ibragim Todashev, before he was shot dead by a Boston FBI agent, told investigators that he was with Tamerlan when they tied up the victims and killed them so brutally that it took more than an hour to clean up the blood. Todashev, of course, lived with Matanov the taxi driver at the time but fled Boston that same day for Florida. A dead man did tell tales after all, only right before he was riddled with bullets. The detail was kept classified until a month before Dzhokhar's appeal would be heard in a Boston federal court on December 12, 2019.

Many marathon victims have asked me whether a competent investigation into the Waltham triple murder could have prevented the Boston Marathon bombing. It's a tricky question to answer. Tamerlan was identified by the slain victims' friends as someone who should have been looked at as a person of interest after the September 11, 2011, triple murder, but inexplicably wasn't, even though it took place in the same month the FSB began warning American counterterrorism officials that he was becoming "increasingly radicalized." The nature of the slayings — victims nearly decapitated, the Jewish victims sexually mutilated — on the ten-year anniversary of the deadliest terror attack our nation has ever witnessed should have been checked against the information cops gathered about the one guy who didn't show up at the memorial service, the same guy who worked for Gerry's Italian Kitchen: Tamerlan Tsarnaev.

The other lingering mystery revolves around Katherine Russell / Karima Tsarnaeva, Tamerlan's wife. Despite being present the night the brothers celebrated the atrocity on Patriots' Day 2013, despite Google searches that included stories on the Waltham murders and "rewards for the wife of the mujahideen," she was never charged with anything — unlike the wife of Omar Mateen, the Pulse nightclub shooter who gave Tamerlan a shout-out during his bloody rampage in Orlando.

During the trial for Mateen's wife, Noor Salman, court documents were filed by her defense attorneys about her husband's father, Seddique Mateen. In it was a blunt statement: Her father-in-law was "a confidential human source at various points in time between January 2005 and June 2016." That relationship between the bureau and the elder Mateen hindered the FBI's investigation into Omar in 2013, when he should have been arrested for stockpiling ammunition after a tip from a gun store owner, Salman's attorneys argued. She was acquitted by the jury in a Florida federal trial in 2018.

It's clear that Katherine Russell / Karima Tsarnaeva knew at least as much about her husband's actions as Salman knew about Omar's. She wasn't even called as a witness in the trial, even as her mother was. To this day no one in the US Attorney's Office will say why. I accidentally found her on Facebook a couple of years ago — after one of her Facebook friends publicly threatened me on the platform — and she is still covered, but slender, living in New Jersey. Multiple sources have since told me that she was prohibited from being anywhere near the Boston Marathon and in fact was told to stay out of Massachusetts entirely. But once in a while, the sources confirm, she would taunt investigators who were tasked with following her by driving along the edge of Massachusetts from Connecticut to Rhode Island, daring them to arrest her. They never have.

Working on this new epilogue to my book, I came across something I hadn't previously noticed: Janet Napolitano, the Boston FBI field office, and the CT agent assigned to Tamerlan's initial investigation, as well as the inspector general, had all referenced the inaccurate dates of birth given by the FSB to American officials in the FBI and CIA as a possible reason they felt the Russians might have the wrong Cambridge guy. But upon closer inspection of Tamerlan's A-file I realized that his green card listed a birth date of October 21, 1988 — the same date the FSB had given their US counterparts. His Massachusetts driver's license listed the same birth date as his death certificate — October 21, 1986. How does someone granted political asylum have a green card with the wrong birth date?

A lot of friends have asked me why I am still working so hard on this investigation, for virtually no money, and at great expense to my personal life. The answer is simple: The truth matters.

— MICHELE R. MCPHEE
November 21, 2019

Acknowledgments

The gathering of evidence is a long, steep road, and some people close to me argued that trying to wangle answers out of members of the federal intelligence community would prove exhausting and thankless. I will admit it was a tremendous undertaking, and I could not have done it without the support of countless law enforcement sources, both on and off the record; court employees (they know who they are); and those who trusted me enough to slip me the sensitive information that helped connect some dots. These valued sources have become trusted friends.

It was humbling for me to work alongside the best investigative journalists in the country at the ABC News Brian Ross Investigative Unit. Working with Brian and his vaunted team made me a better reporter, and the team's leaders — Brian Ross and Rhonda Schwartz — have become friends. Also, I had incredible editors at *Newsweek* and *Boston* magazines, Bob Roe and Chris Vogel, who shepherded the cover stories that first inspired much of the reporting in these pages. I cannot say enough about their expertise.

Many of the brave law enforcement officers from police departments throughout the Commonwealth of Massachusetts, federal prosecutors, defense attorneys, federal agents, and first responders from the Boston Fire Department and EMS who saved countless lives that day and also assisted my reporting cannot be named. For the guidance they gave me or the Freedom of Information Act requests they answered, however, I am able to thank: the entire Boston Fire Department, BPD spokesman Lieutenant Detective Mike McCarthy and his staff, Massachusetts State Police department spokesman David Procopio, FBI spokesperson Kristen

Setera, former Watertown Police Chief Ed Deveau and current Watertown Police Chief Ed Long, Cambridge Police Department spokesman Jeremy Warnick, US Attorney's Office spokeswomen Christina Sterling and Elizabeth McCarthy, US Marshals Service spokesman Kevin Neal, retired Somerville Police Chief Tom Pasquarello, retired Police Chief Joseph Cafarelli, Massport fire-fighter Michael Ward, and others who I hope know my gratitude. I am especially grateful to the late Mayor of Boston Thomas M. Menino, whom I adored, and his staff, among them Dot Joyce. Since the first inception of this book, Massachusetts Governor Charlie Baker and Boston Mayor Marty Walsh have been support-ive and encouraging.

Writing any book is a complicated task, and I leaned on a lot of people. Most recently I have relied on the incredible editing of Chip Fleischer, who believed in my reporting and has since spun it into the narrative here. I have the utmost respect for the hard work Chip put into these pages, and Steerforth Press is lucky to have him. I also want to thank Joel Gotler and Murray Weiss, members of my creative team who helped me find him.

My family has always pushed me to write, since I was a little girl scribbling notes in my little locked diary. To my sisters Erin Donovan and Shannon Thompson; my godparents, Joan and the late, but great, Dick Dennis; and my father, Bruce: Thank you. You all knew that my nosy nature might come in handy one day. So did former Massachusetts Senator Jarrett Barrios, who gener-ously opened his Los Angeles home to me as a writer-in-residence of sort and allowed me the space and time to re-create my life. I'm also grateful to his partner, Danny Feldman. And of course, Nate. And Ricky. Also, thank you to my screenwriting collaborator and showrunner, David Graziano, who is teaching me how to tell truths through lies. In other words, let loose and create.

I dedicate this book to the victims: Martin Richard, Krystle Marie Campbell, Lingzi Lu, and Sean Collier, who died at the hands of the Tsarnaev brothers; the seventeen victims whose limbs were torn from their bodies and yet overcame, continuing to inspire all of us to turn tragedy into triumph; and the loved ones whose lives were turned upside-down caring for their critically injured family members. I must also mention the ones who have become honored friends: Rebekah Gregory-Varney, Liz Norden, and Roseann Sdoia.

Notes

Author's Note

1 Lorenzo Vidino and Seamus Hughes, "ISIS in America: From Retweets to Raqqa," accessed September 18, 2016, https://cchs.gwu.edu/sites/cchs.gwu.edu/files/downloads/ISIS%20in%20America%20-%20Full%20Report_o.pdf.

2 House of Representatives Homeland Security Committee, *The Road to Boston: Counterterrorism Challenges and Lessons from the Boston Marathon Bombings*, March 2014, accessed August 9, 2016, https://homeland.house.gov/files/documents/Boston-Bombings-Report.pdf.

3 *United States v. Dzhokhar Tsarnaev*, defense motion filed March 14, 2014.

4 Boston medical examiner's death certificate for Tamerlan Tsarnaev, dated April 19, 2013.

5 Stephen Silva testimony, transcript from the trial of Dzhokhar Tsarnaev, March 17, 2015.

6 The report noted: "Indeed after 19 hijackers demonstrated the relative ease of obtaining a U.S. visa and gaining entrance to the United States, border security is still not considered a cornerstone of national security. We believe, for reasons we discuss in the following pages, that it must be made one." National Commission on Terrorist Attacks upon the United States, *9/11 Commission Report* (Washington, DC: Government Printing Office, 2004), 168.

Prologue

1 According to the "Action Report for the Response to the 2013 Boston Marathon Bombings," released by the Massachusetts Emergency Management Agency in December 2014.

2 Author interview with Boston Police Department Sergeant Dan Keeler, May 27, 2016.

3 Steven Woolfenden testimony, transcript from the trial of Dzhokhar Tsarnaev, April 23, 2015. All quotes attributed to Woolfenden are taken from his trial testimony.

4 Boston Police Department Officer Thomas Barrett testimony, transcript from the trial of Dzhokhar Tsarnaev, March 5, 2015. All quotes attributed to Barrett are taken from his trial testimony.

5 According to the "Action Report for the Response to the 2013 Boston Marathon Bombings," released by the Massachusetts Emergency Management Agency in December 2014.

6 Boston EMS Chief James Hooley testimony, transcript from the trial of Dzhokhar Tsarnaev, March 9, 2015. All quotes attributed to Hooley are taken from his trial testimony.

7 Danling Zhou testimony, transcript from the trial of Dzhokhar Tsarnaev, March 9, 2015. All quotes attributed to Zhou in the prologue are taken from her trial testimony.

8 Boston Police Department Officer Thomas Barrett testimony, transcript from the trial of Dzhokhar Tsarnaev, March 5, 2015.

9 William Richard testimony, transcript from the trial of Dzhokhar Tsarnaev, March 5, 2015. All quotes attributed to Richard in the prologue are taken from his trial testimony.

10 Adrianne Haslet-Davis testimony, transcript from the trial of Dzhokhar Tsarnaev, March 9, 2015. All quotes attributed to Haslet-Davis in the prologue are taken from her trial testimony.
11 Karen Rand-McWatters testimony, transcript from the trial of Dzhokhar Tsarnaev, March 5, 2015. All quotes attributed to Rand-McWatters are taken from her trial testimony.
12 The photograph was a government exhibit shown to the jury but not released publicly during the trial of Dzhokhar Tsarnaev.
13 Rebekah Gregory testimony, transcript from the trial of Dzhokhar Tsarnaev, March 9, 2015. All quotes attributed to Gregory are taken from her trial testimony or multiple author interviews conducted with Gregory in 2015 and 2016.
14 Nicole Gross testimony, transcript from the trial of Dzhokhar Tsarnaev, March 9, 2015. All quotes attributed to Gross are taken from her trial testimony.
15 Gillian Reny testimony, transcript from the trial of Dzhokhar Tsarnaev, March 4, 2015. All quotes attributed to Reny are taken from her trial testimony.
16 Celeste Corcoran testimony, transcript from the trial of Dzhokhar Tsarnaev, April 21, 2015. All quotes attributed to Corcoran — including the quotes she attributed to her husband — are taken from her trial testimony.

Chapter 1

1 Assistant US Attorney Steven Mellin, closing argument, transcript from the trial of Dzhokhar Tsarnaev, May 13, 2015. All quotes attributed to Mellin in this chapter are from that transcript.
2 Multiple author interviews with Boston Police Department Commissioner William Evans in 2014–2016. Evans, a BPD deputy superintendent at the time of the bombings, was promoted to commissioner in 2014.
3 Federal Bureau of Investigation, "A Byte Out of History: 1975 Terrorism Flashback: State Department Bombing," January 29, 2004, accessed September 18, 2016, https://archives.fbi.gov/archives/news/stories/2004/january/weather_012904.
4 David Abel, "Apologetic in the End, William Gilday Dies," *Boston Globe*, September 16, 2011, http://archive.boston.com/news/local/massachusetts/articles/2011/09/16/william_lefty_gilday_dies_at_82.
5 Author interview with retired Boston Police Department Captain Frank Armstrong, June 2016.
6 Homeland Security Secretary Janet Napolitano testimony at a Senate Judiciary Committee hearing on April 23, 2013.
7 I was at the FBI press conference, covering it for ABC News.
8 ABC News special report "Five Days, the Hunt for the Marathon Bombers," an ABC Ross Investigative Unit web series with multiple producers including the author, Michele McPhee. The series was posted in a five-day sequence beginning on April 15, 2016.
9 Letter from Senator Charles E. Grassley to FBI Director Robert Mueller on October 15, 2013 (I was given a copy of the letter).
10 FBI, "Joint Release from Massachusetts Law Enforcement Agencies," October 18, 2013, accessed September 20, 2016, https://archives.fbi.gov/archives/boston/press-releases/2013/joint-release-from-massachusetts-law-enforcement-agencies.
11 According to the "Action Report for the Response to the 2013 Boston Marathon Bombings" released by the Massachusetts Emergency Management Agency in December 2014.

Chapter 2

1 "Five Days, the Hunt for the Marathon Bombers," an ABC News special report.
2 From the transcript of my notes from the prayer service.
3 Multiple author interviews with FBI Special Agent Vincent Lisi, the agent in charge of the bureau's Boston field office, in 2012, 2014, and 2015.

4 MIT Police Chief John DiFava testimony, transcript from the trial of Dzhokhar Tsarnaev, March 11, 2015. All quotes attributed to DiFava are taken from his trial testimony.

5 911 call placed to the MIT Police Department, played in court at the trial of Dzhokhar Tsarnaev, March 11, 2015.

6 MIT Police Sergeant Clarence Henniger testimony, transcript from the trial of Dzhokhar Tsarnaev, March 11, 2015. All quotes attributed to Henniger are taken from his trial testimony.

7 Medical Examiner Renee Robinson testimony, transcript from the trial of Dzhokhar Tsarnaev, March 12, 2015.

8 Aaron Swartz, "Guerilla Open Access Manifesto," July 2008, accessed September 18, 2016, https://archive.org/stream/GuerillaOpenAccessManifesto/Goamjuly2008_djvu.txt.

9 *United States of America v. Aaron Swartz*, September 12, 2012, accessed September 18, 2016, https://archive.org/stream/UsaV.AaronSwartz-CriminalDocument53/UsaV.AaronSwartz-CriminalDocument53_djvu.txt.

10 Carmen M. Ortiz, "Statement of United States Attorney Carmen M. Ortiz Regarding the Death of Aaron Swartz," January 16, 2013, accessed September 18, 2016, https://www.justice.gov/usao-ma/pr/statement-united-states-attorney-carmen-m-ortiz-regarding-death-aaron-swartz.

11 Josiah Ryan, "Anonymous Hacks MIT Website to Avenge Reddit Founder's Suicide," *Campus Reform*, January 24, 2013, accessed September 18, 2016, http://www.campusreform.org/?ID=4573.

12 Rebecca Baird-Remba, "Anonymous Threatens to Leak Sensitive Records if the Feds Don't Reform an Anti-Hacking Law," *Business Insider*, January 28, 2013, accessed September 18, 2016, http://www.businessinsider.com/anonymous-hacks-us-sentencing-commission-2013-1.

13 MIT News Office, "Israel Ruiz Writes to MIT Community Regarding Recent Hoax," March 1, 2013, accessed September 18, 2016, http://news.mit.edu/2013/letter-to-the-community-ruiz-0228.

14 Quoted in Milton Police Department Deputy Chief Charles Paris statement, March 16, 2013.

15 Statement by US Attorney Carmen Ortiz released by her spokesperson, Christina Sterling, March 16, 2013.

16 Quoted in *United States v. Aaron Swartz* government motion, filed March 23, 2013.

17 *United States v. Aaron Swartz* government motion, filed March 23, 2013.

18 Dun Meng testimony, transcript from the trial of Dzhokhar Tsarnaev, March 12, 2015. All quotes attributed to Meng in this chapter are taken from his trial testimony.

Chapter 3

1 Dun Meng testimony, transcript from the trial of Dzhokhar Tsarnaev, March 12, 2015. All quotes attributed to Meng in this chapter are taken from his trial testimony.

2 The law enforcement officers agreed to an author interview but did not want to be identified.

3 911 call from the clerk at the gas station played in court at the trial of Dzhokhar Tsarnaev, March 12, 2015.

Chapter 4

1 Transcript of Cambridge Police Department transmission over police radios.

2 Boston Police Department Officer Michael Nickerson testimony, transcript from the trial of Dzhokhar Tsarnaev, March 12, 2015.

3 Watertown Police Department Officer Joseph Reynolds testimony, transcript from the trial of Dzhokhar Tsarnaev, March 16, 2015. All quotes attributed to Reynolds in this chapter are taken from his trial testimony.

4 Watertown Police Department Sergeant John MacLellan testimony, transcript from the trial of Dzhokhar Tsarnaev, March 16, 2015. All quotes attributed to MacLellan in this chapter are taken from his trial testimony.
5 Watertown Police Department Sergeant Joseph Pugliese testimony, transcript from the trial of Dzhokhar Tsarnaev, March 16, 2015.
6 Multiple author interviews with Watertown Police Department Sergeant Jeffrey Pugliese and his testimony, transcript from the trial of Dzhokhar Tsarnaev, March 16, 2015.
7 Watertown Police Department Sergeant Jeffrey Pugliese testimony, transcript from the trial of Dzhokhar Tsarnaev, March 16, 2015. All subsequent quotes attributed to Pugliese in this chapter are taken from his trial testimony.
8 Boston Police Department incident summary report on the injuries suffered by Officer Dennis Simmonds, April 19, 2013.
9 Letter Massachusetts State Police Trooper Chris Dumont wrote about his actions in Watertown on April 18–19, 2013, and sent to his superiors (copy on file), corroborated by author interviews with MSP officials.
10 Heather Studley testimony, transcript from the trial of Dzhokhar Tsarnaev, March 16, 2015. All quotes attributed to Studley in this chapter are taken from her trial testimony.
11 Michael Sullivan testimony, transcript from the trial of Dzhokhar Tsarnaev, April 29, 2015.
12 Boston medical examiner's death certificate for Tamerlan Tsarnaev, dated April 19, 2013.
13 Multiple author interviews with FBI Special Agent Vincent Lisi, the agent in charge of the bureau's Boston field office; and the assistant agent in charge, Special Agent Kiernan Ramsey, in 2014 and 2015.
14 MSP Trooper David Cahill testimony, transcript from the trial of Dzhokhar Tsarnaev, March 24, 2015.
15 "Action Report for the Response to the 2013 Boston Marathon Bombings," released by the Massachusetts Emergency Management Agency in December 2014.
16 Transcript of the press conference held by Massachusetts Governor Deval Patrick, April 19, 2013.
17 "Saudi Similar to [Boston] Marathon Suspect Speaks About Raid on His Apartment," *Saudi Today*, April 25, 2013, accessed September 19, 2016.
18 Author interview with retired Somerville Police Department Chief Thomas Pasquarello, June 2016.

Chapter 5

1 *United States v. Dzhokhar Tsarnaev*, indictment, filed June 27, 2013.
2 Multiple author interviews with Boston Police Department Lieutenant Detective Michael McCarthy in 2013–2016.
3 Multiple author interviews with FBI Special Agent Kiernan Ramsey, the assistant agent in charge of the bureau's Boston field office. Some of the contents of those interviews appeared in "Five Days, the Hunt for the Marathon Bombers."
4 Multiple author interviews with Roseann Sdoia in 2013–2016.
5 Jessica Kensky testimony, transcript from the trial of Dzhokhar Tsarnaev, May 13, 2015.
6 Frank Chiola testimony, transcript from the trial of Dzhokhar Tsarnaev, March 5, 2015.
7 Sydney Corcoran testimony, transcript from the trial of Dzhokhar Tsarnaev, March 4, 2015.
8 Jeffrey Bauman testimony, transcript from the trial of Dzhokhar Tsarnaev, March 5, 2015.
9 Multiple author interviews with Carlos "the Cowboy" Arrendondo in 2013–2015.
10 Author interview with FBI Special Agent Jeffrey Rowland, March 2016. All quotes attributed to Rowland in this chapter are taken from this interview, which appears in "Five Days, the Hunt for the Boston Marathon Bombers."

Notes

Chapter 6

1 A transcript of the note Tsarnaev wrote on the boat was read to the jury during his trial.

2 Robert McCarthy testimony, transcript from the trial of Dzhokhar Tsarnaev, March 18, 2015. All quotes attributed to McCarthy in this chapter are taken from his trial testimony.

3 Edward Knapp testimony, transcript from the trial of Dzhokhar Tsarnaev, March 26, 2015.

4 David Henneberry testimony, transcript from the trial of Dzhokhar Tsarnaev, March 17, 2015.

5 Multiple author interviews with Boston Police Department Commissioner William Evans in 2014–2016.

6 Transcript of police radio scanner feed, recorded during the hunt for Dzhokhar Tsarnaev in Watertown, April 18–19, 2013.

7 Multiple author interviews with Revere Police Department Chief Robert Cafarelli in September 2016.

8 Transcript of police radio scanner feed, recorded during the hunt for Dzhokhar Tsarnaev in Watertown, April 18–19, 2013.

9 Transcript of police radio scanner feed, recorded during the hunt for Dzhokhar Tsarnaev in Watertown, April 18–19, 2013, and multiple author interviews with BPD Commissioner William Evans in 2014–2016.

10 Multiple author interviews with Everett Police Department Officer Matt Cunningham, September 2016.

11 Laura Lee testimony, transcript from the trial of Dzhokhar Tsarnaev, April 29, 2015. All quotes attributed to Lee in this chapter are taken from her trial testimony.

12 Boston Police Department tweet, posted April 19, 2013, accessed September 19, 2016, https://twitter.com/bostonpolice/status/325413032110989313.

13 I attended the press conference on April 19, 2013, to announce the arrest of Dzhokhar Tsarnaev.

14 Author interview with BPD Commissioner William Evans, 2016.

15 *United States v. Dzhokhar Tsarnaev*, motion to suppress statements, filed by federal prosecutors May 7, 2014.

Chapter 7

1 Raisat Suleimanova testimony, transcript from the trial of Dzhokhar Tsarnaev, May 4, 2015. All quotes attributed to Suleimanova in this chapter are taken from her trial testimony.

2 House of Representatives Homeland Security Committee, *The Road to Boston: Counterterrorism Challenges and Lessons from the Boston Marathon Bombings*, March 2014, accessed August 9, 2016, https://homeland.house.gov/files/documents/Boston-Bombings-Report.pdf.

3 Sam Lipson testimony, transcript from the trial of Dzhokhar Tsarnaev, April 28, 2015. All quotes attributed to Lipson in this chapter are taken from his trial testimony.

4 Graham E. Fuller, "About," accessed September 21, 2016, http://grahamefuller.com/about.

5 Author email exchange with Graham E. Fuller in June 2016.

6 House of Representatives Homeland Security Committee, *The Road to Boston: Counterterrorism Challenges and Lessons from the Boston Marathon Bombings*, March 2014, accessed August 9, 2016, https://homeland.house.gov/files/documents/Boston-Bombings-Report.pdf.

7 The quote is from Tamerlan Tsarnaev's US Citizenship and Immigration Services alien file, a DHS record of all paperwork pertaining to his asylum request and naturalization processing, obtained by the author through a Freedom of Information Act request in 2016. https://www.uscis.gov/sites/default/files/USCIS/About%20Us/Electronic%20Reading%20Room/A-Files%20of%20Interest%20-%20Static%20Files/Tamerlan_Tsarnaev.pdf.

255

8 Multiple author phone interviews with Ruslan Tsarni in 2013 and 2014. All quotes attributed to Tsarni in this chapter are taken from these interviews.

9 Lauren Sher, "Marathon Bombing Suspects' Uncle: 'We Are Ashamed,'" ABC News, April 19, 2013, accessed September 19, 2016, http://abcnews.go.com/blogs/headlines/2013/04/marathon-bombing-suspects-uncle-we-are-ashamed.

10 According to court records filed in Middlesex District Probate and Family Court.

11 Boston Police Department incident summary report by Detective Robert Kenney, filed in South Boston District Court, pertaining to a charge that Ailina Tsarnaeva refused to cooperate with investigators in connection with a counterfeit money case.

12 Quoted in a criminal complaint filed by the Manhattan District Attorney's Office in August 2014 after Ailina Tsarnaeva was accused of threatening the father of her youngest child's ex-girlfriend.

13 I was present at Ailina Tsarnaeva's hearing in South Boston District Court and heard this statement in the hallway.

14 Cambridge Police Department incident report pertaining to the arrest of Tamerlan Tsarnaev on a domestic battery charge dated July 10, 2009.

15 Amanda Ransom testimony, transcript from the trial of Dzhokhar Tsarnaev, April 27, 2015.

16 Judy Russell testimony, transcript from the trial of Dzhokhar Tsarnaev, April 27, 2015. All quotes attributed to Russell in this chapter are taken from her trial testimony.

17 Author interview with Imam Taalib Mahdee from the Masjid Al-Qur'aan mosque in Boston, 2013.

18 The quote is from notebooks recovered from 410 Norfolk Street during the execution of search warrants and entered into evidence in the trial of Dzhokhar Tsarnaev by the government.

19 Author Michele McPhee, "Boston Bomb Suspect Eyed in Connection to 2011 Triple Murder," ABC News, April 22, 2013, accessed September 19, 2016, http://abcnews.go.com/Blotter/boston-bomb-suspect-eyed-connection-2011-triple-murder/story?id=19015628.

Chapter 8

1 National Commission on Terrorist Attacks upon the United States, *The 9/11 Commission Report* (Washington, DC: Government Printing Office, 2011).

2 *New York Times*, "The 9/11 Tapes: The Story in the Air," September 7, 2011, accessed September 19, 2016, http://www.nytimes.com/interactive/2011/09/08/nyregion/911-tapes.html?_r=0.

3 "Rest in Peace Brendan Mess," January 12, 2012, accessed September 19, 2016, http://www.youtube.com/watch?v=-ampMMBT7j4.

4 Author interview with friends of Brendan Mess on background, 2013.

5 *United States v. Safwin Madarat*, transcript of preliminary hearing, May 13, 2011.

6 US Attorney's Office, Massachusetts, "Individuals Charged with Federal Drug, Extortion and Money Laundering Charges, Former Watertown Officer Charged with Impeding a Federal Investigation," May 24, 2011, accessed September 20, 2016, https://www.justice.gov/archive/usao/ma/news/2011/May/MadaratiSafwan.html.

7 US Immigration and Customs Enforcement, "Former Massachusetts Police Officer Named in Federal Indictment," May 24, 2011, accessed September 20, 2016, https://www.ice.gov/news/releases/former-massachusetts-police-officer-named-federal-indictment.

8 Cambridge Police Department incident report pertaining to the 2010 arrest of Brendan Mess on charges of aggravated assault and battery, resisting arrest, and disorderly conduct on August 10, 2010.

9 The quote is from an off-the-record author interview.

10 I was on the scene when the neighbor spoke to reporters.

11 Author Michele McPhee, "What Happened on Harding Avenue," ABC News, September 2011.

12 Author Michele McPhee, "Boston Bomber Suspect Eyed in Connection to 2011 Triple Murder," April 22, 2013, accessed September 20, 2016, http://abcnews .go.com/Blotter/boston-bomb-suspect-eyed-connection-2011-triple-murder/ story?id=19015628.
13 Background author interview.
14 Transcript of Middlesex District Attorney Gerry Leone's press conference, September 12, 2011. All quotes attributed to Leone in this chapter are taken from this transcript.
15 Author phone interview with Waltham City Councilor Gary Marchese, September 2011.
16 Author interview with Scott Wood, April 2013.
17 Author interview with Dylan Mess, April 2013.

Chapter 9
1 Author interview with Congressman William Keating after his return from Russia on June 2, 2013.
2 Unclassified summary of information handling and sharing prior to the April 15, 2013, bombings, prepared by the inspectors general for the Central Intelligence Agency, Department of Justice, and DHS, released April 10, 2014.
3 Unclassified summary of information handling and sharing prior to the April 15, 2013, bombings, prepared by the inspectors general for the Central Intelligence Agency, Department of Justice, and DHS, released April 10, 2014.
4 Department of Homeland Security, "Privacy Impact Assessment Update for the TECS System: CBP Primary and Secondary Processing (TECS) National SAR Initiative," August 5, 2011, accessed September 21, 2016, https://www.dhs.gov/ xlibrary/assets/privacy/privacy-pia-cbp-tecs-sar-update.pdf.
5 Boston FBI field office press release, September 23, 2010, posted on the FBI website: https://www.fbi.gov/newyork/press-releases/2010/nyfo092310.htm.
6 Defense motion filed on behalf of Dzhokhar Tsarnaev in *United States v. Dzhokhar Tsarnaev* CASE #: 1:13-cr-10200-GAO-1, March 28, 2014.
7 Boston FBI field office press release, April 19, 2013, posted on the FBI website: https://archives.fbi.gov/archives/news/pressrel/press-releases/2011-request-for -information-on-tamerlan-tsarnaev-from-foreign-government.
8 Boston FBI, "Aafia Siddiqui Sentenced in Manhattan Federal Court to 86 Years for Attempting to Murder U.S. Nationals in Afghanistan and Six Additional Crimes," September 23, 2010, accessed September 20, 2016, https://www.fbi.gov/newyork/ press-releases/2010/nyfo092310.htm.
9 FBI, "Tarek Mehanna Sentenced in Boston to 17 Years in Prison on Terrorism-Related Charges," April 12, 2012, https://archives.fbi.gov/archives/boston/press -releases/2012/tarek-mehanna-sentenced-in-boston-to-17-years-in-prison -on-terrorism-related-charges.
10 Quoted in the transcript from the trial of Dzhokhar Tsarnaev, April 29, 2015.
11 Nadia Suleimanova testimony, transcript from the trial of Dzhokhar Tsarnaev, May 4, 2015.
12 Elmirza Khuozhugov testimony via video from the US embassy in Almaty, Kazakhstan, transcript from the trial of Dzhokhar Tsarnaev, May 6, 2015.
13 Jamestown Foundation, "Jamestown Foundation Responds to False Izvestia Article About Tsarnaev Link," April 26, 2013, accessed September 21, 2016, http://www.jamestown.org/single/?tx_ttnews%5Btt_news%5D=40797&tx_ ttnews%5BbackPid%5D=381#.V-Oh2PArLIV.
14 Brian Glyn Williams, accessed September 21, 2016, http://www.brianglynwilliams .com.
15 Steve Urbon, "UMass Dartmouth Professor: 'I Hope I Didn't Contribute,'" *South Coast Today*, April 19, 2013, accessed September 20, 2016, http://www.south coasttoday.com/apps/pbcs.dll/article?AID=/20130419/NEWS/130419860.
16 Alexander Niss testimony, transcript from the trial of Dzhokhar Tsarnaev, May 5, 2015. All quotes attributed to Niss in this chapter are taken from this transcript.

17 Quoted in Boston Police Department incident summary report, August 8, 2009.
18 The client agreed to an author interview but did not want to be identified.
19 Elmirza Khuozhugov testimony, transcript from the trial of Dzhokhar Tsarnaev, May 6, 2015.
20 Quoted in the transcript from the trial of Dzhokhar Tsarnaev, April 29, 2015.
21 Stephen Silva testimony, transcript from the trial of Dzhokhar Tsarnaev, March 17, 2015.
22 "Yahoo Emails Between Dzhokhar and Tamerlan Tsarnaev," exhibit filed in the trial of Dzhokhar Tsarnaev.
23 Quoted in the transcript from the trial of Dzhokhar Tsarnaev, April 29, 2015.
24 *United States v. Dzhokhar Tsarnaev*, transcript of sidebar conversation between his defense team and federal prosecutors, April 27, 2015.

Chapter 10

1 Simon Shuster, "The Boston Bomber Trail: Fresh Clues in Rurual Dagestan," *Time*, April 29, 2013, accessed September 20, 2016, http://world.time.com/2013/04/29/picking-up-the-boston-bomber-trail-in-utamysh-russia.
2 Stewart Bell, "The Canadian Who Converted to Islam: Boxer Turned Militant Killed in Dagestan," *National Post*, August 20, 2012, http://news.nationalpost.com/news/canada/dagestan.
3 FBI Director James Comey, Statement Before the Senate Committee on Homeland Security and Governmental Affairs, Washington, DC, "Threats to the Homeland," October 8, 2015, https://www.fbi.gov/news/testimony/threats-to-the-homeland.
4 FBI Director James Comey, speech about ISIS given at the National Association of Attorneys General, February 25, 2015, available online at https://www.washington post.com/posttv/world/national-security/comey-extremists-exist-in-all-50-states/2015/02/25/8bb6a716-bcfd-11e4-9dfb-03366e719af8_video.html.
5 Stewart Bell, "Canadian Jihadist's Disturbing Video Shows Fanaticism of Rebels Who May Have Inspired the Boston Bomber," *National Post*, May 1, 2013, http://news.nationalpost.com/news/canadian-jihadists-video-may-have-been-inspired-boston-bombings.
6 National Commission on Terrorist Attacks upon the United States, *The 9/11 Commission Report* (Washington, DC: Government Printing Office, July 22, 2004).
7 Anton Troianovski, "Lost Son," *Wall Street Journal*, May 24, 2013, http://www.wsj.com/articles/SB10001424127887323975004578501360359119672.
8 This statement and story were posted on Kavkaz.org. After the death of founder Doku Umarov, this site was taken down. http://www.kavkaz.org.uk/eng/content/2012/07/16/16472.shtml.

Chapter 11

1 Simon Shuster, "A Dead Militant in Dagestan: Did This Jihadi Meet Tamerlan Tsarnaev," *Time*, May 1, 2013, accessed September 20, 2016, http://world.time.com/2013/05/01/a-dead-militant-in-dagestan-did-this-slain-jihadi-meet-tamerlan-tsarnaev.
2 Representative William Keating and others, testimony to the House Homeland Security Committee, July 10, 2013.
3 Video of standoff between Mahmoud Nidal and Russian counterterrorism officials, posted by UmaraskmaM on May 22, 2012, https://www.youtube.com/watch?v=nEt3k2Pgryg.
4 Representative William Keating testimony, transcript from a Homeland Security Committee hearing on the Boston Marathon attacks, July 9, 2010.
5 Author interview with Joanna Herlihy, June 2013.
6 "Tsarnaevs' News Conference: A Transcript," *New York Times*, April 26, 2013.
7 Transcript of Department of Homeland Security Secretary Janet Napolitano's testimony before a Senate committee on immigration reform, April 23, 2013.

8 Tamerlan Tsarnaev, US Citizenship and Immigration Services A-file, posted on the DHS reading room website February 2016 pursuant to a Freedom of Information Act Request: https://www.uscis.gov/sites/default/files/USCIS/About%20Us/ Electronic%20Reading%20Room/A-Files%20of%20Interest%20-%20Static%20 Files/Tamerlan_Tsarnaev.pdf.

9 Transcript of phone calls between Omar Mateen and the Orlando Police Department's Crisis Negotiation Team, released by the OPD September 23, 2016, after a court order prompted by multiple Freedom of Information Act requests by news media outlets.

10 Unclassified summary of information handling and sharing prior to the April 15, 2013, bombings, prepared by the inspectors general for the Central Intelligence Agency, Department of Justice, and DHS, released April 10, 2014.

11 Unclassified summary of information handling and sharing prior to the April 15, 2013, bombings, prepared by the inspectors general for the Central Intelligence Agency, Department of Justice, and DHS, released April 10, 2014.

12 Quoted in *United States v. Dzhokhar Tsarnaev*, indictment, filed June 27, 2013.

Chapter 12

1 Press release by US House Homeland Security Committee, "Bipartisan Support in Congress to Counter Violent Extremism," July 17, 2016, https://homeland.house .gov/press/bipartisan-support-congress-counter-violent-extremism.

2 Quoted in *United States v. Alexander Ciccolo*, motion to detain, July 15, 2015.

3 Quoted in *United States v. Alexander Ciccolo*, indictment, July 23, 2015.

4 Author interview with Boston Police Department Commissioner William Evans, July 2015.

5 City of Boston press release regarding a Department of Homeland Security grant of $17.7 million, posted February 19, 2016, a reduction from $18 million in FY 2015: http://www.cityofboston.gov/news/Default.aspx?id=20520.

6 Author interview with Rene Fielding, Boston Office of Emergency Management, and Boston Mayor Marty Walsh, February 2016.

7 Columbia University Law School, "Illusions of Justice: Human Rights Abuses in US Terrorism Prosecutions," 2014, accessed September 21, 2016, https://www.hrw .org/sites/default/files/reports/usterrorism0714_ForUpload_0_0_0.pdf.

8 American Civil Liberties Union, "Fact Sheet: The NYPD Muslim Informant Program," accessed September 21, 2016, https://www.aclu.org/other/factsheet-nypd -muslim-surveillance-program.

9 New York Police Department, "Radicalization in the West: The Homegrown Threat," 2009.

10 *United States v. Dzhokhar Tsarnaev*, defense motion, filed March 28, 2014.

11 *United States v. Dzhokhar Tsarnaev*, defense motion, filed March 28, 2014.

12 Unclassified summary of information handling and sharing prior to the April 15, 2013, bombings, prepared by the inspectors general for the Central Intelligence Agency, Department of Justice, and DHS, released April 10, 2014.

13 Letter from Senator Charles E. Grassley to FBI Director Robert Mueller on October 15, 2013 (I was given a copy of the letter).

Chapter 13

1 Braintree Police Detective Matt Heslam report detailing the interview of Khairullozhon Matanov on April 19, 2013.

2 FBI 302 proffer reports between federal investigators and Khairullozhon Matanov.

3 FBI 302 proffer reports between federal investigators and Khairullozhon Matanov.

4 Dzhokhar Tsarnaev, April 15, 2013, tweet entered into evidence by US Attorney's Office. Trial exhibit.

5 Author interview with Edward Hayden, attorney for Khairullozhon Matanov, September 2014.

Notes

Chapter 14

1 FBI Special Agent John Walker testimony, transcript from the trial of Dzhokhar Tsarnaev's college friend Robel Phillipos, May 14, 2014.
2 FBI Special Agent John Walker testimony, transcript from the trial of Dzhokhar Tsarnaev's college friend Robel Phillipos, May 14, 2014.
3 Transcript of Dzhokhar Tsarnaev text messages entered into evidence by US Attorney's Office. Trial exhibit.
4 FBI Special Agent John Walker testimony, transcript from the trial of Dzhokhar Tsarnaev's college friend Robel Phillipos, May 14, 2014.
5 Azamat Tazhayakov testimony, transcript from the trial of Dzhokhar Tsarnaev's college friend Robel Phillipos, October 8, 2014.
6 Author interview with retired Somerville Police Chief Tom Pasquarello, September 2016.
7 FBI Special Agent Stephen Kimball testimony, transcript from the trial of Dzhokhar Tsarnaev, March 10, 2015.
8 Mark Preble, chief financial officer at University of Massachusetts–Dartmouth, testimony, transcript from the trial of Dzhokhar Tsarnaev, May 24, 2015. Copy of form entered into evidence by US Attorney's Office. Trial exhibit.
9 Elizabeth Zamparelli testimony, transcript from the trial of Dzhokhar Tsarnaev, May 5, 2015.

Chapter 15

1 FBI Special Agent John Walker testimony, transcript from the trial of Dzhokhar Tsarnaev's college friend Robel Phillipos, May 14, 2014.
2 Receipt, Target store in Watertown, for two backpacks purchased April 14, 2013. Trial exhibit entered into evidence by *United States v. Dzhokhar Tsarnaev*.
3 Defense brief filed in US Appellate Court, Memoranda in Support of Motion to Dismiss, April 11, 2014, in *United States v. Robel Phillipos*.
4 US Magistrate Justice Marianne Bowler at the bedside arraignment of Dzhokhar Tsarnaev, transcript, filed in *United States v. Dzhokhar Tsarnaev*, April 23, 2013.

Chapter 16

1 FBI Special Agent Tim McElroy testimony, transcript of detention hearing and arraignment of Khairullozhon Matanov in US District Court, June 4, 2014.
2 Author Michele McPhee and Aaron Katersky, "Mystery Aircraft Spied on Mass. Man After Bombing," ABC News, June 4, 2015, http://abcnews.go.com/blogs/headlines/2014/06/mystery-aircraft-spied-on-mass-man-after-boston-bombing.
3 Author Michele McPhee, "Boston Bomb Suspect Eyed in Connection to 2011 Triple Murder," ABC News, April 22, 2013, http://abcnews.go.com/Blotter/boston-bomb-suspect-eyed-connection-2011-triple-murder/story?id=19015628.
4 FBI 302 proffer reports between federal investigators and Khairullozhon Matanov.
5 Press release from the Nixon Peabody law firm, "Middlesex Massachusetts District Attorney to Join Nixon Peabody LLP," effective April 29, 2013, http://www.nixonpeabody.com/Middlesex_District_Attorney_Gerry_Leone_Joins_Nixon_Peabody.
6 Ed Hannon, "DA Tells Nashoba Grads: Exceed Your Potential," *Lowell Sun*, June 3, 2012, http://www.lowellsun.com/rss/ci_20772373/da-tells-nashoba-grads-exceed-your-potential.
7 FBI 302 proffer reports between federal investigators and Khairullozhon Matanov.
8 FBI 302 proffer reports between federal investigators and Khairullozhon Matanov.
9 FBI 302 proffer reports between federal investigators and Khairullozhon Matanov.
10 Office of the Florida State Attorney General Jeffrey Ashton report on the investigation into the fatal shooting of Ibragim Todashev, released March 25, 2014.
11 Office of the Florida State Attorney General Jeffrey Ashton report on the investigation into the fatal shooting of Ibragim Todashev, released March 25, 2014.
12 Boston Police Department incident report dated February 11, 2010 (copy on file).

13   Office of the Florida State Attorney General Jeffrey Ashton report on the
     investigation into the fatal shooting of Ibragim Todashev, released March 25, 2014.

14   Ibragim Todashev, US Citizenship and Immigration Services A-file, posted on the
     DHS reading room website February 2016 pursuant to a Freedom of Information
     Act request: https://www.uscis.gov/sites/default/files/USCIS/About%20Us/
     Electronic%20Reading%20Room/A-Files%20of%20Interest%20-%20Static%20
     Files/Ibragim_Todashev.pdf.

15   Office of the Florida State Attorney General Jeffrey Ashton report on the
     investigation into the fatal shooting of Ibragim Todashev, released March 25, 2014.

16   Office of the Florida State Attorney General Jeffrey Ashton report on the
     investigation into the fatal shooting of Ibragim Todashev, released March 25, 2014.

17   Office of the Florida State Attorney General Jeffrey Ashton report on the
     investigation into the fatal shooting of Ibragim Todashev, released March 25, 2014.

18   Kirit Radia, "FBI 'Bandits' Executed Friend of Boston Marathon Suspect, Dad
     Says," ABC News, May 30, 2013, http://abcnews.go.com/blogs/headlines/2013/05/
     fbi-bandits-executed-friend-of-boston-suspect-dad-says.

19   Council on American-Islamic Relations press release, "Ibragim Todashev's Father
     Writes to Obama Over Son's Death in Connection with Marathon Bombings,"
     posted January 2, 2014, https://www.cairflorida.org/blog/ibragim_todashevs_father_
     writes_to_obama_over_sons_death_in_connection_to_boston_bombings.html.

20   Maria Sachetti, "FBI Shooter Had Stormy Record as Officer," *Boston Globe*, May 14,
     2014, https://www.bostonglobe.com/metro/2014/05/13/fbi-shooter-had-stormy
     -record-officer/7zJ1ha78Z0SpfDey0PBuJJ/story.html.

21   Council on American-Islamic Relations press release, "Cair-FL Says FBI Denied
     Todashev Friend the Right to an Attorney," March 15, 2015, http://www.cair.com/
     press-center/press-releases/12165-cair-fl-says-fbi-denied-todashev-friend-the
     -right-to-an-attorney.html.

22   Office of the Florida State Attorney General Jeffrey Ashton report on the
     investigation into the fatal shooting of Ibragim Todashev, released March 25, 2014.

Chapter 17

1   Assistant United States Attorney Aloke Chakravarty, closing argument in the trial
    of Dzhokhar Tsarnaev, transcript, April 6, 2015.

2   FBI Special Agent Chad Fitzgerald testimony, transcript from the trial of Dzhokhar
    Tsarnaev, March 11, 2015.

3   Assistant United States Attorney William Weinreb to the court, transcript from the
    trial of Dzhokhar Tsarnaev, April 28, 2015.

4   Vishkan Vakhabov interview with FBI Special Agent Jeffrey Hunter conducted on
    April 20, 2013, at his Boston apartment, entered into evidence as defense exhibit,
    transcript from the trial of Dzhokhar Tsarnaev, April 28, 2015.

5   Magomed Dolokov interview with FBI Special Agents Timothy Brown and
    William Filbert conducted on May 21, 2013, at his Cambridge apartment, entered
    into evidence as defense exhibit, transcript from the trial of Dzhokhar Tsarnaev,
    April 28, 2013.

6   Defense attorney Miriam Conrad sidebar conversation with US District Court
    Judge George O'Toole and prosecutors, transcript from the trial of Dzhokhar
    Tsarnaev, April 28, 2015.

Chapter 18

1   Topsfield Police court filings pertaining to the arrest of Daniel Morley in June 2013,
    filed in the Newburyport District Court (copy on file).

2   Government's Opposition to Defendant's Motion to Suppress Statements, filed in
    the trial of Dzhokhar Tsarnaev, May 21, 2014. Unsealed in January 2016.

3   Government's Opposition to Defendant's Motion to Suppress Statements, filed in
    the trial of Dzhokhar Tsarnaev, May 21, 2014. Unsealed in January 2016.

4 Topsfield Police court filings pertaining to the arrest of Daniel Morley in June 2013, filed in the Newburyport District Court (copy on file).

5 Author interview with Daniel Morley's associate Marc Pascuito, who recalled the conversation, September 2014.

6 Gavin Aronsen, "N.H. City Wants a 'Tank' to Use Against Occupiers and Libertarians," *Mother Jones*, August 6, 2013, http://www.motherjones.com/politics/2013/08/occupy-free-state-project-dhs-police-concord.

7 Evidence collected from the home of Daniel Morley after his June 2013 arrest included various Free State materials and printed propaganda (copy on file).

8 Author interview with David Bloss at his Topsfield home, September 2013.

9 Author interview with David Bloss at his Topsfield home, September 2013.

10 Statement released to the author by the Essex County District Attorney's Office in December 2014.

11 Multiple author interviews with Marc Pascuito in 2013 and 2014.

12 *United States v. Dzhokhar Tsarnaev*, court filing regarding evidence filed August 8, 2014.

13 *United States v. Dzhokhar Tsarnaev*, indictment, filed June 27, 2013.

14 Author interview with David Bloss in Topsfield and interviews with law enforcement sources close to the case.

Chapter 19

1 Author Michele McPhee, "Mom Comforts Two Sons Who Each Lost a Leg in Boston Bomb Blasts," ABC News, April 16, 2013, accessed September 21, 2016, http://abcnews.go.com/US/mom-comforts-sons-lost-leg-boston-blasts/story?id=18969625; and multiple author interviews with Liz Norden, 2013–16. All quotes attributed to Norden in this chapter are taken from these sources.

2 Arraignment of Dzhokhar Tsarnaev before US Magistrate Justice Marianne Bowler, transcript from July 10, 2013, initial appearance at US District Court.

3 I was present as Ed Fucarile addressed reporters outside federal court, July 10, 2013.

4 Author interview with MIT Police Chief John DiFava, July 10, 2013.

5 US Marshal Kevin Roche testimony, transcript from the trial of Dzhokhar Tsarnaev, May 6, 2015.

6 Assistant US Attorney Nadine Pelligrini argument, transcript from the trial of Dzhokhar Tsarnaev, April 21, 2015.

7 Defense attorney Miriam Conrad, cross-examination question to US Marshal Kevin Roche, transcript from the trial of Dzhokhar Tsarnaev, April 21, 2015.

8 Roche testimony, transcript from the trial of Dzhokhar Tsarnaev, May 6, 2015.

Chapter 20

1 Stephen Silva testimony, transcript from the trial of Dzhokhar Tsarnaev, March 17, 2015.

2 Federal indictment of Stephen Silva filed by US Attorney Carmen Ortiz, July 14, 2014.

3 Federal indictment of Stephen Silva filed by US Attorney Carmen Ortiz, July 14, 2014.

Chapter 21

1 Author interview with Congressman William Keating, October 2013.

2 National Commission on Terrorist Attacks upon the United States, *The 9/11 Commission Report* (Washington, DC: Government Printing Office, July 22, 2004).

3 Unclassified summary of information handling and sharing prior to the April 15, 2013, bombings, prepared by the inspectors general for the Central Intelligence Agency, Department of Justice, and DHS, released April 10, 2014.

4 ACLU, Lawyers' Committee for Civil Rights, Mayer Brown report, "Muslims Need Not Apply: How USCIS Secretly Mandates the Discriminatory Delay and Denial

of Citizenship and Immigration Benefits to Aspiring Americans," released August 2013 (copy on file).

5   Boston medical examiner's death certificate for Tamerlan Tsarnaev, dated April 19, 2013.

6   Tamerlan Tsarnaev, US Citizenship and Immigration Services A-file, posted on the DHS reading room website February 2016 pursuant to a Freedom of Information Act request: https://www.uscis.gov/sites/default/files/USCIS/About%20Us/Electronic%20Reading%20Room/A-Files%20of%20Interest%20-%20Static%20Files/Tamerlan_Tsarnaev.pdf.

7   Author interview with Phantom Fireworks store assistant manager Megan Kearns, April 2013. Confirmed by multiple law enforcement sources.

8   Trial exhibits entered into evidence by federal prosecutors in the trial of Dzhokhar Tsarnaev included photos of items seized from 410 Norfolk Street.

Chapter 22

1   Jessica Kensky testimony, transcript from the trial of Dzhokhar Tsarnaev, May 13, 2015.

2   Shane O'Hara testimony, transcript from the trial of Dzhokhar Tsarnaev, March 4, 2015.

3   Roseann Sdoia testimony, transcript from the trial of Dzhokhar Tsarnaev, March 5, 2015.

4   Lynn firefighter Matt Patterson testimony, transcript from the trial of Dzhokhar Tsarnaev, March 9, 2015.

5   Nadia Suleimanova testimony, transcript from the trial of Dzhokhar Tsarnaev, May 4, 2015.

6   Shakhurzat Suleimanova testimony, transcript from the trial of Dzhokhar Tsarnaev, May 4, 2015.

7   Raisat Suleimanova testimony, transcript from the trial of Dzhokhar Tsarnaev, May 4, 2015.

8   Audio recording made by Tamerlan Tsarnaev during his trip to Russia in 2012, entered into evidence as a trial exhibit by attorneys for Dzhokhar Tsarnaev and played in court on May 4, 2015.

9   Shakhurzat Suleimanova testimony, transcript from the trial of Dzhokhar Tsarnaev, May 4, 2015.

10 Dzhokhar Tsarnaev addresses the court, transcript from the sentencing hearing of Dzhokhar Tsarnaev, June 24, 2015.

11 US District Court Justice George O'Toole to the court, transcript from the sentencing hearing of Dzhokhar Tsarnaev, June 24, 2015.